JOHN LOCKE

ON TOLERATION AND THE UNITY OF GOD

JOHN LOCKE

ON TOLERATION AND THE UNITY OF GOD

by

MARIO MONTUORI

J.C. GIEBEN, PUBLISHERS

AMSTERDAM 1983

© 1983 by J.C. Gieben
ISBN 90 70265 25 7
Printed in The Netherlands

CONTENTS

PREFACE

In this book I have collected and re-published some of my studies on Locke's Toleration and the Unity of God which appeared in the last twenty years.

During this time there have been no reasons for me to make any alterations to my writings, therefore I am publishing them again without any additions or deletions — although I have corrected some misprints which appeared in the preceding Italian editions. To avoid causing extrinsic revisions I have left my writings in their original version, as it responds to the moment in which they were conceived. On the other hand it is all too clear that the chronological course which embraces a rather extensive period of time, in itself involves a progressive revision of the writings here published, through the discussion of them with other editors, scholars and critics of Locke. For this reason I have left the date of redaction and publication at the bottom of each of them.

The first of the writings collected in this book is my critical edition of Locke's celebrated *Epistola de Tolerantia*, published by Martinus Nijhoff, The Hague, 1963, with the title *John Locke. A Letter concerning Toleration. Latin and English texts revised and edited with variants and an introduction.*

The Socinianism of Locke and the English edition of the Letter Concerning Toleration was published as *Proceedings* of the Accademia di Scienze Morali e Politiche della Società Nazionale di Scienze, Lettere ed Arti, vol. LXXVIII, Naples, 1967, under the title *Il Socinianesimo di Locke e l'edizione inglese dell'Epistola sulla tolleranza.*

Locke's Epistola on Toleration from the translation of Popple to that of Gough appeared in Giornale Critico della Filosofia Italiana, II, 1969, pp. 206-221, as *L'Epistola Lockiana sulla tolleranza dalla traduzione di Popple alla traduzione di Gough.*

On Klibansky and Locke's Epistola de Tolerantia appeared in Il Cannocchiale 1/2, 1978, pp. 155 ff. with the title: *Di Klibansky e l'Epistola lockiana sulla tolleranza.*

The *Three letters from Locke to Limborch on the Unity of God* were published in the *Proceedings* of the Accademia Pontaniana,

Naples, n.s. vol. XXIII, Naples, 1974, pp. 287-312, with the title *Tre Lettere di Locke a Limborch sull'Unità di Dio*.

The Correspondence of John Locke was published in Giornale Critico della Filosofia Italiana, ff. III-IV (LIX), 1978, pp. 534-538, with the same title.

The Rational Evidence of the Unity of God in the Correspondence of Locke was published in 'Discorsi,' I, I (1980), pp. 109-112, as *Le prove razionali dell'unità di Dio nella corrispondenza di J. Locke*.

I would like to express my sincere gratitude to all those who helped me in the preparation of this edition and, in particular, to Mr. John Muir to whom I am indebted for the invaluable favour he did me in undertaking the translation of my Italian writings, and to the publisher Mr. J.C. Gieben for the speed and care with which he has published this book.

London, Summer, 1981   M.M.

A LETTER CONCERNING TOLERATION

LATIN AND ENGLISH TEXTS REVISED AND EDITED WITH VARIANTS AND AN INTRODUCTION

FOREWORD

Two different editions of Locke's famous letter on the Toleration which the various Christian churches should show among themselves appeared in 1689: one in Gouda, in Holland, where Limborch, under the title *Epistola de tolerantia* published the Latin manuscript entrusted to him by Locke; the other in London, where Popple published the translation of the Latin text of the *Epistola* under the title *A Letter concerning Toleration*.

Locke accepted the first of these two editions, owning himself the author of the Latin text. Regarding the English translation, he declared, in the codicil to his will, that it had been made 'without my privity'. This expression was interpreted by Coste, and by many subsequent editors of Locke, as meaning 'à l'insû de Mr Locke'.

The two versions of the first letter on Toleration have in the course of centuries had a very different history from that which it would have been permissible to expect. It has happened in fact, that the Latin text of the *Epistola*, apart from the fine edition by Hollis recently reprinted in Italy, has been neglected by the editors of Locke. On the other hand the English translation by Popple, printed in the first edition of Locke's works, has since then always been included in succeeding editions, and more and more often in a separate edition by itself. This has happened in spite of the fact that Popple was regarded as not entirely reliable as a translator, and in spite of the reserve with which the English translation is commonly regarded.

But is it in fact true that Popple's translation is not altogether faithful to the original Latin text? A reply to this question depends not so much on a comparison between

v

Limborch's edition and Popple's translation, as on whether it is true that Popple translated the *Epistola* into English 'à l'insû de Mr Locke', and consequently whether Locke was right or wrong in saying that the translation was made 'without my privity'.

Long research into documents hitherto unpublished, or little known, or badly used, has persuaded me that Locke not only knew that Popple had undertaken to translate the Gouda Latin text, but also that Locke followed Popple's work very closely, and even that the second English edition of 1690 was edited by Locke himself. In these circumstances it does not seem possible to speak of an original text, that in Latin, and an English translation; rather they are two different versions of Locke's thoughts on Toleration.

The accusations of unreliability levelled at Popple therefore fall to the ground, and the Latin and English texts acquire equal rights to our trust, since they both deserve the same place among Locke's works.

Consequently the expression 'without my privity', which a number of people had seen as revealing an innate weakness in Locke's moral character, reacquires its precise meaning: testifying to Locke's profound modesty and integrity.

In my researches I delved deep into the history of the composition and translation of the *Epistola*, and also into a whole chapter of Locke's biography; at the same time I did not ignore the text itself. Indeed in many places the text has been clarified by the reconstruction of its history, and in particular by the reconstruction of the times and the environment in which the *Epistola* was conceived and written. The same remarks apply to the form of the *Epistola*. It was still not certain whether it was a personal letter addressed to Limborch or whether it was a real tractate on Toleration written in the form of a letter.

Because it seems to me, as I have said, that the English text deserves the same respect as that accorded to the Latin text, and because the two texts deserve the same place in Locke's

works, I have thought it appropriate to print the two texts side by side. In doing this, however, I have not limited myself to printing any one edition of each of the two texts, but I have attempted a reconstruction of each of them which is as far as possible faithful to the spirit and letter of what Locke wrote. To this end I have collated the most trustworthy editions, accepting or at times proposing the reading which seemed to me to be most accurate and closest to the original Latin version and to the English version edited by Locke.

The two texts, Latin and English, of Locke's first *Letter concerning Toleration* are therefore here presented for the first time free of the errors which accumulated in them during the course of various editions. At the same time I have made a few small changes in the form of the *Letter's* writing which I hope will make it easier to read this fundamental document on Locke's social and political thought: the most acute and topical which we can read today on the problem of religious toleration.

I would like to thank all those who have so kindly helped me in the preparation of this edition. In particular Mr O. D. Elliott and Mrs Valérie Minogue; also the Library of the University of Leyden and the Bodleian Library in Oxford which, among other valuable assistance, kindly put at my disposal many photo-copies of texts and of documents.

The Hague, Spring 1961   **M.M.**

ABBREVIATIONS

(a) Manuscripts

MSS. R. L.   Remonstrants' Manuscripts in the University Library, Amsterdam.

BL. MSS. Locke   Locke's Manuscripts in the Bodleian Library, Oxford.

Note: The letters of Locke and of his correspondents are dated according to two different calendars in use at that time.
To avoid confusion I have followed the system used by Cranston, p. XII, transcribing in Roman type dates according to the Julian or Old Style calendar, and in italic type dates according to the Gregorian or New Style calendar.

(b) Libraries

ALB   Academia Lugduni Batavorum
BLO   The Bodleian Library, Oxford
KBsG   Koninklijke Bibliotheek, 's-Gravenhage
ULA   The University Library, Amsterdam

(c) Bibliography
Only those books frequently quoted have been included.

Aaron   *John Locke* by Richard I. Aaron. Second Edition. Oxford, 1955

Bayle, *Dictionnaire*   *Dictionnaire Historique et Critique* de Pierre Bayle. Nouvelle Edition. 16 Volumes. Paris, 1820

IX

Bayle, *Lettres*	*Lettres Choisies* de Mr Bayle avec des remarques. 3 Tom. Rotterdam, MDCCXIV (KBsG. 482–J.10)
Bayle, *Oeuvres*	*Oeuvres Diverses* de Pierre Bayle. 4 tom. La Haye, 1727–1731. (ALB. 379 A 10–13)
Bibliothèque	*Bibliothèque Universelle et Historique* de l'année MDCLXXXIX. Tome XV. Amsterdam, MDCXC. Art. XIV: *Epistola de Tolerantia* ecc. pp. 402–412. (ALB. 542 G 15)
Bonno	*Lettres Inédites de Le Clerc à Locke*, edited with an introduction and notes, by Gabriel Bonno. Berkeley and Los Angeles, 1959.
Bourne	*The Life of John Locke* by H. R. Fox Bourne. Two Volumes. London, 1876.
Coste, *Avertissement*	*Essai Philosophique concernant L'Entendement Humain* [...] par M. Locke. Traduit de l'Anglois par M. Coste. Troisiéme édition [...] Amsterdam, MDCCXXXV. *Avertissement du Traducteur*, pp. IX–XVIII.
Coste, *Eloge*	*Eloge de M. Locke*, par P. Coste, in *Nouvelles de la Republique des Lettres*, Mois de Fevrier 1705, p. 154 ff. Reprinted in: Coste, *Avertissement*, pp. XXI–XXIX.
Cranston	*John Locke. A Biography* by Maurice Cranston. Longmans, London, 1957.
Christophersen	*A Bibliographical Introduction to the Study of John Locke*, by H. Christophersen. Oslo, 1930. In *Skrifter utgitt av Det Norske Videnskaps-Akademi i Oslo*, 1930. II *Historisk-Filosofisk Klasse*. 2 Bind. Oslo, 1931.
Ebbinghaus	*John Locke, Ein Brief über Toleranz*. Englisch-deutsch. Übersetzt, eingeleitet und in Anmerkungen erläutert von Julius Ebbinghaus. Hamburg, 1957
Eloge	*Eloge Historique de feu Mr Locke*, par J. Le Clerc in *Bibliothèque Choisie*, Tome VI,

	1705, p. 342 ff. First reprinted in *Oeuvres Diverses de Mr. Locke*, Rotterdam, 1710 and afterwards in *Oeuvres Diverses de Mr Locke. Nouvelle Edition considérablement augmentée.* 2 Volumes. Amsterdam, MDCCXXXII. Vol. I, pp. IX–CXIX. (KBsG. 1138 B. 57)
Familiar Letters	*Some Familiar Letters between Mr Locke and several of his Friends.* Printed for A. and J. Churchill, London, 1708.
Gough	*John Locke's Political Philosophy. Eight Studies* by J. W. Gough. Oxford, 1950
Gough, *Introduction*	*The Second Treatise of Government* [....] *and A Letter Concerning Toleration* by John Locke. Edited with an Introduction by J. W. Gough. Blackwell, Oxford, 1956.
King	*The Life of John Locke with Extracts from his Correspondence, Journals and Commonplace Books* by Lord King. New Edition. Two Volumes. London, 1830.
Klibansky	*John Locke, Lettera sulla Tolleranza.* Testo latino e versione italiana. Premessa di R. Klibansky. Introduzione di Ernesto De Marchi. Traduzione di Lia Formigari. Firenze, 1961.
Laslett, *Introduction*	*Locke's Two Treatises of Government.* A critical edition with an introduction and apparatus criticus by Peter Laslett. Cambridge, 1960.
Lettres Inédites	*Lettres Inédites de John Locke à ses amis Nicolas Thoynard, Philippe van Limborch et Edward Clarke,* publiées [...] par M. Henry Ollion [et] T. J. De Boer. La Haye, Martinus Nijhoff, 1912.
Mémoires	*Mémoires pour servir à l'Histoire Litteraire des Dix-sept Provinces des Pays-Bas, de la Principauté de Liege et de quelques contrées voisines.*

	3 Tom. A Louvain, MDCCLXV. (ALB. 2667 A 1–3.)
Moreri	*Le Grand Dictionaire Historique ou Le mélange Curieux de l'Histoire Sacrée et Profane* [.....] par Louis Moreri. Dix-huitieme edition. Amsterdam, MDCCXL. 8 Tomes.
Oeuvres Diverses	*Oeuvres Diverses de Mr Locke. Nouvelle Edition considérablement augmentée.* 2 Volumes. Amsterdam, MDCCXXXII. (KBsG. 1138 B. 57)
Trevelyan, *England*	G. M. Trevelyan, *England under the Stuarts.* Penguin Books, 1950.
Trevelyan, *Revolution*	*The English Revolution 1688–1689* by G. M. Trevelyan. London, 1939
Viano	C. A. Viano, *John Locke. Dal razionalismo all'illuminismo.* Einaudi Editore, 1960
Voltaire, *Siècle*	*Oeuvres Complètes de Voltaire.* 45 volumes. Paris, MDCCCXVII. *Siècle de Louis XIV.* Tomes 13–14.
v. Leyden, *Introduction*	John Locke, *Essay on the Law of Nature* [....] edited by W. von Leyden. Oxford, 1954.

(d) Collated Works
For the Latin text.

LG.	*Epistola de Tolerantia ad Clarissimum Virum T.A.R.P.T.O.L.A. Scripta a P.A.P.O.I.L.A.* Goudae, apud Justum ab Hoeve. MDCLXXXIX [Limborch's edition. In 12°, pp. 96] (ALB. 512 G.2.1.)
ML.	*Letters concerning Toleration,* by John Locke. London. Printed for A. Millar, H. Woodfall et alii. 4° ed. MDCCLXV. [*Epistola de Tolerantia,* Hollis's edition, pp. 3–28] (ALB. 1368 D.22)
HE.	*The Works of John Locke. In four volumes. The*

seventh edition. London. H. Woodfall et
alii. 4° ed. MDCCLXVIII.
[The *Epistola de Tolerantia,* Hollis's edition,
is in the second vol. pp. 317–343] (ULA.
1160–B.15/18)

For the English text.

PE.   *A Letter concerning Toleration.* London.
Printed for Awnsham Churchill. 4° ed.
MDCLXXXIX. pp. 61. [Popple's edition]
(BLO. 4° S.70.Th [11])

SE.   *A Letter concerning Toleration. The second
edition corrected.* London. Printed for
Awnsham Churchill. In 8°. MDCXC.
pp. 87. [Locke's edition?] (BLO. 8°P.260.
Th [3])

CM.   *The Works of John Locke Esq. In Three Volumes.*
London. John Churchill and Sam.
Manship. In folio. MDCCXIV.
[*A Letter concerning Toleration* is in the second
vol. pp. 230–256] (BLO. H.1.5.Th)

HL.   *Letters concerning Toleration,* by John Locke.
London. Printed for A. Millar, H. Wood-
fall et alii. 4° ed. MDCCLXV.
[*A Letter concerning Toleration,* Hollis's edition, pp. 31–66] (ALB. 1368 D.22)

LW.   *The Works of John Locke. In Four Volumes. The
Eighth Edition.* London. Printed for W.
Straham, etc. 4° ed. MDCCLXXVII.
[*A Letter concerning Toleration,* Law's edition,
is in the second vol. pp. 313–350] (BLO.
4° BS. 363)

GH.   *The Second Treatises of Government* [....] and
A Letter concerning Toleration, by John
Locke. Edited with an Introduction by
J. W. Gough. Blackwell. Oxford, 1956.

Notes:

(1) The copy LG which I have used belonged to Prosper Marchand who gave it, with other books and manuscripts, to the University Library of Leyden. This copy bears on the title page: 'Ex Legato Cl. Viri Prosperi Marchandi'. In reproducing the title page these words have been deleted.

With this copy is bound an *Abregé de la Doctrine de la Tolérance Civile. Suivant la Copie de Londres.* A Rotterdam. Chez Barent Bos, Marchand Libraire auprès la Bourse. 1691.

There are two other copies of the *Epistola* in Dutch libraries: one in Amsterdam, ULA 410 G 10, and one in The Hague, KBsG 1175 F 12.

(2) The copy ML (= HL) of the ALB bears the following autograph dedication: 'An Englishman, a Lover of Liberty, civil and religious, is desirous of having the honor to present this book to the University of Leyden, ancient and renoumed.' London, Jan. 1, 1765. This dedication is typical of those used by Thomas Hollis when making donation of his editions of Locke. There is one, more or less the same, on the copy of Hollis's edition dated 1763 of *Two Treatises of Government* given to the Library of University of Leyden (ALB. 1365 E 43). The same applies to the copy given to Christ's College Library (see: Laslett, *Introduction*, p. 154).

There is another copy of ML (= HL) in the KBsG 142 B 5.

(3) PE in the BLO is the copy given by Locke to the Bodleian Library and mentioned in the codicil to his will. It is in a volume of miscellaneous works which bears the inscription: 'Ex Dono Celeberrimi Viri Joannis Lock' (sic) and includes as well as the *First* also the *Second* and the *Third Letter concerning Toleration.*

(4) PE, SE, CM, LW are not found in libraries in Holland. For these texts I used photo-copies kindly made available to me by the Bodleian Library.

INTRODUCTION

Locke's famous *Epistola* on toleration was, according to Le Clerc,[1] written in Amsterdam between the first days of November and the second half of December in the year 1685.[2] That is, in the tragic autumn when the revocation of the Edict of Nantes,[3] and the Jacobite attempt to repeal the Test Act,[4] which together put the non-Catholic churches

[1] *Eloge*, p. LII, and there is a valuable confirmation in Limborch's letter to Lady Masham of *March 24th 1705*, in MSS.R.L. III D. 16–54. The *Eloge* of Le Clerc has served as a basis for every serious biography of Locke. In composing it, Le Clerc had at his disposition not only his own personal knowledge of Locke, *Eloge*, p. X, Bonno, *Introduction*, but also two letters, MSS.R.L. J. 20. and J. 57., sent to him by the two people closest to the philosopher in the last years of his life: the third Lord Shaftesbury and Lady Masham. Of these letters, the *Eloge*, as Bourne has revealed, p. VI, is 'little more than a translation.' On Le Clerc, there is a very accurate and detailed bio-bibliographical article in *Mémoires*, III, pp. 445–478. An excellent study of Le Clerc and his place in the vast movement of ideas from the seventeenth to the eighteenth century is that by Annie Barnes, *Jean Le Clerc et la République des Lettres*, Paris, Droz, 1938.

[2] So also Bourne, II. p. 34, 51.
According to Christophersen, p. 15, n. 1, however, the *Epistola* was written 'during a short stay at Cleve'; while Cranston, p. 259, gives 'during 1686' 'in Utrecht.' It is curious that neither Cranston nor Christophersen indicates the sources for these statements.

[3] The Edict of Nantes, which in 1598 had granted religious toleration to the Huguenots, was formally repealed by the Edict of Fontainebleau, on October 18th 1685: the last act in a drama of destruction played out with ever-increasing fury over a period of twenty-five years.

[4] The Test Act, passed by Parliament in 1673, obliged all those about to hold any office or appointment to take an oath renouncing the Catholic doctrine of transubstantiation. Catholics were thus virtually excluded from public life. Despite the Test Act, James II had appointed

with their backs to the wall, seemed destined to make possible, in France as in England, the triumph of the most odious political and religious absolutism. There seems to me to be no doubt that Locke thought again about the problem of religious toleration under the impulse of the feelings roused in him by the incredible moral and material violence suffered in France by the Huguenots who were determined to adhere to their faith,[1] and by the fear that the political madness of catholicising the country [2] might lead James II to establish in England the brutal rule of the *dragonnades*.[3]

as officers many of the Catholics recruited in the army raised against Monmouth's insurrection.

When Parliament, in November 1685, demanded that since the revolt had been suppressed the Catholics should now be dismissed, the King contemptuously rejected the request. The Tory Parliament, in consequence, refused to grant the funds which James sought for the maintenance of the army. The conflict between the King and Parliament on these two points: James' demand for the abolition of the Test Act, and Parliament's demand for the disbanding of the army, is at the root of that series of events which led to the revolution of 1688.

[1] For the cruelty exercised against the Huguenots, see: Voltaire, *Siècle*, vol. XIV, p. 123 seqq. The most deplorable and infamous practice was that 'd'arracher les enfants aux prétendus réformés, pour les remettre entre les mains des plus proches parents catholiques.' p. 125.

For the reactions of the French refugees in Holland towards these acts of cruelty, see: P. Bayle: *Ce que c'est que la France toute catholique sous le règne de Louis-le-Grand*. Amsterdam, 1686, in which Bayle replied to the chorus of praise then being raised by the Catholics in honour of Louis XIV, who, 'en détruisant l'hérésie' had made 'la France toute catholique.' Also by Bayle, there is the celebrated but very little read *Commentaire philosophique sur ces paroles de Jésus Christ, Contrains-les d'entrer*, in Bayle, *Oeuvres*, vol. II, pp. 355-496.

[2] For James II's politics, and his attempt to impose a Catholic preponderance in England, see: Trevelyan, *England*, ch. 13 and Trevelyan, *Revolution*, ch. III.

[3] The *croisade dragonne* or *conversions à la dragonne*, or simply *la dragonnade*, were the terms adopted to describe the excesses of Louvois' dragoons in France, where they were quartered in the homes of Protestants. James II's obstinate determination to maintain an army of 30,000 men and to fill it with Catholics gave grounds for fearing that the brutalities of

In fact, the dramatic tone of the introduction to the *Epistola*, the deeply-felt references to 'those that persecute, torment, destroy, and kill other men upon pretence of religion' (SE3), to the 'infidels [...] converted by force' (SE6) and to those recalcitrant persons dissuaded from error by the brutality of soldiers (ibid), demonstrate clearly that Locke does not speak in abstract terms, but that his thesis was inspired by events which occurred and were all too well-known in the last months of 1685.[1]

At this time Locke, who had been accused of favouring the designs of the Duke of Monmouth,[2] and was required for extradition,[3] was hiding under a false name [4] in the

the *dragonnades* might be repeated in England. Trevelyan, *England*, p. 415, seqq., *Revolution*, p. 54.

[1] It is interesting to note that the Latin text, LG. 9, reads *suae* [...] *cohortes*, whilst in the English text, SE. 7, one finds *His dragoons*, thus making more explicit and immediate the reference to the appalling reputation of the *dragonnes* unleashed against the Protestants.

[2] James Scott, Duke of Buccleuch and Monmouth, was the recognised natural son of Charles II. Shaftesbury's Whigs, basing themselves on a spurious rumour that Charles had married Monmouth's mother, made him their candidate for the Stuart throne. When the Whigs fell Monmouth fled to Holland, in the spring of 1685. There, with the support of the Amsterdam magistrates, acting against the wishes of the Stadtholder, he prepared for the ill-fated enterprise of overthrowing 'not only the Popish King but the Anglican Church.' Trevelyan, *Revolution*, p. 50. He disembarked in June 1685 at Lyme Regis, had himself proclaimed King at Taunton, but was routed at Sedgemoor by Churchill and Lord Feversham. Trevelyan, *England*, p. 413. He was captured and executed at Tower Hill. His followers were ruthlessly massacred.

It is likely that Locke was in touch with Monmouth's supporters while the latter was preparing to return to England *armata manu*, but, according to Cranston, p. 252, it is quite untenable that Locke subscribed to the fund which Monmouth opened for the acquisition of the ship which was to bring him and his followers back to England.

[3] Le Clerc, *Eloge*, pp. XLIX–L, gives this account of the request for extradition: 'Au printemps de l'année 1685, le Duc de Monmouth étoit en Hollande avec plusieurs Anglois, mécontents du Governement, et il se préparoit à l'entreprise qui lui réussit si mal. Le Roi d'Angleterre en étant averti, fit demander aux Etats par Mr Skelton, son Envoyé

house of Dr. Veen.[1] The frequent visits of the theologian
Philip van Limborch,[2] to whom Locke had been tied by
bonds of affectionate friendship since the first days of his

à La Haye, le 17 May, quatre vingts quatre personnes, entre lesquelles
étoit Mr. Locke. [...] Il étoit le dernier de tous; et je me souviens d'avoir
ouï dire alors que son nom n'étoit point dans la liste venue d'Angleterre,
mais que le Consul Anglois, qui étoit alors ici, le fit ajouter. Je crois
– adds Le Clerc – au moins, que l'on peut assurer que Mr Locke n'avoit
aucune liaison avec le Duc de Monmouth, qu'il n'estimoit pas assez,
pour s'en promettre aucun bien. Il n'étoit d'ailleurs aucunement
brouillon, et plutot timide que courageux.'

The 'Mémoire présenté par Monsieur Schelton, Envoyé Extraordinaire
de Sa Majesté de la Grande Bretagne à Messeigneurs les Etats Généraux'
which bore the request for the extradition of the 84 suspected of com-
plicity with Monmouth, is reported by King, II, pp. 286–288.

[4] On his return to Amsterdam from Cleve, where he had stayed
from early September till the beginning of November, 1685, Locke had
prudently taken the name of *Dr. Van der Linden.*

[1] Egbertus Veen (1629–1709) 'l'un des plus habiles et des plus heureux
praticiens' of Amsterdam, *Eloge,* XLV, was Locke's host for some time,
offering him his house as a place of concealment. 'Ce fut chez lui qu'il
[Locke] composa la lettre latine de la Tolérance qui fut ensuite imprimée
à Tergou, et qui est intitulée *Epistola de Tolerantia.' Eloge,* p. LIII, Moreri,
Locke.

[2] Philip van Limborch was born in 1632 in Amsterdam, and died
there in 1712. The grand-nephew of Episcopius, and brought up in the
Arminian tradition, he was appointed as Remonstrant minister at
Gouda in 1657, that at Amsterdam in 1667, where, in the following year,
he replaced Isaac Pontanus in the Chair of Professor of Theology in the
Remonstrants' Seminary. He edited the works of Episcopius (1661)
and Etienne de Courcelle (1675), and was himself the author of a *Theologia
Christiana ad praxin pietatis ac promotionem pacis Christianae unice directa.* Amster-
dam, 1686 (ALB N.H.K. 334), which is the most lofty and complete ex-
pression of Arminian theological thought. There is a complete review
of the works of Limborch, seen from a Catholic point of view, in *Mémoires,*
I, 553–557. See also Le Clerc, *Oratio funebris in obitum reverendi et clarissimi̱ viri
Phil. A. Limborch, S. Theologiae apud Remonstrantes Professoris, Defuncti d. XXX
Aprilis, Anno MDCCXII. Habita a Joanne Clerico, d. VI Maii, quo sepultus est.*
Amstelaedami [...] anno 1712 (ALB. 435–F. 32). Le Clerc also wrote the
Limborch entry for the great dictionary of Moreri. De Boer has given a
brief perceptive outline of the character of Limborch in *Lettres Inédites,*
p. 149 seqq. The relationship between Locke and Limborch has been well
reconstructed by Bourne, and by Cranston.

exile in Holland,[1] were comforts in his solitude. Those visits, as Limborch himself recalled many years later, were opportunities for long and impassioned discussions.[2] It is easy to suppose that in the atmosphere created by the dramatic events which occurred during that autumn in France and England, the problem of toleration between the various churches, and thus the problem of the relations between the State and the Church in matters of religious liberty, was the crux of the discussions between the latitudinarian philosopher and the Arminian theologian.[3] This is all the more likely because both Locke and Limborch, each by himself, had already long thought about the problem of religious toleration,[4] but in another mood and in other circumstances.

[1] For the curious circumstances which led to the first meeting between Locke and Limborch, *Eloge*, p. XLV.

For Locke's attitude to Limborch, see the letter Locke wrote to the theologian immediately after his return to England, in Aaron, p. 24.

[2] Limborch to Lady Masham, *March 24th 1705*, MSS. R. L. III. D. 16–54: '[...] often visited him [Locke] in his solitude and conversed with him for many hours at a time.' Translated by Bourne and quoted by Cranston, p. 253.

[3] In the same letter to Lady Masham. MSS. R. L. III. D. 16–54, Limborch recalls that his conversations with Locke turned mainly on religious questions.

On the influence which these conversations had on the thought of both Locke and Limborch, see Viano, p. 378, seqq.

[4] Religious toleration is an essential and characteristic feature of the thought of the Remonstrants, from Coornhert, who went so far as to banish the term 'heresy' which is not found in the Gospels, in order to allow the widest possible religious freedom; and Arminius, for whom all religions have a common rational nucleus; to Episcopius, who allowed the possibility of divergence on certain articles of faith without consequent exclusion or condemnation; and Limborch, who 'comme tous les Remonstrants, étoit grand partisan de la tolérance et [...] a rempli ses écrits du fiel le plus amer contre l'Eglise Catholique, qui fait gloire d'être la plus intolérante de toutes les Sociétés qui prennent le nom de Chrétiennes,' according to the curious comment on him in *Mémoires*, I, 557.

Precisely on the question of toleration Limborch had published in 1661 in Amsterdam a short treatise in Dutch in the form of a dialogue:

Now the same problem, to which each of the two men had already found his own solution, had to be examined and resolved again in a new and unexpected political and religious situation. During their discussions it is not improbable that Limborch urged his friend to write down 'in a conversational way' [1] the thoughts which Locke had developed, as Limborch himself had already done on another occasion.[2]

Be that as it may, this is what Locke did, in writing the Latin treatise which to-day we know under the title *Epistola de Tolerantia.*

Thus the *Epistola*, written, as we have seen, in the autumn

Korte wederlegginge van 't boexken onlangs uytgegeven by Iacobus Sceperus genaemt Chrysopolerotus. Waer in onder anderen gehandelt wert van de Onderlinge Verdraegsaemheyt, by forme van t' samen-sprekinge tusschen een Remonstrant en Contraremonstrant te samen gestelt door Philippus van Limborch, Predicant in de Remonstrantsche gemeente tot Gouda. Tot Amsterdam, By Jan Rieuwertsz, Boeckverkooper in Dirck van Assen-steegh in 't Martelaersboeck 1661. [6] + 196 p. 8°. (ULA 402 G. 32).

Locke, for his part had in the same year drawn up a series of notes on toleration, reproduced by King, p. 75, seqq, in preparation for his later essays: *Question: whether the Civil Magistrate may lawfully impose and determine the use of indifferent things in reference to Religious Worship.* (1660); *An magistratus civilis possit res adiaphoras in divini cultus ritus asciscere easque populo imponere? Affirmatur.* (1661–1662); *An essay concerning Toleration* (1667). For Locke's first two Essays see von Leyden, *Introduction*, pp. 22–30. These works of Locke's on toleration have been recently edited and translated into Italian, by C. A. Viano: *John Locke, Scritti editi e inediti sulla tolleranza*, Torino, Taylor, 1961. See also: Viano, pp. 29 ss: 277 seqq.

[1] An apt hypothesis of Bourne's, II, p. 35. But it is quite out of the question that Locke, in response to a request from Limborch, decided to rewrite 'his old arguments' of the *Essay concerning Toleration.* ibid. The *Epistola* presupposes the *Essay* but does not reproduce it. Between the *Essay* and the *Epistola* lie not only the repeal of the Edict of Nantes, and the Jacobite attempt to overthrow the Test Act, but also, the bitter reflections of the *Second Treatise of Government*, in the light of which, the arguments of the *Epistola*, even if they recall certain of 'his old arguments' of the *Essay*, acquire a new and different significance. For the time of composition of the *Second Treatise of Government*, see Laslett, *Introduction*, p. 65.

[2] In the above-mentioned dialogue in Dutch on toleration.

E P I S T O L A

de

TOLERANTIA

ad

Clariffimum Virum

T. A. R. P. T. O. L. A.

Scripta à

P. A. P. O. I. L. A

G O U D Æ,
Apud JUSTUM AB HOEVE
CIƆ IƆC LXXXIX.

of 1685, was published by Limborch in Gouda between the end of April and the first few days of May in the year 1689, the printer being Justus van den Hoeve.[1]

In a letter dated *6th May* Limborch gave news of the publication to Locke, who had by then been back in England for a few months: 'Prodiit hic hisce diebus libellus elegantissimus de Tolerantia, per modum epistolae scriptus, non expresso authoris nomine.' [2]

This anonymous 'libellus', however, carried with the title *Epistola de Tolerantia* on the title-page this 'inscription singulier': [3] '*ad Clarissimum Virum T.A.R.P.T.O.L.A. Scripta a P.A.P. O.I.L.A.*' According to Limborch himself, in a letter written to Lady Masham in 1705, these mysterious initials, which hide the names of the addressee and the sender, denote that the letter was written to '*Theologiae apud Remonstrantes Professorem, Tyrannidis Osorem, Libertatis Amantem*' by '*Pacis Amante, Persecutionis Osore, Joanni Lockio, Anglo.*' [4]

[1] A volume in XII°, of 12,50 × 8 cms., pp. 96, incl. title page and blank verso. The title page is reproduced elsewhere.

[2] Limborch to Locke, *May 6th 1689*, MSS. R. L. III D. 16 f. 195, reproduced in *Lettres inédites*, p. 187, n. 1.

The correspondence between Locke and Limborch was conducted in Latin, since the former knew no Dutch, and the latter no English; even though Limborch understood French quite well, he did not know it well enough for the purposes of writing.

[3] This is how Prosper Marchand defines it in: Bayle, *Lettres Choisies*, III, p. 861, n. 3.

[4] Limborch to Lady Masham, *March 24th 1705*, MSS. R. L. III D. 16–54. Although Limborch's letter to Lady Masham is very well known, it still seems to me that insufficient attention has been paid to Limborch's explanation of the mysterious initials which accompany the *Epistola*. It differs from that given by Le Clerc, *Eloge*, p. LII; *Oeuvres Diverses, Avertissement*, p. IV–V; Moreri, art. *Locke*, which is commonly followed. In place of *Libertatis Amantem* Le Clerc, in fact, gives *Limburgium Amstelodamensem*. This divergence is, to say the least, strange, when we bear in mind that it was Limborch himself who supplied Le Clerc with the key to the mystery of the initials. It is difficult to understand why Limborch gave a different interpretations to Lady Masham and Le Clerc. Unless we wish to suppose, with Bourne, II, p. 151 n. 2, that Limborch himself was the

It is a fact that in writing to Lady Masham Limborch explained the *Epistola* as if it had been originally conceived and written as a personal letter, with the title *Epistola de Tolerantia*, ('eximiam illam de tolerantia epistolam ad me scripsit') addressed by Locke to Limborch while the latter was present and aware of what Locke was doing, ('me solo conscio') in 1685 ('illa hieme'), and with those same initials concealing the names of Limborch and Locke ('voluitque nomina nostra sub literis cum titulo insertis habere').[1]

But, without wronging the good Dutch theologian, it seems extremely improbable that a man like Locke, who was noted for his character 'plutôt timide que courageux',[2] who had already been accused of uttering seditious libels,[3] and who was under the threat of extradition, should have decided to address to Limborch, in that very autumn of 1685, a letter on a subject of such dangerous topicality that it denounced, among other matters, the taking of a clear position against the cause of James II on both political and religious grounds.

It would not have escaped a man as prudent as Locke that

author 'of the ingenious and eccentric wording, or rather initialing of the title-page.'

[1] Limborch to Lady Masham, *March 24th 1705*, MSS. R. L. III D. 16–54. The whole passage runs as follows: 'Illa hieme, in aedibus D. Venii, me solo conscio, eximiam illam de Tolerantia epistolam ad me scripsit, voluitque nomina nostra sub literis cum titulo insertis habere, quibus indicatur epistolam esse scriptam ad Theologiae apud Remonstrantes Professorem, Tyrannidis Osorem, Libertatis Amantem a Pacis Amante, Persecutionis Osore, Joanne Lockio Anglo.'

[2] *Eloge*, p. L.

[3] 'Il n'y avoit pas un an que Mr. Locke étoit sorti d'Angleterre' writes Le Clerc 'lorsqu'on l'accusa à la Cour d'avoir fait certains petits livres contre le Gouvernement, que l'on disoit être venus de Hollande. Cela lui fit perdre la place qu'il avoit dans le Collège de l'Eglise de Christ à Oxford.' *Eloge*, p. XLVI.

In the face of this accusation, Locke solemnly protested his innocence in a letter to Lord Pembroke, dated December 8th 1684: 'I am suspected to [have] writ divers scandalous seditious libels.' [...] 'I here solemnly protest in the presence of God, that I am not the author, not only of

these strange initials would in fact excite, rather than deflect, the curiosity of anybody into whose hands the manuscript happened to fall. An imprudence on the part of Limborch, who in fact proved to be less silent than the grave,[1] could have meant disaster for Locke, and he would certainly not have exposed himself to this risk.

To have an idea of the paroxysms induced in Locke by his mania for secrecy it is enough to reflect that even in 1692, when sending his first two Letters on Toleration to Le Clerc from England, Locke not only concealed from his friend the fact that he was the author of the letters, but even went to the lengths of avoiding writing the word toleration at all, referring to the letters as treatises περὶ τῆς τ.[2]

If it is possible to hazard a guess, it seems more probable that Locke, threatened, as I have said, by the constant danger of extradition, and having resolved to make a will and to entrust its execution to Limborch,[3] gave to his friend, with other papers and valuables, the manuscript of the 'libellus de Tolerantia', so that it could be jealously preserved among his secret papers. It is very likely that Limborch regarded this manuscript, which was the result of his discussions with Locke, as belonging in part to him, or as something over which he had certain rights, and asked Locke, when his friend was preparing to leave Holland for England, for permission to publish the *Epistola* anonymously (non expresso

any libel, but not of any pamphlet or treatise whatsoever in print ...'
Quoted by Cranston, p. 248.

[1] In the spring of 1690, Limborch, repeatedly asked by Guenelon whether Locke were the author of the *Epistola*, decided to reveal the secret which still concealed his name. Informed of this by Limborch himself, BL. MSS. Locke, *April 25th 1690* C.14 f.44 Latin, Locke had hard words for the friend whose indiscretion could have such disastrous consequences for him. BL. MSS. Locke, April 22nd 1690 C.24 f.155 Latin.

[2] Le Clerc to Locke, dated *January 20th* and *April 11th 1692* in: Bonno, p. 49, 50.

[3] Limborch to Lady Masham, *March 24th 1705*, MSS. R. L. III D. 16–54.

authoris nomine). Limborch intended to use it in support of the propaganda of the Remonstrants [1] who had not forgotten the former condemnations and persecutions suffered at the hands of the intransigent Calvinists.[2]

It is a fact that Locke granted Limborch's request, and authorised him to publish the treatise on Toleration which he had written four years earlier. Locke was, indeed, as he himself acknowledged, particularly sensitive to requests from friends he respected to publish one of his works, even though it was not intended for printing, if they considered it would be of some use.[3] It is perhaps not unlikely, that because of

[1] As an indication of the use to which the Remonstrants put Locke's *Letters*, Le Clerc's words to Locke, referring to the first two letters on toleration are highly significant: 'J'ai [...] quelques livres anglois de la Tolérance, que je ferai valoir comme il faut contre nos Persécuteurs.' Bonno, p. 44.
It is worth noticing that here Le Clerc writes plainly 'Tolérance'; but when Locke, not realising that Le Clerc was referring to his own *Letters*, sent the latter to him, calling them 'traités περὶ τῆς τ.,' Le Clerc in his reply adopted the same covert form used by Locke. Bonno, pp. 49, 50.
[2] At the Synod of Dordrecht, in 1619, the intransigent Calvinists proposed and obtained the condemnation of Arminianism and the banishment of Remonstrant ministers from the United Provinces. In 1620, a new decree banished even those ministers who had renounced the 'Remonstrantie.' Only towards 1630 were the Remonstrants granted any widespread freedom of worship in Holland, and then not in Leyden, which was the stronghold of the Gomarists. However, the latter never dropped their attitude of open hostility to the Arminians. As a testimony to, and in memory of, the persecution endured, Limborch, together with Chrétien Hartsoeker, published in Amsterdam in 1660 a collection of letters of Remonstrants persecuted as a result of the sentence passed by the Synod of Dordrecht: *Praestantium ac Eruditorum Virorum Epistolae ecclesiasticae et theologicae varii argumenti, inter quas eminent eae, quae a Jac. Arminio, Conr. Vorstio, Sim. Episcopio, Hug. Grotio, Casp. Barleo conscriptae sunt.* Amsterdami, 1660, (ALB. 342 D. 1)
In 1684, Limborch brought out a second augmented edition (ALB. 591 A. 7) and in 1704 the whole collection appeared, in the third edition. (ALB. 591 A. 8)
[3] In the letter to Edward Clarke of Chipley, containing the dedi-

the profit the Remonstrants might derive from it, Locke then allowed himself to be persuaded to add to the *Epistola* the *Postcriptum*, which is nothing if not an open defence of the arguments put forward by the Arminians against the continual accusations of schism and heresy levelled against them by their bitter adversaries the Gomarists.[1] It was probably only when Locke finally delivered the manuscript to Limborch for publication that he added the 'inscription singulier', which perhaps in his heart he meant to be a way of dedicating to his friend a 'libellus' intended for printing rather than an address on a personal letter.[2]

These observations allow us, in my opinion, to set right the judgement common among biographers, critics, and editors of Locke, that the *Epistola* was conceived and written as a personal letter addressed to Limborch.[3] But it should be

cation of *Some Thoughts concerning Education*, Locke expresses his inability to resist the persuasion of people he esteems highly when they entreat him to publish some writing of his, which, they maintain, though not intended for publication, would, if published, prove useful to its readers. Locke adds that this is an argument to which he will always be susceptible: 'will always be very prevalent with me': and that *always* seems to imply that he has already had occasion to yield to the persuasion of friends. And it is our view that this is precisely what occurred in the case of the *Epistola*, and Limborch's entreaty to be allowed to publish it.

[1] Gomarists, intransigent Calvinists, or Counter-Remonstrants were the names used to designate the followers of François Gomarus, who, born in Bruges in 1563, died at Groningen in 1641. Professor of Theology in several Dutch Universities, he had Arminius as a colleague at Leyden. The positions maintained by Arminius on the subjects of grace and predestination provoked fierce opposition from Gomarus. At the Synod of Dordrecht Gomarus played a decisive part in the formulation of the measures adopted against the Arminians.

[2] This of course is only a hypothesis. Limborch's statement: letter to Lady Masham *March 24th 1705*, MSS. R. L. III D. 16–54: is too explicit to be entirely rejected: 'voluitque nomina nostra sub literis cum titulo insertis habere.' But it is unlikely, not to say out of the question, that Locke prefixed that strange inscription to the *Epistola* in 1685, when, that is, the *Epistola* was written.

[3] This is the view, for instance, of Bourne, II, p. 34; Aaron, p. 22; Cranston, p. 259, not to mention others.

xxv

noted that in the Locke-Limborch correspondence there is nothing in favour of this supposition. The only evidence is that given by Limborch himself in the letter to Lady Masham, already quoted, written twenty years after the *Epistola*. When writing to Locke, on the other hand, Limborch, as we have seen, speaks of the *Epistola* as a *libellus de Tolerantia per modum epistolae scriptus*, and Locke himself, in writing to Limborch on the 6th June 1689 [1] refers to it as a *libellus* or *tractatus de Tolerantia:* thus showing that the *Epistola* was not, in spite of what Limborch later loved to claim, a personal letter.

It seems to me that we can conclude that the letter on Toleration, although born of a conversation between Locke and Limborch, was not, unlike the *Thoughts concerning Education*, written as a personal letter reproducing or recalling the arguments advanced in a private conversation between friends, but was a discourse intended, then or later, for printing as a real 'libellus de Tolerantia per modum epistolae scriptus', and therefore different, as much in intention as in tone and style, from a personal letter.[2]

To support this not unfounded conjecture one could advance the fact that in the play of the conversation, studded with frequent 'dices' and 'respondeo', the arguments are certainly not those held and discussed by Locke and Limborch. To the interlocutor in the *Epistola* are attributed polemical objections which Limborch could not have held, and which certainly he would not have been pleased to see attributed to him. In the conversation between the Dutch theologian and the English philosopher which was the origin of the *Epistola* the two took the same stand; while the interlocutor in the *Epistola* is assigned a negative and polemical stand against which Limborch's principles and opinions are

[1] MSS. R.L. Ba 256 L.

[2] Locke himself in the above-mentioned dedicatory letter to Edward Clarke, in: *Some Thoughts concerning Education*, posits a substantial difference in tone and style between the 'private conversation of two friends' and 'a discourse designed for publick view.'

allied with Locke's. Locke, then, does not merely speak with Limborch; but speaks also for Limborch in defence of the same arguments in favour of toleration. Did Limborch then lie to Lady Masham? It is not for me to say so. It seems to me, rather, that when twenty years after the *Epistola* had been written Limborch gave Lady Masham an account, not of the history of the *Epistola* but of the circumstances of Locke's life in Holland and of their friendly intercourse, Limborch fell into one of those common errors of transposition of time in which what actually happened is confused with the expectation: thus presenting the *Epistola* which Locke probably dedicated to him in 1689 as a letter addressed to him in 1685.

In Holland, a country freely open to all religions and 'grande arche des fugitifs'[1] but, because of this, extremely sensitive to the problem of mutual toleration among churches, the *Epistola* was received with a lively interest, even if with varying reactions. If the Catholics could not congratulate themselves on the anonymous treatise of Gouda which denied them the right to toleration, the non-Catholics, persecuted in France, threatened in England, attacked elsewhere, found in the *Epistola* an effective document in favour of the toleration which they invoked for their churches. Because the *Postscriptum* re-echoed the old arguments of Coornhert, revived by Arminius and supported by the Remonstrants in order to defend themselves against the accusation of having dismembered the Reformed Church,[2] the responsibility for publishing the *Epistola*, if not for its paternity, was attributed to the Remonstrants. Furthermore, the fact that the *Epistola* had been printed in Gouda by

[1] Bayle, *Dictionnaire*, art.: *Kuehline*.
[2] This was the accusation hurled at the Remonstrants at the Synod of Dordrecht by Gomarus and Hall. Thereafter the Remonstrants were regarded as schismatics and heretics. See: *Praestantium ac Eruditorum virorum Epistolae Ecclesiasticae et Theologicae*, 1704 (II ed. Limborch), p. 515. The arguments used by Hall and Gomarus are given in Hall, *Epîtres Mêlées*, Genève, 1627, tr. Jaquelot, pp. 501–507.

Iustus van den Hoeve, Limborch's publisher,[1] gave rise to the
belief that Limborch, chief pastor and theologian of the
Remonstrants, was not unconnected with its publication.[2]
But Limborch, pressed on all sides to reveal the name of the
author, parried the questions by saying that he did not know
a Remonstrant capable of writing such good Latin.[3] But even
if Limborch denied any active part in the publication of the
Epistola, it was clear that the author was to be found, if not
among the Dutch Remonstrants, then certainly among the
refugees sheltered by the Remonstrants. Basnage de Beauval in
recording the *Epistola* in his *Histoire des Ouvrages des Sçavans*,[4] gave

[1] Gouda or Tergou was Limborch's first pastoral seat, occupied by
him from 1657 to 1667.

At Gouda, Limborch had published in 1664 a *Lykpredicatie over het salig'*
afsterven d. Joannes Owens dien. J. Chr. in de remonstr. gem. tot Gouda in den Heere
ontslapen den 19en Juni 1664. Gouda, Bij Corn. Dijvoort, 1664.

At the Van den Hoeve Press, after 1671, Limborch had published first,
a *Korte historie van het Synode van Dordrecht, Vervattende eenige aenmerkelijke en*
noyt voor-henen ontdekte bijsonderheden: begrepen in brieven van Mr. John Hales en
Dr. Walter Balcanqual van den Koning van Groot-Brittanie gesonden op de gemelde
Synode; geschreven aan den Heere Dudley Carlton Ambassadeur des selven Konings aen
hare Hoog-Mog. Vertaelt uyt het Engelsch. Gouda, W. v. d. Hoeve, 1671; and in
1687, the *De veritate religionis christianae amica collatio cum erudito Judaeo.* Goudae,
Apud Justum ab Hoeve, 1687. (ULA.2454.0.14).

[2] Limborch to Locke, B. L. MSS, Locke, *April 25th 1690*, C. 14 f. 44–45 l.,
in which Limborch referred to the pressure Guenelon brought to bear
on him to reveal the name of the author of the *Epistola*, asking whether
it were not Limborch himself: 'ille me urgebat, primo an ego autor
[sic] essem.'

[3] Limborch to Locke, B. L. MSS, Locke, *June 15th 1689*, C. 14 f. 24 l.

[4] Henri Basnage de Beauval (1656–1710), was born at Rouen, and fled
to Holland a few years before the Edict of Nantes. In 1687, Bayle, now ill
and exhausted by the enormous task he had undertaken, entrusted

Introduction

the author simply as Jacques Bernard, cousin of Le Clerc, who had repaired to Holland after the revocation of the Edict of Nantes and had been received as Protestant minister in Gouda. Very soon, particularly among the circle of Limborch's friends, Locke also began to be mentioned as the author. However the secret was not destined to last long: an indiscretion on the part of Limborch [1] allowed Guenelon to make the name of the author as well-known in Holland as he thought it was in England.[2] Locke's indignation at Limborch's lack of discretion [3] persuaded his Dutch friends

him with the continuation of his *Nouvelles de la République des Lettres* which de Beauval took over under the title: *Histoire des Ouvrages des Sçavans*, printed by Leers in Rotterdam. In the Sept.-Nov. 1689 issue of the *Histoire*, de Beauval, himself the author of a *Tolérance des Réligions*, Rotterdam, 1684. (KBsG 1114 F. 12) gave a graceful summary of the *Epistola*, pp. 20–26, noting a point of contact with Bayle's *Commentaire*, pp. 23–24, and attributing the *Epistola* to Jacques Bernard.

Bayle, in note F under the *Sainctes* heading in his *Dictionnaire*, referring to certain contemporary writings on Toleration, records among others 'la lettre latine imprimée à Tergou l'an 1689. M. de Beauval la donna à M. Bernard, ministre français fort connu par ses ouvrages, et très capable d'avoir fait un livre d'un raisonnement si bien poussé; mais on a su très-certainement qu'il n'en était point l'auteur, et l'on croit qu'il la faut donner à un Anglais.' It is not unlikely that, once the secret was out, Bayle had been informed of the true identity of the author of the *Epistola*. In which case, only his personal respect for Locke, Bayle, *Lettres Choisies*, III, p. 861, can have prevented him from disclosing his name either in the first or second edition of the *Dictionnaire*. Bayle makes mention of the *Epistola* in Bayle, *Oeuvres Diverses*, II p. 729; IV, p. 850.

A list of references to Locke in the works of Bayle, in: *Pierre Bayle, Le Philosophe de Rotterdam. Etudes et Documents, publiées sous la direction de Paul Dibon.* Elsevier, Amsterdam, 1959, p. 96.

[1] See above, p. XXIII, n. 1.

[2] This was what Guenelon wrote to Locke, *April 18th 1690*, B. L. MSS. Locke C. 11. f. 32 French.

[3] Locke to Limborch, April 22nd 1690, B. L. MSS Locke. C.24. f.155, Latin: 'Rumours are abroad about this pamphlet which, having troubled me not at all when its authorship was unknown, now threaten to ruin me...' Cranston, p. 332.

to make prudent use of Locke's name,[1] and to try to keep a secret which was now no longer hidden from anybody.

The *Epistola* was made known outside the borders of Holland, although the English translation had already appeared, by an abridged version which the Remonstrant Le Clerc inserted in Volume XV of the *Bibliothèque Universelle et Historique* of December 1689. 'On a peu vu de livres qui aient traité ce sujet en si peu de mots, et avec tant de netteté et de force que celui-ci' concluded Le Clerc in his report.[2] In order to excite the interest of readers in the anonymous Latin treatise on toleration Le Clerc was the first to send to the 'République des Lettres' the announcement that the *Epistola* had already been translated and published in English and in Dutch, and that it would perhaps be translated also into French.[3]

The *Epistola* was translated into English by William Popple [4]

[1] Limborch to Locke, *May 12th 1690*, B. L. MSS. Locke. C. 14 f. 46 Latin. Guenelon to Locke, *June 20th 1690*, ibid. C. 11 f. 34 French. See also King, II, 306 seqq., 310 seqq.

[2] *Bibliothèque*, Art. XIV, pp. 402–412.

[3] 'Ce livre a si fort plu en Angleterre, et ici, qu'on l'a traduit d'abord en Anglois, et en Flamand. Il est déjà imprimé en ces deux langues, et peut être qu'on le verra encore en François.' *Bibliothèque*, p. 412. That volume XV of the *Bibliothèque* came out after Popple's English translation is made clear by what Le Clerc himself writes: 'On avoit résolut de mettre ce petit Ouvrage dans le Tome précédent, mais l'ayant oublié, je ne sais pas comment, on le met ici.' p. 402. To the *abrégé* of vol. xxv, which had already been prepared, Le Clerc had prefixed this brief statement, excusing the delay, and at the end, had put as a sort of concluding note, the announcement of the appearance of the English translation. We must remember that vol. XV only appeared in the winter of 1690.

[4] William Popple, an English merchant, avowed Socinian, author of a *Rational Catechism*, 1687, and other Unitarian works. When Locke was appointed as a Commissioner for Trade in 1696, Popple was appointed Secretary of the Board of Trade. Contrary to Bourne's supposition, Bourne II, p. 154, Popple's friendship with Locke must date from before the translation of the *Epistola*, and must therefore go back to the years before Locke's exile.

A

LETTER

CONCERNING

Toleration :

Humbly Submitted, *&c.*

By A: Lock

LICENSED, *Octob.* 3. 1689.

LONDON,

Printed for *Awnsham Churchill,* at the *Black*
Swan at *Amen-Corner.* 1689.

and published in London by A. Churchill with the title *A Letter concerning Toleration* in the month of November 1689, having been licensed by the censor on 3rd October of the same year.[1]

There are two differences worthy of mention between the Gouda edition and the English translation of the *Epistola:* the addition in the English translation of a preface *To the Reader*, and the deletion of the 'inscription singulier' which had appeared on the title-page of the Latin edition. I will have to return to these two points later.

The translation by Popple renders very faithfully the sense of the original,[2] and in no case, or so it seems to me, does Popple distort Locke's thoughts. In any case Locke followed Popple's work very closely, and we can be sure that he was

[1] It is perfectly possible that the *Letter* only came out in 1690. Le Clerc, in fact, both in the *Eloge*, p. LII, and in the *Avertissement* to the *Oeuvres Diverses*, p. IV, and later in Moreri, *Locke*, repeats that the *Epistola*, 'traduit en Anglois... fut imprimée deux fois à Londres en 1690'; 'il s'en fit deux éditions à Londres en 1690.' This hypothesis is not refuted by Le Clerc's announcement of the English translation of the *Epistola* in vol. XV of the *Bibliothèque* of the year 1689. First, because vol. XV only appeared in the winter of 1690, and secondly because the announcement of the translation is a later addition to the *abrégé*, already prepared, of vol. XIV. Besides, even if the *Letter* had come out in January or even February, Jonas Proast still had quite enough time – in a month and more – to write the 28 pages he devoted to the refutation of the *Letter: The Argument of the Letter concerning Toleration, Briefly consider'd and Answer'd.* Oxford, Printed at the Theatre, for George West, and Henry Clement, Book-sellers in Oxford. A.D. 1690., hence he could very well date the letter of dedication: *To my very Worthy Friend Mr. ......* March 27th 1690 and have the *Imprimatur* of Jonathan Edwards, Vice-Can. Oxoniense April 9th 1690.

[2] Bourne, II, p. 54, is of the same opinion, though nowadays there is a tendency to question the faithfulness of the translation to the Latin text. Ebbinghaus, p. VII, writes: 'Dagegen ergab der Vergleich mit der lateinischen Originalausgabe von 1689 eine ganze Reihe von Abänderungen und Fehlern in Popples Arbeit.' Certainly, if we make a word-by-word comparison of the English and Latin texts, it is not difficult to discover some inaccuracies and a few liberties, but it does not appear that Popple's translation 'in alcuni casi' distorts 'il senso originale' as is claimed by Klibansky, p. VIII.

not unconnected with the translation.[1] That afterwards Locke stated that this translation was made 'without *his* privity', is another question. In a codicil to his will, by which he bequeathed to the Bodleian Library in Oxford those of his works which had appeared anonymously or under a pseudonym, Locke in fact wrote that the *Epistola* had been translated into English 'without *his* privity'.[2] However this declaration is disproved by other evidence which can be deduced from the Locke-Limborch correspondence.

I have already said that in a letter dated *6th May 1689* Limborch gave Locke the news that the *Epistola* had been published.[3] In the same letter Limborch promised to urge the booksellers to send copies of the *Epistola* and of *De Pace Ecclesiastica* by Samuel Strimesius to England as soon as possible; but that in the meantime he was trying to send Locke a few copies of both books by the first ship leaving for London. Having received them Locke thanked Limborch on 6th June: 'gratias tibi ago pro exemplaribus tractatus de Tolerantia et Pace Ecclesiastica quae mihi misisti'. But immediately afterwards

[1] See the argument given at greater length in the following pages.
[2] Here is the passage from the codicil concerning the donation of the three *Letters concerning Toleration* to the Bodleian Library: 'I do hereby give to the public library of the University of Oxford, these following books; that is to say: three letters concerning Toleration, the first whereof I writ in Latin, and was published at Tergou in Holland 1689, under the title *Epistola de Tolerantia*, and afterwards translated into English, without my privity. 2nd. *A second Letter concerning Toleration*, printed for Awnsham and John Churchill, 1690. 3rd. *A Third Letter for Toleration, to the author of the third letter concerning Toleration*, printed for Awnsham and John Churchill, 1692...' B. L. MSS. Locke, b. 5/14, dated September 15th 1704. The codicil of Mr. Locke's will relating to his works is reproduced by King, II, 51–53. Coste, *Eloge*, XXVIII, says of the *Epistola* that it was 'traduit quelque temps après en Anglois à l'insû de M. Locke.' Locke's statement, confirmed by Coste, has given grounds for believing that the *Epistola* was translated into English 'without Locke himself knowing.' Christophersen, p. 15.
[3] See p. XXI, n. 2.

he made this unexpected revelation to Limborch: 'In vertendo de Tolerantia libello aliquem Anglum jam jam occupatum intelligo'.[1] On 10th September the translation was finished: '*Epistola de Tolerantia* jam in anglicanum sermonem versa est'.[2]

Locke therefore knew perfectly well that 'aliquem Anglum' had translated the *Epistola* into 'anglicanum sermonem'. Moreover it was Locke himself who gave Popple the copy used for the translation. In fact, in the same letter of 10th September Locke complained that he could not yet find in the London bookshops the treatise Limborch had promised to send with all dispatch: 'Miror', writes Locke, 'Bibliopolam vestrorum vel nostrorum negligentiam. *Epistolam de Tolerantia* et Strimesium *De Pace Ecclesiastica* apud nos nullibi reperire possum venalem'.

If, therefore, Locke himself gave Popple one of the copies received from Limborch, and if the translation had been made before the *Epistola* could be obtained from the booksellers in England, why did Locke declare that the same translation had been made 'without *his* privity'? Must we believe that the mania for secrecy had made Locke, in this case, 'positively mendacious?' [3] To me it seems more likely that when giving Popple a copy of the *Epistola* to read Locke characteristically did not reveal the fact that he was the author.[4] When Popple, therefore, having finished his reading, told Locke of his intention to translate the *Epistola* into English, Locke,

[1] Locke to Limborch, MSS.R.L. B.a. 256 1. (*Familiar Letters*, p. 331).

[2] Locke to Limborch, MSS.R.L. B.a. 256 0 (*Lettres Inédites*, p. 190.) Rather inaccurately, given the possibilities of confusion in the reader's mind between the finishing of the translation and its publication, Bourne translates this passage: 'The English translation of the *Epistola de Tolerantia* is just appeared.' Bourne, II, p. 159.

[3] Cranston, p. 320.

[4] The secret, presumably, cannot have lasted very long, since when Locke was constrained to reply to Jonas Proast's attack, with the *Second Letter concerning Toleration*, London, A. & J. Churchill, 1690, he could scarcely avoid revealing both to Popple and his publishers the true identity of the author of the *Epistola*.

having refused all rights over the 'libellus' could not then oppose, as in fact he did not oppose, his friend's proposal; even if, for his part, he did not encourage it. If this is the case, as seems probable, Locke was perfectly right in saying that the *Epistola* was translated and published 'without *his* privity', in so far as he did not mean without his knowledge, as Coste says,[1] but without his consent,[2] given that, having denied being the author, he was not called upon to give his consent.

I have already said that Popple's English translation had a short preface which had not appeared in the Gouda Latin edition. That it was Popple who added this preface seems clear from the statement in it 'I have translated it into our language.' This statement also throws on to the translator the responsibility for the famous sentence which Lord King used as the epigraph for his *Life of John Locke:* 'Absolute liberty, just and true liberty, equal and impartial liberty, is the thing that we stand in need of.' It has been said that Locke 'never believed in absolute liberty,' and it follows that he could not have written such a sentence.[3] The appeal for absolute

[1] Coste, *Eloge*, XXVIII, quoted above, p. XXXII, n. 2.

[2] For the interpretation of 'privity' as 'consent' see the word *privity* in *The Oxford English Dictionary*, 1961, Vol. III, in which in Note 5 the words 'privity' and 'consent' are shown as having the same meaning. This was common usage in Locke's time. On the other hand, the term 'privity' is applied, ibid. Note 6, to 'any relation between two parties recognised by law,' and it is clear that no such relation between two parties is possible without a previous agreement and the mutual consent of both.

[3] Gough, p. 191; Cranston, p. 260.

It is generally agreed that it was Popple who added the Preface to the *Letter;* see: *A Letter concerning Toleration, Advertissement* London, 1800; Bourne, II, 154; Aaron, 293, n. 1; Christophersen, p. 15; Gough, *A Letter*, p. X and p. 124, note; Gough, p. 191; Cranston, pp. 260, 327, n. 1; and others. It must however be observed that Locke denies no one the right to profess whatever religion he believes right for the salvation of his soul. Locke would be the last to deny this fundamental right of man. Nor does Locke deny to any church the right to be tolerated by other churches;

religious liberty, or rather for absolute toleration, seems in fact more in conformity with the aspirations of the Unitarian Popple, disappointed by the limitations of the Act of Toleration,[1] than with the convictions of Locke. Moreover, Locke could not deny Popple the right to add to an anonymous treatise which he was putting into English a preface for which Popple himself, in his capacity as translator, took the responsibility. This does not mean that Locke, although denying that he was the author of the *Epistola*, could not advise Popple to delete those strange initials which had appeared in the Gouda edition, and which Locke, in his heart, must have considered too dangerous. The initials in fact did not appear in the English version edited by Popple. Nor is it impossible that Locke, following the work Popple was doing, should have checked the translation and inspired the preface. Of this, in fact, there is incontestable proof.

At the beginning of Popple's preface we read that the *Epistola* 'first printed in Latin this very year, in Holland, has already been translated both into Dutch and French.' Now it cannot be held that French and Dutch translations appeared

he prescribes to all the duty of mutual toleration. The limitation which Locke imposes is possible only on the political level, in so far as the magistrate, in consideration of the ends for which the political society has been constituted, may find himself unable to allow toleration of certain churches, not because of their religious professions, but because of the political implications of these professions. Toleration, therefore, is denied at the point when the interests of the State impinge on those of individuals or groups. But they are excluded from toleration not for their religious convictions – the magistrate having no authority in this sphere – but for the political behaviour resulting from these convictions. Interpreted in this sense, the sentence: Absolute liberty, etc. could equally well be Popple's or Locke's. Hence, perhaps, the caution of certain critics in attributing this famous utterance to Popple.

[1] The Toleration Act of 1689 in fact excluded from toleration, together with the Catholics, all those who denied the Trinity, therefore, expressly, the Socinians or Unitarians. Hence Popple's disappointment, for he was himself a Socinian

between the very early days of May 1689, the time of the publication of the *Epistola*, and 3rd October of the same year, the day on which the English translation with the preface which Popple had added was licensed by the censor.

In fact the French translation did not appear until 1710, the work of Le Clerc, who included it in *Oeuvres Diverses de Monsieur J. Locke*.[1] In the *Avertissement* Le Clerc provided the valuable clarification: 'on a cru rendre service au curieux si l'on joignit ici la fameuse lettre de M. Locke sur la Tolérance, qui n'avait pas encore paru en notre langue.' The fact that the French translation did not appear before 1710 is confirmed by Coste who states unequivocally that the *Epistola* 'a été traduite en français et imprimée à Rotterdam en 1710.' [2]

Some believe that it was Le Clerc's abridgment of the *Epistola* in volume XV of the *Bibliothèque Universelle et Historique* which led Popple to make his mistake.[3] This view is mistaken. Volume XV appeared after Popple's translation, and Le Clerc made it clear that he already knew about this translation: 'Ce livre,' writes Le Clerc, 'a si fort plu en Angleterre, et ici, qu'on l'a traduit d'abord en anglais et en flamand. Il est déjà imprimé en ces deux langues, et, peut-être, qu'on le verra encore en français.' [4] One must therefore reject the view that Popple was referring to Le Clerc's abridgment. If anything it was Popple's preface which led Le Clerc into error. As we

---

1. *Oeuvres Diverses de Mr. Jean Locke*, Rotterdam 1710; *Letter sur la Tolerance*, pp. 1-140. A second edition with additional letters and writings appeared in 1732 under the title *Oeuvres Diverses de Mr. Locke, nouvelle edition considerablement augmentee*, 2 voll. Amsterdam, 1732. The *Lettre sur la Tolerance* appears on pages 1-123 of vol. I. We shall always refer to this edition.

[2] Coste, *Eloge*, p. XXXIII, n. 1.

[3] Christophersen, p. 15.

[4] *Bibliothèque*, p. 412.

have seen Le Clerc makes no mention of the French translation, but following Popple's lead, states that the *Epistola* had been translated into Dutch before it appeared in English. Some years later, in the *Eloge*, Le Clerc rectifies this error by making no mention of the Dutch translation;[1] nor can any reference to this translation be found in the *Avertissement* printed at the beginning of the *Oeuvres Diverses*, in which his French translation appeared. 'Elle, [the *Epistola de Tolerantia*] Le Clerc says merely, n'eut pas plutôt vu le jour qu'un de ses amis la traduisit en anglais.' [2]

Contrary, therefore, to what is written in the *Preface*, neither a French nor a Dutch translation appeared before the English version published by Popple. In my researches in libraries in Holland I did not find a Dutch translation of 1689.

In the University Library of Leyden, however, there is a *Verzameling van eenige Verhandelingen over de verdraagzaamheid en Vrijheid van Godsdienst*, te Amsterdam, bij Jacob ter Beek en Isaak Tirion, boekverkoopers, MDCCXXXIV,[3] in which, with other writings on Toleration, is also the *Epistola: Een Brief Aangaande Verdraagzaamheid. Geschreven door Joannes Locke.* Uit het Latijn vertaald. Tweede Druk.

In his preface the editor says that the *Epistola* was published at Gouda in Latin in 1689 and was 'shortly afterwards translated into Dutch, but since, as is often the destiny of such booklets, it has gone completely out of circulation. Many people who highly esteem the works of Locke know it only by name. This made me decide to reprint this Letter, after having it read and corrected in many places by one of my friends.'

Therefore it would seem that we have finally found, if not the Dutch translation to which Popple refers, at least its second,

---

[1] *Eloge*, p. LII.
[2] See: *Oeuvres Diverses, Avertissement*, p. V; Moreri, art. *Locke*, Le Clerc writes 'On traduisit ce petit Ouvrage en Anglois, et il fut imprimé deux fois à Londres en 1690. On l'a imprimé en François avec ses *Oeuvres Posthumes* en 1710.'
[3] ALB. 597, G. 15.

Introduction

corrected edition, if it were not that a quick glance at this
translation, presented in the *Verzameling*, is sufficient to
show that the reference to the booklet which had gone astray
or become unobtainable, but which is not described even
in the most summary way; and the recourse to the friend
who had revised the old translation, are the usual tricks
once played by publishers and of which Bayle, who knew
them very well, had already found cause to complain.[1]
The Dutch translation of the *Verzameling*, in fact, contrary
to the explicit statement of the editor, is later and not earlier
than the translation of Popple and is based on the English
text, not the Latin one.

This example will suffice.

Latin text: 'Tolerantia eorum qui de rebus religionis
LG. 9   diversa sentiunt Evangelio et rationi adeo
               consona est, ut monstro simile videatur,
               homines in tam clara luce caecutire. Nolo ego
               hic aliorum incusare fastum et ambitionem;
               aliorum intemperiem et zelum caritate et
               mansuetudine destitutum ....'

Dutch text: 'De Verdraagzaamheid der zulken die in zaken
Verz. p. 7-8   van Godsdienst verscheidentlyk gevoelen, komt
               met het Evangelium van Jezus Christus en met
               de reden zo wel overeen, dat het meer dan
               wonder schynt dat de menschen zo blint
               kunnen wezen, dat ze de noodzakelykheit en
               het voordeel daar van niet konnen zien, in
               zulk een helder licht. Ik wil hier de trotsheit
               en eerzucht van zommigen, de quaadaardigheit
               en liefdelozen en onzachtmoedigen yver van
               anderen niet beschuldigen.'

English text: 'The Toleration of those that differ from others
SE. p. 7   in matters of religion, is so agreeable to the
               Gospel of Jesus Christ, and to the genuine
               reason of mankind, that it seems monstrous

[1] Bayle, *Dictionnaire*, II, 469; II, 476; III, 479; V, 146, VI, 235; etc.

for men to be so blind as not to perceive the necessity and advantage of it in so clear a light. I will not here tax the pride and ambition of some, the passion and uncharitable zeal of others.'

Forty years after the *Verzameling* there appeared, again in Amsterdam, another collection of works on toleration under the title: '*De Vrijheid van Godsdienst in de Burgerlijke Maatschappij... door de zeer vermaande mannen Locke, Noodt, Barbeyrac, Hoadly en Drieberge*. Amsterdam, By J. Andoll, MDCCLXXIV.[1] Here also, when dealing with the *Epistola*, which comes first in the collection, the editor states that it was translated into Dutch immediately after it had been published in Gouda and that in 1734 it appeared in the first edition of the collection.[2] But having traced this first edition in the University Library of Leiden,[3] I found out that it is but a second edition of the *Verzameling* of 1734, of which it repeats the title: *Verzameling van eenige Verhandelingen over de Verdraagzaamheit en Vrijheid van Godsdienst. Bijeengebracht door Isaac Tirion*. Amsterdam 1734. [...] *J. Locke. Een Brief Aangaande Verdraagzaamheit. Uit het Latijn vert. 2° dr.* Nor is the Dutch translation of the *Epistola*, presented in the edition of 1774, more than a reprint of the one published in 1734,[4] as appeared from a confrontation of the texts. We have already seen that the translation of the *Verzameling* of 1724, contrary to the statements of the Editor, is not the

[1] ULA. 291 F 24.

[2] *De Vryheid van Godsdienst* etc. *Bericht van den uitgever:* 'ook wordt dezelve terstond in 't Nederduitsch overgezet en uitgegeven; welke uitgave in den jare 1734, verbeterd en in de eerste uitgave der Verzamelinge, die we thans herhalen, weder in 't licht kwam.'

[3] ALB. 597, G. 15.

[4] Bayle, *Dictionnaire*, art. *Paréus*, still on the subject of the 'finesses' of the book-sellers, writes: 'Mais combien de fois s'émancipent-ils de rafraîchir la première page de leurs livres, afin de les faire passer pour nouveaux? Quelquefois même ils osent marquer que c'est une nouvelle édition...'

second corrected edition of the Dutch translation of the *Epistola*, but a translation based on the English text of Popple. We have reason to believe, therefore, that notwithstanding the devices of the editors of the *Verzameling* of 1734 and of the *Vrijheid* of 1774, no Dutch translation of the *Epistola* appeared before 1734.

Furthermore, just as Bayle was on the alert against the tricks of the editors, so Le Clerc, making amends for the error into which he had fallen, both in the *Eloge* and in the *Avertissement* of the *Oeuvres Diverses*, no longer refers to a Dutch translation. Nor does Coste mention it. This seems sufficient to exclude the fact that the French and Dutch translations of the *Epistola* appeared before the English translation.

Who, therefore, gave Popple cause to say in his preface that the *Epistola* had been already translated into French and Dutch? Locke, and none other than Locke. In his letter of 10th September to Limborch, in which he informed his friend that the English translation had just been finished, Locke asked Limborch to send him the French and Dutch translations: 'Traductionem et Gallicam et Belgicam quaeso mittas:' [1] a clear sign that Limborch had informed Locke that these two translations had appeared, or at least had led him to believe that they would appear soon. Very probably Limborch was referring to the abridgments which were due to be published. In any case Locke understood 'traductionem' and asked that they should be sent to him. In the meantime he mentioned them to Popple, and Popple included the information in the preface.

The observations I have made allow us to conclude that Locke not only gave Popple the copy sent to him by Limborch and on which Popple based the English translation, but also that Locke followed Popple's work very closely and certainly checked Popple's translation.

[1] Locke to Limborch, September 10th 1689, MSS.RL. B.a 256 0; *Lettres Inédites*, p. 190.

Popple's English version therefore deserves, in my opinion, the same, if not even more, respect and confidence as the Gouda Latin edition. The Latin text was written in a language which only a few years later Locke regretted he did not know very well,[1] and was published by Limborch in Locke's absence, Locke having then been back in England for some months. Popple's translation on the other hand restored the *Epistola* to Locke's mother tongue, was made under Locke's eyes, and was without doubt published after checking by Locke himself. It is a fact that Le Clerc, a good latinist and a good translator from English, preferred to base his French translation on Popple's English version rather than on the Latin text published in Gouda. I repeat in this case the example already given.

Latin text: LG. 9	'Tolerantia eorum qui de rebus religionis diversa sentiunt Evangelio et rationi adeo consona est, ut monstro simile videatur, homines in tam clara luce caecutire. Nolo ego hic aliorum incusare fastum et ambitionem; aliorum intemperiem et zelum caritate et mansuetudine destitutum....'
French text: O.D. p. 10–11	'La Tolérance en faveur de ceux qui diffèrent des autres en matière de Réligion, est si conforme à l'Evangile de Jésus-Christ, et au sens commun de tous les Hommes, qu'on peut regarder comme des monstres ceux qui sont assez aveugles, pour n'en voir pas la nécessité et l'avantage, au milieu de tant de lumière qui les environne. Je ne m'arrêterai pas ici à taxer l'orgueil et l'ambition des uns, la passion et le zèle peu charitable des autres.'
English text: SE. p. 7	'The Toleration of those that differ from others in matters of religion, is so agreeable to the Gospel of Jesus Christ, and to the genuine

[1] *Familiar Letters*, in *L.'s W.* III[1] p. 625.

XLI

reason of mankind, that it seems monstrous for men to be so blind as not to perceive the necessity and advantage of it in so clear a light. I will not here tax the pride and ambition of some, the passion and uncharitable zeal of others.'

It appears to me that the fact that Le Clerc preferred Popple's English translation to the original Gouda text published by Limborch is indicative of the fact that even in the circle of the Dutch Remonstrants, dominated by the authority of Limborch who maintained he was the addressee of the *Epistola*, the English version immediately took the place of the Latin text, as it evidently seemed a more suitable vehicle of Locke's style and thought. In any case Le Clerc knew quite well that the *Epistola* 'n'eut pas plutôt vu le jour qu'un de ses amis la traduisit en Anglais;' [1] it could therefore not have been difficult for him to imagine, knowing from personal experience the care with which Locke followed the translations which his friends made of his writing;[2] how much more care Locke must have devoted to following the translation of the

[1] *Oeuvres Diverses, Avertissement*, p. V. This statement of Le Clerc's confirms what we said above, p. XXX, n. 4, on the subject of the friendship between Locke and Popple, that it must certainly antedate the translation of the *Epistola*.

[2] In the *Bibliothèque Universelle et Historique de l'année 1688*, vol. VIII, pp. 49–142, Le Clerc published an *Extrait d'un Livre Anglois qui n'est pas encore publié, intitulé Essai Philosophique concernant l'Entendement, où l'on montre quelle est l'étendue de nos connoissances certaines, et la manière dont nous y parvenons. Communiqué par Monsieur Locke*, a translation of an abridgement of the *Essay concerning Human Understanding* made by Le Clerc under the careful guidance of Locke himself, who had a good knowledge of French. Coste, too, *Avertissement*, p. X, states that in translating the *Essay* into French, he enjoyed the assistance of Mr. Locke 'qui a eu la bonté de revoir ma traduction,' and adds: 'si j'ai pris quelque liberté [...] ç'a toujours été sous le bon plaisir de Mr. Locke.' p. XIV.

Our hypothesis that Locke concealed his authorship of the *Epistola* from Popple is not contradicted by the fact that Locke followed and revised his translation.

Epistola from an acquired language to his own mother tongue. To support this is the fact that while Le Clerc took a number of liberties with the abridgment of the *Essay on Human Understanding* which he translated under Locke's eyes, and which Locke must have authorised,[1] he took no similar liberties with the translation of the *Letter* made after Locke's death. In this he kept scrupulously to the English text, translating it carefully word for word.

But if this observation, which may seem superficial and debatable, is not enough to support what I have said above, we can bring to mind two other very relevant facts.

In the codicil to his will, in which Locke bequeathed to the University Library in Oxford those of his works which had appeared anonymously or under a pseudonym, one can read:

'I do hereby give to the public library of the University of Oxford, these following books; that is to say: three letters concerning Toleration, the first whereof I writ in Latin, and was published at Tergou in Holland 1689, under the title *Epistola de Tolerantia*, and afterwards translated into English, without my privity. 2nd. *A second Letter concerning Toleration*, printed for Awnsham and John Churchill, 1690. 3rd. *A third*

[1] It is sufficient to compare the first sentence of the *Extrait* published by Le Clerc with that of the *Abstract of the Essay* published by King, II, p. 231, seqq., from Locke's manuscript:

Abstract, 'Lib. 1. In the thoughts I had had concerning the Understanding, I have endeavoured to prove that the mind is at first *rasa tabula*.'

Le Clerc translates:

Extrait, 'Livre Premier. Dans les pensées que j'ai eues, concernant nôtre Entendement, j'ai tâché d'abord de prouver que nôtre Esprit est au commencement ce qu'on appelle *tabula rasa*; c'est à dire, sans idées et sans connoissance.'

Accepting Coste's account of the matter, *Avertissement*, p. X, quoted above, p. XLII, n. 2, we must believe that these liberties taken by Le Clerc were authorized by Locke himself, who, evidently, so long as the original sense of his writing was respected, did not deny his translators a certain independence of interpretation and style, always necessary in the translating of another's thought into a different language.

Letter for Toleration, to the author of the third Letter concerning Toleration, printed for Awnsham and John Churchill, 1692. *Two Treatises of Government...* [1]

But John Churchill, Awnsham Churchill's heir, with whom his name had been connected since the time of the printing of the *Second Letter concerning Toleration,* quoted the passage concerning the three letters on toleration in these terms in the *Preface* to his 1st Collected Edition of Locke's Works published in 1714: 'I do hereby further give to the public Library of the University of Oxford, these following books; that is to say: *Three Letters concerning Toleration; Two Treatises of Government...*' [2]

The reference to the English translation which had been completed without Locke's privity is therefore entirely deleted by Churchill. This alteration in the sense of Locke's will would seem irresponsible if it did not, on the other hand, respect a truth of which John Churchill was aware. There is no doubt in fact that the part played by Locke in the publication of the first *Letter concerning Toleration* was no longer a secret in the Black Swan printing shop in Ave-Mary-Lane; [3] particularly after Locke had been obliged to reply to the attack by Jonas Proast [4] and had thus revealed to Popple

[1] BL. Mss. Locke. b 5/14. We have already reproduced the relevant passage from the codicil of Locke's will, in note 3, p. XXXII.
[2] *The Works of John Locke Esq., in Three Volumes.* London. John Churchill and Sam. Manship, MDCCXIV, in folio. vol. I. *To the Reader.*
[3] In 1690 Locke was well established in Churchill's printing house. Immediately after the first edition of the *Letter,* there came from Churchill's presses, in the space of a very few months, the *Two Treatises of Governement,* then the second corrected edition of the *Letter* (there is in fact a mention of the *Two Treatises* in the list of *Books lately printed for Awnsham Churchill* added at the end of the *Letter,* second edition) and finally the *Second Letter concerning Toleration,* which bears for the first time, beside the name of Awnsham, that of his heir and successor, John Churchill.
[4] Jonas Proast attacked the *Epistola* in an anonymous pamphlet: *The Argument of the Letter concerning Toleration, Briefly consider'd and Answer'd,* Oxford, Printed at the Theatre for George West, and Henry Clements, Booksellers in Oxford A.D. 1690. Under the pseudonym of Philantropus, Locke replied to Proast in *A second Letter concerning Toleration, to the author of*

A

LETTER

Concerning

TOLERATION.

by John Locke

LICENSED, *Octob.* 3. 1689.

The Second Edition Corrected.

LONDON, Printed for *Awnsham Churchill* at the *Black Swan* in *Ave-Mary Lane.*
MDCXC.

and to Churchill the secret which up to then had still hidden the identity of the *Letter*'s author.[1]

Indeed I venture to go so far as to suggest that when his secret had been revealed Locke decided to prepare personally a second edition of the *Letter* [2] intended, after Proast's attack, for wider circulation. This edition would include the amendments which Locke, a scrupulous editor,[3] thought necessary, but which Popple could no more include on his own initiative.

In any case it seems that the change in the codicil to Locke's will as quoted by John Churchill was not an irresponsible omission, but rather a timely clarification of fact which Locke himself seemed to have intended to remain únclarified.

In any case, even if Popple had translated the *Epistola* 'à l'insû de Mr. Locke' it is a fact that Locke did not repudiate this translation. In spite of the brief reference in his will, so different from the minute description of the other two

the *Argument of the Letter concerning Toleration, Briefly considered and answered.* London, Printed for Awnsham and John Churchill, at the Black Swan in Ave-Mary-Lane, near Pater-Noster-Row, MDCXC. Jonas Proast responded with *A Third Letter concerning Toleration, In Defence of the Argument of the Letter concerning Toleration, briefly consider'd and Answer'd.* Oxford, printed by L. Lichfield, for George West, and Henry Clements, Booksellers in Oxford, 1691. Locke replied once again with *A Third Letter for Toleration to the Author of the Third Letter concerning Toleration.* London. Printed for Awnsham and John Churchill at the Black Swan in Pater-Noster-Row, 1692.

Part of a *Fourth Letter for Toleration* appeared in *Posthumous Works,* London, J. Churchill, 1706, pp. 663–681. For a part omitted in the printing of this, see: King, II, 229–230. For the Locke-Proast controversy, see Bourne, II, 181–184, and Christophersen, p. 16 seqq.

[1] We have put forward the hypothesis that Locke at first concealed from both Popple and Churchill his authorship of the *Epistola.*

[2] Everything leads one to believe that this appeared in May–June 1690, that is, after Proast's pamphlet which had the *imprimatur* of April 9th 1690, and before the *Second Letter* of Locke, licensed on June 24th, 1690.

[3] It is sufficient to recall the enormous care with which he undertook the preparation of a definitive and corrected edition of the *Essay concerning Human Understanding* and the *Two Treatises of Government;* See: Laslett, *Introduction,* p. 10.

letters, Locke gave the Bodleian Library not only a copy of the *Epistola* [1] but also a copy of the first edition of the *Letter* translated by Popple. Still to-day in the famous Bodleian Library there is a volume of collected works, (shelfmark No. S 70 Th 1–5), bearing the inscription 'ex dono celeberrimi Viri Joannis Lock' (*sic*) which includes the three *Letters* on toleration numbered respectively 1, 3, 5, and intercalated with the replies of Jonas Proast. Locke would certainly have repudiated the translation of one of his books if it had been made without his knowledge or against his wishes, or if the translation had not faithfully reflected his thoughts and style. That Locke in fact recognised it confirms, in my opinion, the interpretation I gave of the expression 'without my privity', and proves, without a shadow of a doubt, that Popple's translation, supervised and approved by Locke, is rather a new edition in English language of the Latin 'tractatus' on toleration than an unauthorized translation of it.

THE LATIN TEXT

The Latin text of the *Epistola* which is printed here is the result of a collation of the text edited by Limborch (LG) and the text established by Hollis (ML) and immediately thereafter reproduced in the seventh edition of Locke's Works (HE). The former is clearly out-of-date and in places incorrect, but was taken direct from Locke's manuscript, even if we do not know how far Limborch was a faithful editor; the latter is more modern and correct but introduces a number of amendments which can only be justified and rendered acceptable by a careful comparison with LG. In comparing the two texts I found 136 variants, although for the most part the differences are slight. The present edition therefore does not reproduce either of these texts, but is based on a collation of both, with a view to establishing a version which is correct and accurate. This is not to say that I have made no amend-

[1] Still to be seen in the Bodleian Library, N. 67. Th.

XLVI

LETTERS CONCERNING TOLERATION

BY IOHN LOCKE

LONDON, PRINTED FOR A. MILLAR, H. WOOD-
FALL, I. WHISTON AND B. WHITE, I. RIVINGTON,
L. DAVIS AND C. REYMERS, R. BALDWIN, HAWES
CLARKE AND COLLINS, W. IOHNSTON, W. OWEN,
S. CROWDER, T. LONGMAN, B. LAW, C. RIVINGTON,
E. DILLY, R. WITHY, C. AND R. WARE, S. BAKER,
T. PAYNE, A. SHUCKBURGH, M. RICHARDSON
MDCCLXV

—— FOR ON EARTH,
WHO AGAINST FAITH AND CONSCIENCE CAN BE HEARD
INFALLIBLE? YET MANY WILL PRESUME:
WHENCE HEAVIE PERSECUTION ——

ments to the text, but I have kept such amendments to a minimum, and where I have felt it necessary I have noted them in foot-notes. At the same time I avoided burdening the notes with the modifications I have made in the spelling and punctuation. For these I hope the following notes will suffice as explanation.

So far as spelling is concerned I have discarded the frequent contractions found in LG such as *ę* for *ae* and *verū* for *verum;* to the forms *Quum, quodcunque, utcunque* I preferred *Cum, quodcumque, utcumque;* I have written *auctor, auctoritas, caritas* in place of *author, authoritas, charitas;* in place of the abbreviated forms such as *Resp., Respub.* I have written *Respondeo* and *Res pubblica,* (written always as two words). I have written *se ipsis* in place of *seipsis;* but I have preferred *quidni* to *quid ni,* and, on the other hand, *eo usque* to *eousque.*

I have left as they are all words formed in the post classical period such as *charactere, cerevisiam, authoritativa, carithativa, mahumedano, Lutheranorum* etc, or derived from the Greek in later years, such as *methodus, hypocrisis, theopneusta, porismata, idiosincrasia, adiaphoras, synaxi.*

The difference between LG and ML = HE in the use of diphthongs is noteworthy. In LG we usually find *paena, caetus, faeneratur, infaelicis* etc., in ML = HE on the other hand we find *coelum, coecus, foeneratur, infoelicis* etc. I have made corrections where necessary using the correct spelling according to the authority of A. Ernout et A. Meillet, *Dictionnaire Etymologique de la Langue Latine. Histoire des mots.* Paris, Klincksieck, 1959.[4]

I have deleted signs of quantity and accents.

I have given uniformity to the rather improper use of capital and small letters: leaving capital letters for adjectives formed from proper nouns such as *Christiana,* but spelling *haeretica* with a small letter. I have used a capital for *Numen* where it stands clearly for *Deus,* and I have used a capital for direct speech after a colon.

I have made amendments only where I felt it necessary

to make the sentence lighter and the reading easier.

In all cases I have retained the brackets of the Gouda text as these seem to me to reflect the intention and the style of Locke's writing. In the same way I have retained the italics of LG, reproduced in ML and HE, as the abundant use of this print is typical of Locke's works.

I have at times found it necessary to write differently, but not to change, the numeration of paragraphs, substituting where necessary the ordinal numbers for the cardinal and vice-versa. In such cases I have written the number in square brackets.

The footnotes refer only to the most noteworthy variants met with in the collation of LG with ML, HE, or existing between these editions and earlier ones.

As HE is an exact reproduction of ML, I have referred only to the latter, except in the very rare cases when HE differs from ML.

Other small modifications or corrections are not mentioned in the notes. They do not prejudice the fidelity of the text.

I have abstained from correcting the frequent liberties taken by Locke with grammar and syntax, nor have I thought it necessary to refer to them in the notes. What good would it do? Locke's Latin, we know, was not faultless,[1] but we are interested in how Locke wrote, and not how he should or could have written.

In the margins I have given the page numbers of LG and ML. The reader will therefore have in front of him at one and the same time this edition, the variants between it and the editions of Limborch and Hollis, and the page-numbers of LG and HL.

THE ENGLISH TEXT

There are two textual traditions of the *Letter concerning Toleration*: one founded on the first edition of 1689 established

[1] W. von Leyden, *Introduction*, p. 89.

by CM and followed by GH; the other founded on the second edition of 1690 and followed by HL and LW.

Comparing PE, SE, CM, HL,LW, GH, I found 98 variants without counting those of little importance. Most of the variants are common to a group of texts, such as PE, CM, GH on the one hand, and SE, HL, LW on the other; the others appear in only one of the texts compared.

The present edition for the most part follows SE, which I have reason to consider reflects most faithfully Locke's style and thought, and benefits from a number of amendments from HL and LW. At the same time I have in some places preferred to follow PE, CM, GH. In some other places I have preferred to use my own reading, but in such cases I have given a reference in the notes.

I have also followed SE for typography. I have reproduced exactly, wherever it appears, the italic print frequently used by Locke, but not always reproduced in HL, and entirely deleted by LW and by GH.

I have retained the use of brackets; but I have put back into the text the biblical references which PE and SE put in the margin.

I have corrected a number of obvious printing errors found through the various texts, and I have brought up-to-date, where I thought it necessary, the spelling and punctuation, without making any reference in the notes. As in the Latin text I have brought some order to the abuse of capitals found in PE and SE.

I have deleted the passage from Cicero, *De Officiis*: 'Ea est summa ratio et sapientia boni civis commoda civium non divellere, atque omnes aequitate eadem continere' which does not appear in PE and SE, but appears as an inscription in CM and GH.

In the foot-notes I have referred only to the most important differences found between all the texts and the present edition, and also between the present edition and individual texts.

As I did in the Latin text, I have placed in the margins the

XLIX

page numbers of the basic editions of the English text, i.e. PE, SE, HL.

I have not thought it opportune to point out the differences, although existing, between the Latin text and its English translation. First of all because on no occasion do these differences alter the sense of the original Latin text; secondly because this sort of remark could be multiplied to infinity without any useful result. Locke's Latin, in fact, is certainly not of the most correct, whereas Popple's English has nuances which differ from those of modern English. Although today we can understand either of them, we would risk, when confronting the two texts word for word basing our comparison *not* on the Latin and English of learned men at the end of the 17th century, but on our actual knowledge of Latin and English. This is exactly what happened to Ebbinghaus. He reproached Popple with having translated *enim* by *but* (p. 129, n. 14), thinking precisely of the limited and limitative sense which this conjunction has today, and not of the much more extensive meaning which it had at the time of Popple, when it stood not only for the adversative *sed*, as well as *verum, autem, tamen* etc. and the prepositions *praeter, nisi, nisi vero* etc., but also for the coordinate causal conjunctions *nam, enim* etc. It is sufficient to open at random his *Two Treatises of Government* to see how Locke himself uses and abuses *but* in all these meanings.

On the other hand nobody can pretend that a translation should be a close copy of the original, and after all, as long as the intention of the author is not altered we cannot deny a minimum of liberty to the translator *car on ne peut pas s'en passer*, as observed Coste: an accurate though inelegant translator of Locke.

EPISTOLA DE TOLERANTIA

A LETTER CONCERNING TOLERATION

For the explanation of the abbreviations of works collated used in footnotes to the Latin and English texts, see pp. XII–XIII.

TO THE READER

The ensuing Letter concerning Toleration *first printed in* Latin *this* PE1/SE1
very year in Holland, *has already been translated both into* Dutch *and* HL32
French. *So general and speedy an approbation may, therefore, bespeak its*
favourable reception in England. *I think, indeed, there is no nation under*
heaven in which so much has already been said upon that subject as ours. But
yet, certainly, there is no people that stand in more need of having something
further both said and done amongst them, in this point, than we do. |

    Our government has not only been partial in matters of religion; but those PE11
also who have suffered under that partiality, and have therefore endeavoured
by their writings to vindicate their own rights and liberties, have for the most
part done it upon narrow principles, suited only to the interests of their own
sects.

    This narrowness of spirit, on all sides, has undoubtedly been the principal
occasion of our miseries and confusions. But, whatever have been the occasion,
it is now high time to seek for a thorough cure. We have need of more generous
remedies than what have yet been made use | *of, in our distemper. It is neither* SE11
Declarations of Indulgence *nor* Acts of Comprehension, *such as*
have yet been practised or projected amongst us, that can do the work. The
first will but palliate, the second increase our evil. |

    Absolute liberty, just and true liberty, equal and impartial liberty, is the PE111
thing that we stand in need of.* Nor, though this has indeed been much talked
of, I doubt it has not been much understood; I am sure not at all practised,
either by our governors towards the people in general, or by any dissenting
parties of the people towards one another.

    I cannot, therefore, but hope that this Discourse, *which treats of that sub-*
ject, however briefly, yet more exactly than any we have yet seen, demonstrating

---

* HL, LW: ABSOLUTE ... OF.

To the Reader

both the equitableness and practicableness of the thing, will be esteemed highly seasonable by all men that [1] *have souls large enough to prefer the true interest of the public before that of a party.*

It is for the use of such as are already so spirited, or to inspire that spirit into those that are not, that I have translated | it into our language. But the PEIV *thing itself is so short that it will not bear a longer preface. I leave it, therefore, to the consideration of my countrymen, and heartily wish they may make the use of it that it appears to be designed for.*

[1] LW: who

EPISTOLA DE TOLERANTIA

LG3/ML3 Quaerenti tibi, vir clarissime, quid existimem de mutua
inter Christianos tolerantia, breviter respondeo, hoc
mihi videri praecipuum verae ecclesiae criterium.
Quicquid enim alii jactant de locorum et nominum
antiquitate, vel cultus splendore; alii de disciplinae
reformatione; omnes denique de fide orthodoxa (nam
sibi quisque orthodoxus est), haec et hujusmodi possunt
esse hominum de potestate, et imperio contendentium,
potius quam ecclesiae Christi notae. Haec omnia qui
possidet, si caritate destituatur, si mansuetudine, si
benevolentia erga omnes in universum homines, nedum
LG4 fidem Christianam profitentes, | nondum est Christia-
nus. *Reges gentium dominantur iis; vos autem non sic, Luc.* xxii,
dicit suis Salvator noster. Alia res est verae religionis, non
ad externam pompam, non ad dominationem ecclesiasticam, non denique ad vim; sed ad vitam recte
pieque instituendam natae. Primo omnium vitiis suis,
fastui et libidini propriae bellum debet indicere, qui in
ecclesia Christi velit militare; alias sine vitae sanctimo-
nia, morum castitate, animi benignitate et mansuetudine, frustra quaerit sibi nomen

A LETTER CONCERNING TOLERATION

Honoured Sir

Since you are pleased to inquire what are my thoughts about PE1/SE1
the mutual toleration of Christians in their different professions HL33
of religion, I must needs answer you freely, that I esteem that
toleration to be the chief characteristic mark of the true
church. For whatsoever some people boast of the antiquity of
places and names, or of the pomp of their outward worship;
others, of the reformation of their discipline; all, of the
orthodoxy of their faith (for every one is orthodox to himself):
these things, and all others of this nature, are much rather
marks of men striving for power and empire over one another,
than of the church of Christ. Let any one have | never so true a SE2
claim to all these things, yet if he be destitute of charity,
meekness, and good-will in general towards all mankind, even
to those that are not Christians, he is certainly yet short of
being a true Christian himself. *The kings of the Gentiles exercise*
lordship over them, said our Saviour to his disciples, *but you shall not be*
so, *Luke*, XXII. 25. The business of true religion | is quite another PE2
thing. It is not instituted in order to the erecting of [2] an
external pomp, nor to the obtaining of ecclesiastical dominion,
nor to the exercising of compulsive force, but to the regulating
of men's lives, according to the rules of virtue and piety.
Whosoever will list himself under the banner of Christ, must
in the first place, and above all things, make war upon his own
lusts and vices. It is in vain for any man to usurp the name of

[2] HL, LW: erecting an

7

Christianum. *Tu conversus confirma fratres tuos, Luc.* XXII, dixit Petro Dominus noster. Vix enim quisquam persuadebit, se de aliena salute mire esse sollicitum, qui negligens est suae: nemo sincere in id totis viribus incumbere potest, ut alii fiant Christiani, qui religionem Christi animo suo nondum ipse re vera amplexus est. Si enim Evangelio, si Apostolis credendum sit, sine *caritate,* LG5 sine *fide* | *per amorem,* non per vim, *operante* nemo Christianus esse potest. An vero illi qui religionis praetextu alios vexant, lacerant, spoliant, jugulant, id amico et benigno animo agant, ipsorum testor conscientiam; et tum denique credam, cum zelotas illos videro amicos et familiares suos, contra Evangelii praecepta manifeste peccantes, eundem in modum corrigere; suosque asseclas vitiorum corruptela tactos, et sine mutatione in meliorem frugem certo perituros, ferro et igne aggredi; et amorem suum atque salutis animarum desiderium omni crudelitatis et tormentorum genere testari. Si enim, uti prae se ferunt, caritate et studio erga eorum animas, bonis exuant, corpora mutilent, carcere et paedore macerent, vita denique ipsa privent, ut fideles, ut salvi fiant, cur *scortationem, versutiam, malitiam* et alia quae *ethnicismum* tam aperte sapiunt, testante Apostolo, *Rom. I,* LG6 impune inter suos | grassari permittunt? Cum haec et hujusmodi magis adversentur Dei gloriae,

Christian, without holiness of life, purity of manners, benigni-
ty and meekness of spirit. [3] *Thou, when thou art converted, strengthen
thy brethren,* said our Lord to Peter, *Luke* XXII. 32. It would, indeed,
be very hard for one that appears careless about his own
salvation to persuade me that he were extremely concerned
for mine. For it is impossible that those should sincerely and
heartily apply themselves to make other people Christians,
who have not really embraced the Christian religion in their
own hearts. | If the Gospel and the apostles may be credited, no SE3
man can be a Christian without *charity,* and without *that faith
which works,* not by force, but by *love.* Now, I appeal to the
consciences of those that persecute, torment, destroy, and kill
other men upon pretence of religion, whether they do it out
of friendship and kindness towards them or no? And I shall
then indeed, and not until then, believe they do so, when I
shall see those fiery zealots correcting, in the same manner,
their friends and familiar acquaintance for the manifest sins
they commit against the precepts of the Gospel; when I shall
see them persecute with fire and sword the members of their
own communion that are tainted with enormous vices, and
without amendment are in danger of eternal perdition; and
when I shall see them thus express their love and desire of the
salvation of their souls by the infliction of torments, and
exercise of all manner of | cruelties. For if it be out | of a princi- HL34/PE3
ple of charity, as they pretend, and love to men's souls, that
they deprive them of their estates, maim them with corporal
punishments, starve and torment them in noisome prisons,
and in the end even take away their lives, I say, if all this be
done merely to make men Christians, and procure their
salvation, why then do they suffer *whoredom, fraud, malice, and
such-like enormities,* which (according to the Apostle) *Rom. I.* mani-
festly | relish of heathenish corruption, to predominate so SE4
much and abound amongst their flocks and people? These,
and such-like things, are certainly more contrary to the glory

[3] PE, CM, HL, LW, GH, insert: *Let every one that nameth the name of Christ,
depart from iniquity.* (2 *Tim.* II.19). *Thou, when ....*

9

ecclesiae puritati et saluti animarum, quam erronea quaevis contra decisiones ecclesiasticas conscientiae persuasio, vel in externo cultu defectus cum vitae innocentia conjunctus? Cur inquam zelus ille pro Deo, pro ecclesia, pro salute animarum usque ad vivicomburium ardens, flagitia illa et vitia moralia Christianae professioni, omnibus fatentibus, e diametro contraria, sine castigatione, sine animadversione praeteriens, in corrigendis opinionibus, iisque plerumque de rebus subtilibus, vulgique captum superantibus, vel caerimoniis ingerendis unice haeret et omnes nervos suos ML4 intendit? Quae inter dissidentes | de his rebus sanior sit, quaeve schismatis vel haereseos rea, an dominatrix vel succumbens pars, tum demum constabit, cum de causa separationis judicabitur. Qui enim Christum sequitur LG7 ejusque amplectitur doctrinam, | et jugum suscipit, etiamsi patrem et matrem, patrios ritus, coetum publicum, et quoscumque demum homines relinquat, non est haereticus.

Quod si [1] sectarum divortia adeo adversentur saluti animarum, *adulterium, scortatio, immunditia, lascivia, simulacrorum cultus, et his similia,* non sunt minus opera carnis, de quibus diserte pronuntiat Apostolus, quod *qui talia agunt regni Dei heredes non erunt, Gal. v.* Haec igitur non minore cura et industria, quam sectae, penitus extirpanda, si quis de regno Dei sincere sollicitus in ejus pomeriis ampliandis sibi elaborandum serio judicaverit. Quod si quisquam aliter fecerit, et dum erga diversa sentientes immitis et implacabilis est, peccatis interim et morum vitiis,

[1] LG: se

of God, to the purity of the church, and to the salvation of souls, than any conscientious dissent from ecclesiastical decisions,[4] or separation from public worship, whilst accompanied with innocence of life. Why then does this burning zeal for God, for the church, and for the salvation of souls; burning, I say, literally, with fire and faggot; pass by those moral vices and wickednesses without any chastisement,which are acknowledged by all men to be diametrically opposite to the profession of Christianity, and bend all its nerves either to the introducing of ceremonies, or to the establishment of opinions, which for the most part are about nice and intricate matters, that exceed the capacity of ordinary understandings? Which of the parties contending about these things is in the right, which of them is guilty of schism or heresy, whether those that domineer or those that suffer, will then at last be manifest, when the causes of their separation comes to be judged of. He, certainly, that follows Christ, embraces his doctrine, and bears his yoke, though he forsake both father and mother, separate from the public assemblies and ceremonies of his country, or whomsoever or whatsoever else he relinquishes, will not then be judged a heretic. |

Now, though the divisions that are amongst sects should SE₅ be allowed to be never [5] so obstructive of the salvation of | souls; yet, nevertheless, *adultery, fornication, uncleanliness, lascivi-* PE4 *ousness, idolatry, and such like things, cannot be denied to be works of the flesh,* concerning which the apostle has expressly declared that *they who do them shall not inherit the kingdom of God. Gal.* v. Whosoever, therefore, is sincerely solicitous about the kingdom of God, and thinks it his duty to endeavour the enlargement of it amongst men, ought to apply himself with no less care and industry to the rooting out of these immoralities than to the extirpation of sects. But if any one do otherwise, and whilst he is cruel and implacable towards those that differ from him in opinion, he be indulgent to such iniquities and immoralities

[4] CM, HL, LW: decision   [5] LW: ever

Christiano nomine indignis, parcat, palam demonstrat, quantumvis crepat ecclesiam, se aliud, non Dei regnum quaerere.

LG8 Si quis animam, cujus salutem vehementer | optat, velit per cruciatus etiam nondum conversam, efflari, mirabor sane, et mirabuntur, puto, mecum alii; sed ita tamen, ut nemo uspiam credat hoc ab amore, a benevolentia, a caritate posse proficisci. Si homines igne et ferro ad certa dogmata amplectenda sunt impellendi et ad externum cultum vi cogendi, de quorum tamen moribus nulla omnino sit quaestio; si quis heterodoxos ita convertat ad fidem, ut cogat ea profiteri, quae non credunt, et permittat ea agere quae Evangelium Christianis, fidelis sibi non permittit; illum velle numerosum coetum eadem secum profitentium non dubito; velle autem ecclesiam Christianam, quis est qui potest credere? Non mirandum igitur, si utantur armis militiae Christianae non debitis, qui (quicquid prae se ferunt) pro vera religione et ecclesia Christiana non militant. Si, uti Dux salutis nostrae, sincere cuperent salutem animarum, | illius insisterent vestigiis, et optimum illud principis pacis sequerentur exemplum, qui satellites suos non ferro, non gladio, non vi armatos, sed Evangelio, sed pacis nuntio, morum sanctitate et exemplo instructos, ad subjugandas gentes, et in ecclesiam cogendas emisit. Cui tamen, si vi et armis convertendi essent infideles, si armato milite ab erroribus revocandi caecutientes,[2] vel obstinati mortales, paratior erat caelestium legionum exercitus,

LG9

---

[2] LG: excutientes

as are unbecoming the name of a Christian, let such a one talk
never [6] so much of the church, he plainly demonstrates by
his actions that it is another kingdom he aims at, and not the
advancement of the kingdom of God.

That any man should think fit to cause another man, whose
salvation he heartily desires, to expire in torments, and that
even in an unconverted state, would, I confess, seem very
strange to me, and, I think, to any other also. But nobody,
surely, will ever believe that such a carriage can proceed from
charity, love, or good-will. | If any one maintain that men ought SE6
to be compelled by fire and sword to profess certain doctrines,
and conform to this | or that exterior worship, without any HL35
regard had unto their morals; if any one endeavour to convert
those that are erroneous unto the faith, by forcing them to
profess things that they do not believe, and allowing them to
practise things that the Gospel does not permit, it cannot be
doubted indeed but [7] such a one is desirous to have a numerous assembly joined in the same profession with himself; but
that he principally intends by those means to compose a truly
Christian church, is altogether incredible. It is not, therefore,
to be wondered at if those who | do not really contend for the PE5
advancement of the true religion, and of the church of Christ,
make use of arms that do not belong to the Christian warfare.
If, like the Captain of our salvation, they sincerely desired the
good of souls, they would tread in the steps and follow the
perfect example of that Prince of peace, who sent out his
soldiers to the subduing of nations, and gathering them into
his church, not armed with the sword, or other instruments
of force, but prepared with the Gospel of peace, and with the
exemplary holiness of their conversation. This was his method.
Though if infidels were to be converted by force, if those that
are either blind or obstinate were to be drawn off from their
errors by armed | soldiers, we know very well that it was much SE7
more easy for him to do it with armies of heavenly legions,

[6] CM: ever   [7] CM, HL: that

quam cujvis ecclesiae patrono, quantumvis potenti, suae sunt cohortes.

Tolerantia eorum qui de rebus religionis diversa sentiunt Evangelio et rationi adeo consona est, ut monstro simile videatur, homines in tam clara luce caecutire. Nolo ego hic aliorum incusare fastum et ambitionem; aliorum intemperiem et zelum caritate et mansuetudine destitutum: haec sunt vitia humanis LG10 rebus forsan non eximenda, | sed tamen ejusmodi, ut ea nemo sibi aperte imputari velit; nemo paene est, qui his in transversum actus aliena et honesta specie tectis non quaerat laudem. Ne quis autem persecutioni et saevitiae parum Christianae curam rei publicae et legum observantiam praetexat, et e contra ne alii religionis nomine sibi quaerant morum licentiam et delictorum impunitatem; ne quis, inquam, vel ut fidus principis subditus, vel ut sincerus Dei cultor, sibi vel aliis imponat; ante omnia inter res civitatis et religionis distinguendum existimo, limitesque inter ecclesiam et rem publicam | ML5 rite definiendos. Si hoc non fit, nullus[2b] litibus modus statui potest, inter eos, quibus salus animarum, aut rei publicae, vel re vera cordi est, vel esse simulatur.

Res publica mihi videtur societas hominum solummodo ad bona civilia conservanda promovendaque constituta. |

LG11 Bona civilia voco, vitam, libertatem, corporis integritatem et indolentiam, et rerum externarum possessiones, ut sunt latifundia, pecunia, supellex, etc.

[2b] ML, nullis

14

than for any son of the church, how potent soever, with all his dragoons.

The toleration of those that differ from others in matters of religion, is so agreeable to the Gospel of Jesus Christ, and to the genuine reason of mankind, that it seems monstrous for men to be so blind as not to perceive the necessity and advantage of it in so clear a light. I will not here tax the pride and ambition of some, the passion and uncharitable zeal of others. These are faults from which human affairs can perhaps scarce ever be perfectly freed; but yet such as nobody will bear the plain imputation of, without covering them with some specious colour; and so pretend to commendation, whilst they are carried away by their own irregular passions. But, however, that some may not colour their spirit of persecution and unchristian cruelty with a pretence of care of the public weal and observation of the laws; and that others, under pretence of religion, may not seek impunity for their libertinism and licentiousness; in a word, that none may impose either upon himself or others, by | the pretences of loyalty and obedience PE6 to the prince, or of tenderness and sincerity in the worship of God I esteem it above all things necessary to distinguish exactly the business of civil government | from that of religion, SE8 and to settle the just bound that lie between the one and the other. If this be not done, there can be no end put to the controversies that will be always arising between those that have, or at least pretend to have, on the one side,[8] a concernment for the interest of men's souls, and, on the other side, a care of the commonwealth.

The commonwealth seems to me to be a society of men constituted only for the procuring, preserving, and advancing of [9] their own *civil interests*.

Civil interests [10] I call life, liberty, health, and indolency of body; and the possession of outward things, such as money, lands, houses, furniture, and the like.

[8] CM: ... on the one side, a care of the Commonwealth.
[9] CM, HL, LW, GH: advancing their   [10] LW: interest

15

Harum rerum ad hanc vitam pertinentium possessionem justam omni universim populo et singulis privatim subditis, sartam tectam servare officium est magistratus civilis, per leges ex aequo omnibus positas; quas si quis contra jus fasque violare vellet, illius comprimenda est audacia metu poenae; quae consistit vel in ablatione, vel imminutione eorum bonorum, quibus alias frui et potuit et debuit. Cum vero nemo parte bonorum suorum sponte mulctatur, nedum libertate, aut vita; ideo magistratus ad poenam alieni juris violatoribus infligendam vi armatus est, toto scilicet subditorum suorum robore.

Quod vero ad bona haec civilia unice spectat tota LG12 magistratus jurisdictio, | et in iis solis curandis promovendisque terminatur et circumscribitur omne civilis potestatis jus et imperium; nec ad salutem animarum aut debet aut potest ullo modo extendi, sequentia mihi videntur demonstrare.

Primo. Quia animarum magistratui civili plus quam aliis hominibus non demandatur cura. Non a Deo; quia nusquam apparet Deum hujusmodi auctoritatem hominibus in homines tribuisse, ut possint alios ad suam religionem amplectendam cogere. Non ab hominibus magistratui potest ejusmodi tribui potestas; quia nemo potest ita salutis suae aeternae curam abjicere, ut quam alter, sive princeps sive subditus, praescripserit cultum vel fidem necessario amplectatur. Quia nemo ex alterius praescripto potest, si vellet, credere; in fide autem consistit verae et salutiferae religionis vis et efficacia. Quicquid enim ore profiteris,

16

| It is the duty of the civil magistrate, by the impartial HL36 execution of equal laws, to secure unto all the people in general, and to every one of his subjects in particular, the just possession of these things belonging to this life. If any one presume to violate the laws of public justice and equity, established for the preservation of these [11] things, his presumption is to be checked by the fear of punishment, consisting in [12] the deprivation or diminution of those civil interests, or goods, which otherwise he might and ought to enjoy. But seeing no man does willingly suffer himself to be punished by the deprivation of any part of his goods, and much less of his liberty or life, therefore | is the magistrate SE9 armed with the force and strength of all his subjects, in order to the punishment of those that violate any other man's rights.

Now that the whole jurisdiction of the magistrate reaches only to these civil concernments, and that all civil power, right, and dominion, is bounded and confined to the only care of promoting these things; and that it | neither can nor ought PE7 in any manner to be extended to the salvation of souls, these following considerations seem unto me abundantly to demonstrate.

First. Because the care of souls is not committed to the civil magistrate, any more than to other men. It is not committed unto him, I say, by God; because it appears not that God has ever given any such authority to one man over another, as to compel any one to his religion. Nor can any such power be vested in the magistrate by the *consent of the people*, because no man can so far abandon the care of his own salvation as blindly to leave to the choice of any other, whether prince or subject, to prescribe to him what faith or worship he shall embrace. For no man can, if he would, conform his faith to the dictates of another. All the life and power of true religion consist in the inward [13] and full persuasion of the mind; and faith is not faith without believing. Whatever profession we make, to

[11] PE, CM, GH: those   [12] PE, CM, GH: of
[13] CM, HL: outward

17

LG13 quicquid in cultu externo praestes, | si hoc et verum esse,
et Deo placere tibi intus in corde penitus persuasum
non sit, non modo non prodest ad salutem, verum e
contrario obest; quandoquidem hoc modo aliis peccatis, religione expiandis, addatur cumuli loco ipsius
religionis simulatio Numinisque contemptus, cum eum
Deo O. M. offers cultum quem credis ipsi displicere.

Secundo. Cura animarum non potest pertinere ad
magistratum civilem, quia tota illius potestas consistit
in coactione. Cum autem vera et salutifera religio
consistit in interna animi fide, sine qua nihil apud Deum
valet; ea est humani intellectus natura, ut nulla vi
externa cogi possit. Auferantur bona, carceris custodia,
vel cruciatus poena urgeatur corpus, frustra eris, si
his suppliciis mentis judicium de rebus mutare velis.

Sed dices: Magistratus potest argumentis uti, adeoque
LG14 heterodoxos in veritatem | pertrahere et salvos facere.
Esto; sed hoc illi cum aliis hominibus commune est:
si doceat, si instruat, si argumentis errantem revocet,
facit sane quod virum bonum decet; non necesse est
magistratui vel hominem vel Christianum exuere.
Verum aliud est suadere, aliud imperare; aliud argumentis, aliud edictis contendere. Quorum hoc est po-
ML6 testatis civilis, illud benevolentiae | humanae. Cujvis
enim mortalium integrum est monere, hortari, erroris
arguere, rationibusque in sententiam suam adducere;
sed magistratus proprium est edictis jubere, gladio
cogere. Hoc est igitur quod dico, scilicet quod potestas
civilis non debet articulos fidei, sive dogmata,

whatever outward worship we conform, if we are not | fully SE10
satisfied in our own mind that the one is true, and the other
well pleasing unto God, such profession and such practice, far
from being any furtherance, are indeed great obstacles to our
salvation. For in this manner, instead of expiating other sins
by the exercise of religion, I say, in offering thus unto God
Almighty such a worship as we esteem to be displeasing unto
him, we add unto the number of our other sins those also of
hypocrisy, and contempt of his Divine Majesty.

In the second place. The care of souls cannot belong to the civil
magistrate, because his power consists only in outward force;
but true and saving religion consists in the inward persuasion
of the mind, without which nothing can be acceptable to God.
And such is the nature of the understanding, that it cannot be
compelled to the belief of anything by outward force. Confis-
cation of estate, imprisonment, torments, nothing of that
nature | can have any such efficacy as to make men change the PE8
inward judgment that they have framed of things.

It may indeed be alleged that the magistrate may make use
of arguments, and thereby draw the heterodox into the way
of truth, and procure | their salvation. I grant it; but this is HL37
common to him with other men. In teaching, instructing, and
redressing the erroneous by reason, he may certainly do what
becomes any good man to | do. Magistracy does not oblige SE11
him to put off [14] either humanity or Christianity; but it is one
thing to persuade, another to command; one thing to press
with arguments, another with penalties. This the [15] civil
power alone has a right to do; to the other good-will is
authority enough. Every man has commission to admonish,
exhort, convince another of error, and, by reasoning, to draw
him into truth; but to give laws, receive obedience, and compel
with the sword, belongs to none but the magistrate. And upon
this ground, I affirm that the magistrate's power extends not
to the establishing of any articles of faith, or forms of worship,

[14] PE: of   [15] PE, CM, GH: This civil

vel modos colendi Deum lege civili praescribere. Si enim nullae adjunctae sint poenae, legum vis perit; si poenae intententur, eae plane ineptae sunt et minime ad persuadendum accommodae.

LG15   Si quis ad animae salutem dogma aliquod, | vel cultum amplecti velit, ex animo credat oportet dogma illud verum esse, cultum autem Deo gratum et acceptum fore, hujusmodi vero persuasionem animis instillare poena quaevis minime potest. Luce opus est ut mutetur animi sententia, quam nullo modo feneratur corporis supplicium.

Tertio. Cura salutis animarum nullo modo pertinere potest ad magistratum civilem; quia dato quod legum auctoritas et poenarum vis efficax esset ad convertendas hominum mentes, hoc tamen nihil prodesset ad salutem animarum. Cum enim unica sit vera religio, una quae ad beatas ducit sedes via, quae spes majorem hominum illuc perventurum numerum, si ea mortalibus data esset conditio, ut quisque posthabito rationis et conscientiae suae dictamine, deberet caeca mente amplecti principis sui dogmata, et eo modo Deum colere, prout patriis legibus statutum est? Inter tot varias principum | de religione opiniones necesse esset viam illam strictam portamque angustam, quae ducit in caelum, paucis admodum esse apertam, idque in una solum regione: et, quod maxime hac in re absurdum esset et Deo indignum, aeterna felicitas vel cruciatus unice deberetur nascendi sorti.

by the force of his laws. For laws are of no force at all without penalties, and penalties in this case are absolutely impertinent, because they are not proper to convince the mind. Neither the profession of any articles of faith, nor the conformity to any outward form of worship (as has been already said), can be available to the salvation of souls, unless the truth of the one, and the acceptableness of the other unto God, be thoroughly believed by those that so profess and practise. But penalties are no way capable to produce such belief. It is only light and evidence that can work a change in men's opinions; and that [16] light can in no manner proceed from corporal sufferings, or any other outward penalties. |

In the third place. The care of the salvation of men's souls SE12 cannot belong to the magistrate; because, though the rigour of laws and the force of penalties were capable to | convince PE9 and change men's minds, yet would not that help at all to the salvation of their souls. For there being but one truth, one way to heaven, what hope is there that more men would be led into it if they had no other rule to follow but [17] the religion of the court, and were put under the necessity to quit the light of their own reason, to [18] oppose the dictates of their own consciences, and blindly to resign themselves up to the will of their governors, and to the religion which either ignorance, ambition, or superstition had chanced to establish in the countries where they were born? In the variety and contradiction of opinions in religion, wherein the princes of the world are as much divided as in their secular interests, the narrow way would be much straitened [19]; one country alone would be in the right, and all the rest of the world put [20] under an obligation of following their princes in the ways that lead to destruction; and that which heightens the absurdity, and very ill suits the notion of a Deity, men would owe their eternal happiness or misery to the places of their nativity.

[16] PE, CM, GH: which   [17] PE, CM, GH: had non rule but
[18] PE, CM, GH: and   [19] PE, SE, CM, HL: straitned
[20] SE: world would be put

Haec inter multa alia, quae ad hanc rem afferri pote-
rant, sufficere mihi videntur ut statuamus omnem rei
publicae potestatem versari circa bona illa civilia et intra
rerum hujus saeculi curam contineri, neque ea quae ad
futuram spectant vitam ullatenus attingere.

Nunc videamus quid sit ecclesia. Ecclesia mihi videtur
societas libera hominum sponte sua coeuntium ut
Deum publice colant eo modo quem credunt Numini
acceptum fore ad salutem animarum.

Dico esse *societatem liberam et voluntariam*. Nemo nascitur
alicujus ecclesiae membrum, alias patris avorumque |
LG17 religio jure hereditario simul cum latifundiis ad quem-
que descenderet et fidem quisque deberet natalibus: quo
nihil absurdius excogitari potest. Ita igitur se res habet.
Homo nulli a natura obstrictus ecclesiae, nulli addictus
sectae: illi se sponte adjungit societati ubi veram religionem cultumque Deo gratum credit se invenisse.
Spes vero salutis quam illic reperit, uti unica intrandi in
ecclesiam causa, ita pariter et illic manendi mensura.
Quod si deprehenderit aliquid vel in doctrina erroneum,
vel in cultu incongruum, eadem libertate, qua ingressus
est, semper ipsi pateat exitus necesse est; nulla enim esse
possunt indissolubilia vincula, nisi quae cum certa
vitae aeternae expectatione conjuncta sunt. Ex membris
ita sponte sua et hunc in finem unitis coalescit ecclesia.

Sequitur jam ut inquiramus quae sit ejus potestas,
quibusque legibus subiecta.

LG18   Quandoquidem nulla, quantumvis | libera, aut levi de
causa instituta societas, sive ea fuerit literatorum, ad
ML7 philosophiam; sive mercatorum, ad negotia; | sive
denique feriatorum hominum,

These considerations, to omit many others that might have been urged to the same purpose, seem unto me sufficient to conclude | that all the power of civil government relates only SE13 to men's civil interests, is confined to the care of the things of this world, and hath nothing to do with the world to come.

Let us now consider what a church is. A church, then, I take to be a voluntary society of men, joining themselves together of their own accord in | order to the public worshipping of God HL38 in such manner as they judge acceptable to him, and effectual to the salvation of their souls.

I say it is a free and voluntary society. Nobody is born a member of any church; otherwise the religion of parents would descend unto children by the same | right of inheritance PE10 as their temporal estates, and every one would hold his faith by the same tenure he does his lands, than which nothing can be imagined more absurd. Thus, therefore, that matter stands. No man by nature is bound unto any particular church or sect, but every one joins himself voluntarily to that society in which he believes he has found that profession and worship which is truly acceptable to God. The hope of salvation, as it was the only cause of his entrance into that communion, so it can be the only reason of his stay there. For if afterwards he discover anything either erroneous in the doctrine or incongruous in the worship of that society to which he has joined himself, why should it not be as free for him to go out as it was to enter? No member | of a religious society can be SE14 tied with any other bonds but what proceed from the certain expectation of eternal life. A church, then, is a society of members voluntarily uniting to this [21] end.

It follows now that we consider what is the power of this church, and unto what laws it is subject.

Forasmuch as no society, how free soever, or upon whatsoever slight occasion instituted, whether of philosophers for learning, of merchants for commerce, or of men of leisure for

[21] GH: that

23

ad mutuos sermones et animi causa, subsistere potest, quin ilico dissoluta interibit, si omnibus destituta sit legibus; ideo necesse est ut suas etiam habeat ecclesia: ut loci, temporisque quibus coetus coeant, habeatur ratio; ut conditiones proponantur, quibus quisque in societatem, vel admittatur, vel ab ea excludatur; ut denique munerum diversitas, rerumque constituatur ordo, et his similia. Cum vero spontanea sit (uti demonstratum est) coalitio ab omni vi cogente libera, sequitur necessario, quod jus legum condendarum penes nullum nisi ipsam societatem esse potest, vel illos saltem (quod eodem recidit) quos ipsa societas assensu suo comprobaverit.

Sed, dices, vera esse non potest ecclesia, quae Episco- LG19 pum vel Presbyterium | non habet, gubernandi auctoritate, derivata ab ipsis usque Apostolis, continua et non interrupta successione instructum.

Primo. Rogo ut edictum ostendas, ubi hanc legem ecclesiae suae posuit Christus; nec vanus ero, si diserta in re tanti momenti verba requiram. Aliud suadere videtur effatum illud: *Ubicumque duo vel tres congregantur in meo nomine, ibi ego ero in medio ipsorum.* An coetui, in cuius medio erit Christus, aliquid deerit ad veram ecclesiam, ipse videris. Nihil certe illic deesse potest ad veram salutem: quod ad rem nostram sufficit.

Secundo. Videas, quaeso, illos, qui rectores ecclesiae a Christo institutos et successione continuandos volunt, in ipso limine inter se dissentientes. Lis haec necessario

mutual conversation and discourse, no church or company, I say, can in the least subsist and hold together, but will presently dissolve and break to [22] pieces, unless it be regulated by some laws, and the members all consent to observe some order. Place and time of meeting must be agreed on; rules for admitting and excluding members must be established; distinction of officers, and putting things into a regular course, and such-like, cannot be omitted. But since the joining together of several members into this church-society, as has already been demonstrated, is absolutely free and spontaneous, it necessarily follows that the right of making its laws can | belong to none but the society itself; or, at least (which is the PE11 same thing), to those whom the society by common consent has authorized thereunto. |

Some, perhaps, may object that no such society can be said SE15 to be a true church unless it have in it a bishop or presbyter, with ruling authority derived from the very apostles, and continued down to the present times by an uninterrupted succession.

To these I answer: *In the first place*, let them show [23] me the edict by which Christ has imposed that law upon his church. And let not any man think me impertinent, if, in a thing of this consequence, I require that the terms of that edict be very express and positive: For the promise he has made us, that *wheresoever two or three are gathered together in his name, he will be in the midst of them, Matt.* XVIII. 20, seems to imply the contrary. Whether such an assembly want anything necessary to a true church, pray do you consider. | Certain I am that nothing can be there HL39 wanting unto the salvation of souls, which is sufficient to [24] our purpose.

Next, pray observe how great have always been the divisions amongst even those who lay so much stress upon the divine institution and continued succession of a certain order of rulers in the church. Now, their very dissension unavoidably

---

[22] GH: in   [23] PE, SE, CM, LW: shew   [24] HL, LW: for

permittit eligendi libertatem, scilicet ut integrum sit cujvis ad eam accedere, quam ipse praefert ecclesiam. |

LG20   Tertio. Habeas quem tibi praeponas necessariumque credis hujusmodi longa serie designatum rectorem; dum ego interim me isti societati adjungo, in qua mihi persuasum est repertum iri ea quae ad animae salutem sunt necessaria. Itaque utrique nostrum salva est (quam poscis) ecclesiastica libertas, nec alteruter alium habet quam quem ipse sibi elegerit legislatorem.

Quandoquidem autem de vera ecclesia adeo sollicitus es, obiter hic rogare liceat, an non verae ecclesiae Christi magis conveniat eas communionis conditiones stabilire, quibus illa et illa sola continentur, quae Spiritus Sanctus in Sacra Scriptura clare et disertis verbis docuit, ad salutem esse necessaria; quam sua vel inventa, vel interpretamenta, tamquam legem divinam obtrudere et ea tamquam ad professionem Christianam omnino necessaria legibus ecclesiasticis sancire, de quibus aut nihil prorsus, aut non decretorie saltem pronuntiarunt |

LG21 eloquia divina? Qui ea poscit ad communionem ecclesiasticam, quae Christus non poscit ad vitam aeternam, ille ad suam opinionem et utilitatem forte societatem commode constituit. Sed ea Christi quomodo dicenda, quae alienis institutis stabilitur ecclesia; et ex qua illi excluduntur, quos olim recipiet Christus in regnum caelorum? Sed cum verae ecclesiae notas indagare huius loci non sit, eos saltem qui pro suae societatis placitis tam acriter contendunt et nihil nisi ecclesiam,

puts us upon a necessity of deliberating, and, consequently, allows a liberty of choosing that which upon consideration we prefer.

And, in the last place, I consent that these men have a ruler in [25] their church, established | by such a long series of SE16 succession as they judge necessary, provided I may have liberty at the same time to join myself to that society in which I am persuaded those things are to be found which are necessary to the salvation of my soul. In this manner ecclesiastical liberty will be preserved on all sides, and no man will have a legislator imposed upon him but whom himself has chosen. |

But since men are so solicitous about the true church, I PE12 would only ask them here, by the way, if it be not more agreeable to the church of Christ to make the conditions of her communion consist in such things, and such things only, as the Holy Spirit has in the Holy Scriptures declared, in express words, to be necessary to salvation; I ask, I say, whether this be not more agreeable to the church of Christ than for men to impose their own inventions and interpretations upon others as if they were of divine authority, and to establish by ecclesiastical laws, as absolutely necessary to the profession of Christianity, such things as the Holy Scriptures do either not mention, or at least not expressly command? Whosoever requires those things in order to ecclesiastical communion, which Christ does not require in order to life eternal, he may, perhaps, indeed constitute a society accommodated to his own opinion and his own advantage; but how that can be called the church of Christ | which is established upon laws that are SE17 not his, and which excludes such persons from its communion as he will one day receive into the kingdom of heaven, I understand not. But this being not a proper place to inquire into the marks of the true church, I will only mind those that contend so earnestly for the decrees of their own society, and that cry out continually, the Church, the Church,* with as

---

[25] PE, SE, HL, LW: of   * HL, LW: the CHURCH, the CHURCH

non minore strepitu, et forsan eodem instinctu, quo
olim argentarii illi Ephesii Dianam suam, *Act.* xix;
continuo crepant, unum hoc monitos vellem, Evangelium scilicet passim testari, veros Christi discipulos
expectare, et pati debere persecutiones: veram autem
Christi ecclesiam alios persequi, aut insectari debere; |
ML8 vel vi, ferro et flammis ad fidem et dogmata sua am-
plectenda cogere, non memini me uspiam in Novo
Testamento legisse. |

LG22   Finis societatis religiosae (uti dictum) est cultus
Dei publicus et per eum vitae aeternae acquisitio. Eo
igitur collimare debet tota disciplina; his finibus circum-
scribi omnes leges ecclesiasticae. Nihil in hac societate
agitur, nec agi potest, de bonorum civilium, vel
terrenorum possessione; nulla hic, quacumque de
causa, adhibenda vis, quae omnis ad magistratum
civilem pertinet; bonorumque externorum possessio, et
usus illius subjacet potestati.

    Dices: Quae igitur sanctio leges ecclesiasticas ratas
habebit, si coactio omnis abesse debet? Respondeo: Ea
sane quae convenit rebus, quarum externa professio, et
observantia nihil prodest, nisi penitus animis insideant;
plenumque conscientiae assensum in his obtineant;
nempe hortationes, monita, consilia, arma sunt huius
societatis, quibus membra in officio continenda. Si his
non corrigantur delinquentes, errantesque reducantur
LG23 in viam, nihil aliud restat, nisi ut reluctantes | et obsti-
nati, nullamque melioris frugis de se spem praebentes,
a societate prorsus sejuncti rejiciantur. Haec suprema et
ultima est potestatis ecclesiasticae vis, quae nullam
aliam infert poenam, nisi quod, cessante relatione inter
corpus membrumque abscissum, damnatus desinit [3]
ecclesiae illius esse pars.

[3] ML: definit

much noise, and perhaps upon the same principle, as the *Ephesian* silversmiths did for their *Diana;* this, I say, I desire to mind them of, that the Gospel frequently declares that the true disciples of Christ must suffer persecution; but that the church of Christ should persecute others, and force others by fire and sword to embrace her faith and doctrine, I could never yet find in any of the books of the New Testament.

The end of a religious society (as has already been said) is the public worship of God, and, by means thereof, the acquisition of eternal life. All discipline ought | therefore to tend to that PE13 end, and all ecclesiastical laws to be thereunto confined. Nothing ought nor can be transacted in this society relating to the possession of civil and worldly goods. No force is here to be made use of upon any occasion whatsoever: for force belongs wholly to the | civil magistrate, and the possession of all HL40 outward goods is subject to his jurisdiction. |

But, it may be asked, by what means then shall ecclesiastical SE18 laws be established, if they must be thus destitute of all compulsive power? I answer: They must be established by means suitable to the nature of such things, whereof the external profession and observation, if not proceeding from a thorough conviction and approbation of the mind, is altogether useless and unprofitable. The arms by which the members of this society are to be kept within their duty are exhortations, admonitions, and advices.[26] If by these means the offenders will not be reclaimed, and the erroneous convinced, there remains nothing further to be done but that such stubborn and obstinate persons, who give no ground to hope for their reformation, should be cast out and separated from the society. This is the last and utmost force of ecclesiastical authority. No other punishment can thereby be inflicted, than that, the relation ceasing between the body and the member which is cut off, the person so condemned ceases to be a part of that church.

[26] LW: advice.

His ita constitutis, inquiramus porro quae cujusque sunt circa Tolerantiam officia.

Primo, dico quod nulla ecclesia tenetur tolerantiae nomine eum sinu suo fovere, qui monitus obstinate peccat contra leges in ea societate stabilitas; quas si cui impune violare licet, de societate actum est; cum hae sint et communionis conditiones et unicum societatis vinculum. Verumtamen cavendum est, ne excommunicationis decreto adjiciatur vel verborum contumelia, vel facti violentia, qua vel corpus ejecti, vel bona quoquo modo laedantur. Vis enim tota (uti dictum) magistratus est, nec privato cujvis permissa, LG24 nisi solum ut illatam repellat. Excommunicatio | nihil bonorum civilium, quae aut privatim possidebat, excommunicato aufert, aut auferre potest. Ea omnia ad civilem statum pertinent, et magistratus tutelae subjiciuntur. Excommunicationis vis tota in eo unice consistit, ut declarata societatis voluntate, solvatur unio inter corpus et membrum aliquod, qua cessante relatione necessario cessat quarundam rerum communio, quas membris suis tribuit societas; ad quas nemo jus habet civile. Nulla enim facta est excommunicato civilis injuria, si minister ecclesiae panem et vinum non illius, sed aliena pecunia emptum, illi non dat in celebratione Cenae dominicae.

Secundo, nemo privatus alterius bona civilia quoquo modo invadere, aut imminuere debet, propterea quod a sua religione suisque ritibus alienum se profiteatur. Omnia illi tam humanitatis quam civitatis jura

These things being thus determined, let us inquire, in the next place,[27] how far the duty of toleration extends, and what is required from every one by it .[28]

And, first, I hold that no church is bound, by the duty of toleration, to retain any such person in her bosom as, after admonition, continues obstinately to offend against the laws of the society. For these being | the condition of communion SE19 and the bond of the [29] society, if the breach of them were permitted without any animadversion, | the society would PE14 immediately be thereby dissolved. But, nevertheless, in all such cases care is to be taken that the sentence of excommunication, and the execution thereof, carry with it no rough usage of word or action whereby the ejected person may any wise be damnified in body or estate. For all force (as has often been said) belongs only to the magistrate, nor ought any private persons at any time to use force, unless it be in self-defence against unjust violence. Excommunication neither does, nor can, deprive the excommunicated person of any of those civil goods that he formerly possessed. All those things belong to the civil government, and are under the magistrate's protection. The whole force of excommunication consists only in this, that the resolution of the society in that respect being declared, the union that was between the body and some member comes thereby to be dissolved; and that relation ceasing, the participation of some certain things which the society communicated to its members, and unto which no man has any civil right, comes also to cease. For there is no civil injury done unto the excommunicated person by the church minister's refusing him that bread and wine, in the celebration of the Lord's Supper, which was not | bought with SE20 his but other men's money.

Secondly, no private person has any right in any manner to prejudice another person in his civil enjoyments because he is of another church or religion. All the rights and franchises

[27] GH: place: How   [28] GH: it?   [29] LW: bond of society

31

sancte conservanda: religionis haec non sunt; sive |
LG25 Christianus sit, sive ethnicus, ab omni vi et iniuria
temperandum. Justitiae mensura benevolentiae et
caritatis officiis cumulanda. Hoc iubet Evangelium;
suadet ratio; et, quam conciliavit natura, hominum
inter ipsos communis societas. Si a recto tramite
aberrat, sibi soli errat miser, tibi innocuus; nec igitur
a te male mulctandus debet huius vitae bonis excidere,
quod in futuro saeculo credis periturum. |

ML9 Quod de mutua privatorum hominum inter se de
religione dissidentium tolerantia dixi, id etiam de ecclesiis particularibus dictum volo, quae inter se privatae
quodammodo sunt personae, nec altera in alteram jus
aliquod habet, ne tum quidem, (si forte accidat) cum
magistratus civilis hujus vel illius ecclesiae sit: quandoquidem res publica nullum jus novum tribuere potest
ecclesiae, uti nec vice versa ecclesia rei publicae; siqui-
dem ecclesia, sive magistratus ei se adjungat, sive deserat,
LG26 manet semper eadem, quae ante, libera | et voluntaria
societas; nec accedente magistratu gladii potestatem
acquirit; nec decedente, quam prius habuit docendi
excommunicandive, amittit disciplinam. Hoc sponta-
neae societatis semper erit immutabile jus, ut ex suis,
quos visum fuerit, abalienare possit: nullam vero quo-
rumvis accessione acquirat in alienos jurisdictionem.
Quare pax, aequitas et amicitia inter diversas ecclesias,
uti inter privatos homines, sine juris alicujus praerogativa semper et aequabiliter colenda.
Ut exemplo res clara fiat, ponamus

that belong to him as a man, or as | a denizen,[30] are inviolably HL41
to be preserved to him. These are not the business of religion.
No violence nor injury is to be offered him, whether he be
Christian or Pagan. Nay, we must not content ourselves with
the narrow measures of bare justice; charity, bounty, and
liberality must be added to it. This the Gospel enjoins, this
reason directs, and this that natural fellowship we are born |
into requires of us. If any man err from the right way, it is his PE15
own misfortune, no injury to thee; nor therefore art thou to
punish him in the things of this life because thou supposest he
will be miserable in that which is to come.

What I say concerning the mutual toleration of private
persons differing from one another in religion, I understand
also of particular churches which stand, as it were, in the same
relation to each other as private persons among themselves:
nor has any one of them any manner of jurisdiction over any
other; no, not even when the civil magistrate (as it sometimes
happens) comes to be of this or the other communion. For
the civil government can give no new right to the church, nor
the church to the civil | government. So that whether the SE21
magistrate join himself to any church, or separate from it, the
church remains always as it was before, a free and voluntary
society. It neither requires the power of the sword by the
magistrate's coming to it, nor does it lose the right of instruc-
tion and excommunication by his going from it. This is the
fundamental and immutable right of a spontaneous society;
that it has power to remove any of its members who transgress
the rules of its institution; but it cannot, by the accession of
any new members, acquire any right of jurisdiction over those
that are not joined with it. And therefore peace, equity, and
friendship are always mutually to be observed by particular
churches, in the same manner as by private persons, without
any pretence of superiority or jurisdiction over one another.

That the thing may be made clearer by an example, let us

[30] PE, SE, CM, HL, LW: denison

33

Constantinopoli duas, alteram Remonstrantium, alteram Antiremonstrantium ecclesias. An aliquis dicat alteri earum jus competere, ut dissentientes alios (quod diversa habent, vel dogmata vel ritus) libertate, vel bonis spoliet (quod alibi factum videmus) vel exilio, vel capite puniat? Tacente interim et ridente Turca, dum Christia-LG27 ni Christianos crudelitate et laniena | vexant. Si vero altera harum ecclesiarum in alteram saeviendi habet potestatem, rogo quaenam ex duabus, et quo jure? Respondebitur sine dubio orthodoxa [4] in errantem, vel haereticam. Hoc est magnis et speciosis verbis nihil dicere. Quaelibet ecclesia sibi orthodoxa est, aliis erronea, vel haeretica; siquidem quae credit vera esse credit, quae in diversum abeunt erroris damnat. Itaque de dogmatum veritate, de cultus rectitudine, inter utramque lis aequa est, nulla judicis (qui nullus aut Constantinopoli aut in terris est) sententia componenda. Quaestionis decisio ad supremum omnium hominum judicem unice pertinet, ad quem etiam solum pertinet errantis castigatio. Interim cogitent, quanto gravius illi peccant, qui, si non errori, saltem superbiae addunt injustitiam, dum alieni domini servos, sibi minime obnoxios, temere et insolenter dilacerant.

LG28   Quod si certo constare possit, quaenam | inter dissidentes recte de religione sentiret, non inde accresceret orthodoxae ecclesiae potestas alias spoliandi; cum ecclesiarum in res terrestres nulla sit jurisdictio: nec ferrum et ignis ad errores arguendos, mentesque hominum, aut informandas, aut convertendas idonea sunt instrumenta. Fac tamen alteri parti favere magistratum civilem,

[4] LG: Orthodoxae

suppose two churches, the one of *Arminians*, the other of *Calvinists*, residing in the city of *Constantinople*. Will any one say that either of these churches has a right to deprive the members of the other of their estates and liberty (as we see practised elsewhere), because of their | differing from it in some doctrines PE16 or [31] ceremonies, whilst the *Turks* in the meanwhile silently stand by, and laugh to see with what inhuman cruelty Christians thus rage against Christians? But if one of these | churches SE22 hath this power of treating the other ill, I ask which of them it is to whom that power belongs, and by what right? It will be answered, undoubtedly, that it is the orthodox church which has the right of authority over the erroneous or heretical. This is, in great and specious words, to say just nothing at all. For every church is orthodox to itself; to others, erroneous or heretical. Whatsoever [32] any church believes, it believes to be true; and the contrary unto those things, it pronounces to be error. So that the controversy between these churches about the truth of their doctrines, and the purity of their worship, is on both sides equal; nor is there any judge, either at *Constantinople* or elsewhere upon earth, by whose sentence it can be determined. The decision of that question belongs only to the Supreme Judge of all men, to whom also alone belongs the punishment of the | erroneous. In the meanwhile, let those HL42 men consider how heinously they sin, who, adding injustice, if not to their error, yet certainly to their pride, do rashly and arrogantly take upon them to misuse the servants of another master, who are not at all accountable to them.

Nay, further: if it could be manifest which of these two dissenting churches were in the right way,[33] there would not accrue thereby unto the orthodox any right of destroying the other. For churches have neither any | jurisdiction in worldly SE23 matters, nor are fire and sword any proper instruments wherewith to convince men's minds of error, and inform them of the truth. Let us suppose, nevertheless, that the civil

[31] GH: and   [32] PE, CM, GH: For whatsoever
[33] PE, CM, GH: in the right

suumque illi praebere velle gladium; ut heterodoxos, se
annuente, quocumque velit modo castiget. An a Turca
Imperatore ecclesiae Christianae in fratres jus aliquod
accedere posse quis dixerit? Infidelis, qui sua auctoritate
Christianos ob fidei dogmata punire non potest, societati cujvis Christianae auctoritatem istam minime potest
impertire, nec jus, quod ipse non habet, dare. Eandem
rationem in Christiano esse regno cogita. Potestas civilis
ubique eadem est, nec majorem potest tribuere ecclesiae auctoritatem in manu principis Christiani, quam
LG29 ethnici, id est | nullam. Quamquam hoc observatu
forte dignum est, quod animosiores hi veritatis satel-
lites, errorum oppugnatores, schismatum impatientes,
ML10 zelum istum suum pro Deo, quo toti accenduntur | et
ardent, nuspiam paene expromunt, nisi ubi faventem
sibi habent magistratum civilem. Ubi primum gratia
apud magistratum, adeoque viribus sunt superiores,
violanda ilico pax et caritas Christiana; alias colenda
est mutua tolerantia. Quando robore civili impares
sunt, innoxie et patienter ferre possunt, a quo tantum
sibi et religioni alias metuunt, idololatriae, superstitionis,
haereseos in vicinia contagium. Nec libenter aut fervide
arguendis erroribus, qui aulae et magistratui placent,
impendunt operam; quae tamen vera et sola est
propagandae veritatis methodus,

magistrate inclined to favour one of them, and to put his sword into their hands, that (by his consent) they might chastise the dissenters as they | pleased. Will any man say that PE17 any right can be derived unto a Christian church over its brethren from a Turkish emperor? An infidel, who has himself no authority to punish Christians for the articles of their faith, cannot confer such an authority upon any society of Christians, nor give unto them a right which he has not himself. This would be the case at *Constantinople;* and the reason of the thing is the same in any Christian kingdom. The civil power is the same in every place: nor can that power, in the hands of a Christian prince, confer any greater authority upon the church than in the hands of a heathen; which is to say, just none at all.

Nevertheless, it is worthy to be observed and lamented that the most violent of these defenders of the truth, the opposers of errors, the exclaimers against schism, do hardly ever let loose this their zeal for God, with which they are so warmed and inflamed, unless where they have the civil magistrate on their side. But so soon as ever court favour has given them the | better end of the staff, and they begin to feel themselves the SE24 stronger, then presently peace and charity are to be laid aside. Otherwise they are religiously to be observed. Where they have not the power to carry on persecution and to become masters, there they desire to live upon fair terms, and preach up toleration. When they are not strengthened with the civil power, then they can bear most patiently and unmovedly the contagion of idolatry, superstition, and heresy in their neighbourhood; of which in [34] other occasions the interest of religion makes them to be extremely apprehensive. They do not forwardly attack those errors which are in fashion at court or are countenanced by the government. Here they can be content to spare their arguments; which yet (with their leave) is the only right method of propagating truth, which has no

[34] LW, GH: on

juncto scilicet cum humanitate et benevolentia rationum et argumentorum pondere.

LG30 Nullae igitur sive personae, sive ecclesiae, | sive de-
mum res publicae, jus aliquod habere possunt bona
civilia invicem invadendi seque mutuo rebus mundanis
spoliandi sub praetextu religionis. Qui aliter sentiunt,
velim secum reputent, quam infinitam praebent humano generi litium et bellorum materiem: quantum ad
rapinas et caedes et aeterna odia incitamentum: nec
uspiam securitas aut pax, nedum amicitia inter homines
stabiliri aut subsistere potest, si ea obtineat opinio, Dominium scilicet fundari in Gratia et religionem vi et
armis propagandam.

Tertio. [5] Videamus quid Tolerantiae officium exigit ab
iis, qui a reliquo coetu et gente laica (uti loqui amant)
charactere et munere aliquo ecclesiastico distinguun-
tur, sive sint episcopi, sacerdotes, presbyteri, ministri,
vel quocumque alio nomine veniant. De origine sive
potestatis sive dignitatis clericae jam non est inquirendi
locus; hoc tamen dico: undecumque orta est eorum
LG31 auctoritas, cum | sit ecclesiastica, inter ecclesiae cancel-
los debet coerceri, nec ad res civiles quovis modo potest
extendi: quandoquidem ipsa ecclesia a re publica rebus-
que civilibus prorsus sejuncta est et separata. Fixi et
immobiles sunt utrimque [6] limites. Caelum et terram,
res disjunctissimas, miscet qui has duas societates, origine, fine, materia, toto caelo diversas velit confundere.
Quare nemo, quocumque demum munere ecclesiastico ornatus, potest quemvis hominum, a sua ecclesia
vel fide alienum, vita, libertate, aut quavis bonorum
terrestrium parte mulctare religionis causa. Quod enim
integrae non licitum est ecclesiae,

[5] LG, ML: 3 [6] LG: undique ML: utrique

38

such way of prevailing as when strong arguments and good | reason are joined with the softness of civility and good usage. PE18

Nobody, therefore, in fine, neither single persons nor churches, nay, nor even commonwealths, have any just title to invade the civil rights and worldly goods of each other upon pretence of religion. Those that are of another opinion would do well to consider with themselves how pernicious a seed of discord and war, how powerful a provocation to endless hatreds, rapines, and slaughters they thereby furnish unto | mankind. SE25 No peace and security, | no, not so much as common HL43 friendship, can ever be established or preserved amongst men so long as this opinion prevails, that *dominion is founded in grace* and that religion is to be propagated by force of arms.

In the third place: Let us see what the *duty of toleration requires* from those who are distinguished from the rest of mankind (from the laity, as they please to call us) by some *ecclesiastical character and office;* whether they be bishops, priests, presbyters, ministers, or however else dignified or distinguished. It is not my business to inquire here into the original of the power or dignity of the clergy. This only I say, that whencesoever their authority be sprung, since it is ecclesiastical, it ought to be confined within the bounds of the church, nor can it in any manner be extended to civil affairs, because the church itself is a thing absolutely separate and distinct from the commonwealth. The boundaries on both sides are fixed and immovable. He jumbles heaven and earth together, the things most remote and opposite, who mixes these two [35] societies, which are in their original, end, business, and in everything perfectly distinct and infinitely different from each other. No man, therefore, with whatsoever ecclesiastical office he be dignified, can deprive another man that is not of his church and faith either of liberty or of any part of | his worldly goods upon | SE26 the account of that difference which is between [36] them in reli- PE19 gion. For whatsoever is not lawful to the whole church cannot

[35] SE, HL, LW: these societies
[36] PE, CM, HL, GH: difference between

39

id alicui ejus membro jure ecclesiastico licere non potest.
Nec viris ecclesiasticis satis est a vi et rapina et omni-
moda persecutione abstinere; qui se successorem profitetur Apostolorum, et docendi munus in se suscepit,
tenetur porro monere suos de pacis et benevolentiae
officiis erga omnes homines; tam erroneos quam or-
LG32 thodoxos, | tam secum sentientes quam a fide sua vel
ritibus alienos et cunctos, sive privatos sive rem publicam gerentes (si qui hujusmodi sint in sua ecclesia) ad ca-
ritatem, mansuetudinem, tolerantiam hortari, omnem-
que illam aversationem et contra heterodoxos animi
ardorem compescere et lenire, quem aut suus cujusque
pro sua religione et secta feroculus zelus, aut aliorum
astus in mentibus accenderit. Qui et quantus tam in
ecclesia quam re publica perciperetur fructus, si doctrina pacis et tolerantiae resonarent pulpita, nolo dicere,
nequid gravius a me dictum in eos videatur, quorum
dignitatem a nemine, ne a se ipsis quidem, imminutam
vellem. Verum dico hoc ita fieri oportere, et si quis, qui
se ministrum verbi divini profitetur, et praeconem
MLII Evangelii pacis, alia docet, negotium | sibi demandatum
aut nescit, aut negligit, cujus aliquando principi pacis
reddet rationem. Si monendi sint Christiani, ut a vindic-
LG33 ta abstineant, iteratis | lacessiti injuriis usque ad septua-
gies septies; quanto magis illi ab omni ira et inimica vi
sibi temperare debent, qui nihil ab alio passi sunt; et
cavere maxime ne illos quoquo modo laedant a quibus
nulla in re fuerint laesi; praecipue ne aliis quodvis
intentent malum, qui res suas solum agunt, et de hoc
uno solliciti sunt, ut Deum colant eo modo, quem,

by any ecclesiastical right become lawful to any of its members. *But this is not all.* It is not enough that ecclesiastical men abstain from violence and rapine and all manner of persecution. He that pretends to be a successor of the apostles, and takes upon him the office of teaching, is obliged also to admonish his hearers of the duties of peace and good-will towards all men, as well towards the erroneous as the orthodox; towards those that differ from them in faith and worship as well as towards those that agree with them therein. And he ought industriously to exhort all men, whether private persons or magistrates (if any such there be in his church), to charity, meekness, and toleration, and diligently endeavour to allay and temper all that heat and unreasonable averseness of mind which either any man's fiery zeal for his own sect or the craft of others has kindled against dissenters. I will not undertake to represent how happy and how great would be the fruit, both in church and state, if the pulpits everywhere sounded with this doctrine of peace and toleration, lest I should seem to reflect too severely upon those men whose dignity I desire not to detract from, nor would have it diminished either by | others or themselves. SE27 But this I say, that thus it ought to be. And if any one that professes himself to be a minister of the word of God, a preacher of the gospel of peace, teach otherwise, he either understands not or neglects the business of his calling, and shall one day give account thereof unto the Prince of peace. If Christians are to be admonished that they abstain from all manner of revenge, even after repeated provocations and multiplied injuries, how much more ought they who suffer nothing, who have had no harm done them, to [37] forbear violence and | abstain from all PE20 manner of ill-usage towards those from whom they have | received none! This caution and temper they ought certainly HL44 to use towards those who mind only their own business, and are solicitous for nothing but that (whatever men think of them) they may worship God in that manner which they are

[37] PE, SE, CM, HL, GH: them, forbear

41

neglecta hominum opinione, ipsi Deo maxime acceptum fore credunt, et eam amplectuntur religionem,
quae ipsis maximam spem facit salutis aeternae? Si de
re domestica et facultatibus, si de corporis valetudine
agatur, quid e re sua fuerit apud se consulere cujvis
integrum est, illudque sequi permissum quod suo judicio sit optimum. De vicini sui re familiari male admi-
nistrata nemo queritur; de serendis[*] agris vel locanda
filia erranti nemo irascitur; in popinis decoquentem
nemo corrigit: diruat, aedificet, sumptus faciat suo
more, tacitum est, licitum est; si vero templum publi-
LG34 cum | non frequentet, si illic debito ritu corpus non
flectat; si liberos hujus vel illius ecclesiae sacris initian-
dos non tradat, fit murmur, clamor, incusatio, quisque
tanti criminis paratus est vindex, et a vi et rapina vix sibi
temperant zelotae, dum in jus vocatur, et sententia
judicis vel corpus carceri necive tradat, vel bona hastae
subjiciat. Oratores ecclesiastici cujusque sectae aliorum
errores, qua possunt, argumentorum vi redarguant et
debellent, sed hominibus parcant. Quod si destituantur
rationum momentis, absona et alieni fori instrumenta
ne adsciscant, ecclesiasticis non tractanda; nec in sub-
sidium suae vel eloquentiae vel doctrinae a magistratu
fasces et secures mutuentur, ne forte dum prae se ferunt
veritatis amorem, zelus eorum ferro et igne nimium
effervescens affectatae dominationis [7] fiat indicium.
Haud facile enim persuadebit viris cordatis, se vehe-
menter et sincere cupere fratrem in futuro saeculo ab
LG35 igne gehennae tutum salvumque | fore,

---

[*] LG, ML: semendis
[7] ML: dominionis

persuaded is acceptable to him, and in which they have the strongest hopes of eternal salvation. In private domestic affairs, in the management of estates, in the conservation of bodily health, every man may consider what suits his own convenience, and follow what course he likes best. No man complains of the ill-management of his neighbour's affairs. No man is angry with another for an error committed in sowing his land or in marrying his daughter. Nobody corrects a spendthrift for consuming his substance | in taverns. Let any SE28 man pull down, or build, or make whatsoever expenses he pleases, nobody murmurs, nobody controls him; he has his liberty. But if any man do not frequent the church, if he do not there conform his behaviour exactly to the accustomed ceremonies, or if he brings not his children to be initiated in the sacred mysteries of this or the other congregation, this immediately causes an uproar. The neighbourhood is filled with noise and clamour. Every one is ready to be the avenger of so great a crime, and the zealots hardly have the [38] patience to refrain from violence and rapine so long till the cause be heard, and the poor man be, according to form, condemned to the loss of liberty, goods, or life. Oh, that our ecclesiastical orators of every sect would apply themselves with all the strength of arguments that they are able to the confounding of men's errors! But let them spare their persons. Let them not supply their want of reasons with the instruments of force, which belong to another jurisdiction, and do ill become a churchman's hands. Let them not call in the magistrate's authority | to the aid of their eloquence or learning, lest PE21 perhaps, whilst they pretend only love for the truth, this their intemperate zeal, breathing nothing but fire and sword, betray their ambition and show that what they desire is temporal dominion. For it will be | very difficult to persuade men of SE29 sense that he who with dry eyes and satisfaction of mind can deliver his brother to the executioner to be burnt alive, does

---

[38] SE, HL, LW: have patience

qui siccis oculis et prono animo vivum hic tradit carnifici concremandum.

Quarto. [8] Quae sunt magistratus partes, quae sane circa tolerantiam maximae sunt, ultimo jam loco videndum.

Supra probavimus, ad magistratum non pertinere animarum curam, authoritativam (si ita loqui liceat) volo, quae scilicet legibus jubendo, poenisque cogendo, exercetur; charitativa enim quae docendo, monendo, suadendo consulit, nemini negari potest. Itaque penes quemque animae suae cura est, eique permittenda. Dices: Quid si animae suae curam negligit? Respondeo: Quid si sanitatis? Quid si rei familiaris, quae res propius magistratus imperio subjacent? An magistratus edicto ad eam rem facto cavebit ne pauper vel aeger fiat? Leges quantum fieri potest subditorum bona et sanitatem ab aliena vi vel fraude tueri conantur, non a possidentis incuria vel dissipatione. Nemo ut valeat, ut ditescat, | LG36 invitus cogi potest. Invitos ne quidem Deus servabit. Fac tamen principem subditos ad opes acquirendas, vel corporis robur tuendum velle cogere. Anne solos medicos Romanos consulendos esse lege statutum erit, et ad eorum praescriptum vivere quisque tenebitur? Numquid nullum sumendum vel medicamentum vel obsonium, nisi quod in Vaticano paratum, aut e Genevensi prodierit officina [?] Vel ut subditis domi | suae ML12 abunde sit et laute, anne omnes lege tenebuntur mercaturam vel musicam exercere? An quisque fiet vel caupo, vel faber, quibus artibus aliqui satis commode familiam suam sustentant, opibusque augent? Sed dices: Quaestus mille sunt artes, unica salutis via. Recte sane dictum, ab iis praesertim, qui ad hanc vel

[8] LG ML: 4.

sincerely and heartily concern himself to save that brother from the flames of hell in the world to come.

In the last place. Let us now consider *what is the magistrate's duty* in the business of toleration, which certainly is very considerable.

We have already proved that the care of souls does not belong to the magistrate. Not a magisterial care, I mean (if I may so call it), which consists in prescribing by laws and compelling by punishments. But a charitable care, which consists in teaching, admonishing, and persuading, cannot be denied unto any man. The care, therefore, of every man's soul belongs unto himself, and is to be left unto himself. But what if he neglect the care of his soul? I answer: What if he neglect the care of his health or of his estate, which things are nearlier related to the government of the magistrate than the other? Will the magistrate provide by an express law that such a one shall not become poor or sick? Laws provide, as much as is possible, that the goods and health of subjects be not injured by the fraud and violence | of others; they do not guard HL45 them from the negligence or ill-husbandry of the possessors themselves. | No man can be forced to be rich or healthful SE30 whether he will or no. Nay, God himself will not save men against their wills. Let us suppose, however, that some prince were desirous to force his subjects to accumulate riches, or to preserve the health and strength of their bodies. Shall it be provided by | law that they must consult none but *Roman* PE22 physicians, and shall every one be bound to live according to their prescriptions? What, shall no potion, no broth, be taken, but what is prepared either in the *Vatican*, suppose, or in a *Geneva* shop? Or, to make these subjects rich, shall they all be obliged by law to become merchants or musicians? Or, shall every one turn victualler, or smith, because there are some that maintain their families plentifully and grow rich in those professions? But, it may be said, there are a thousand ways to wealth, but only one way to heaven. It is well said, indeed, especially by those that plead for compelling men into this or

illam cogere vellent; nam si plures essent, ne cogendi quidem inveniretur praetextus. Quod si ego secundum geographiam sacram recta Hierosolymas totis viribis LG37 contendo, | cur vapulo quod non cothurnatus forsan, vel certo modo lotus vel tonsus incedo; quod carnibus in itinere vescor, vel victu utor stomacho et valetudini commodo; quod hinc inde aliqua diverticula vito, quae mihi videntur in praecipitia vel vepreta deducere? Vel inter varios, qui ejusdem viae sunt et eodem tendentis, calles eum seligo qui minime sinuosus caenosusve apparet? Quod illi minus modesti, hi morosiores, visi sunt quam quibus me libenter vellem adjungere comitem; vel quod habeo vel non habeo mitratum vel alba stola indutum itineris ducem? Nam profecto si recte rem reputemus, hujusmodi plerumque sunt minoris momenti res, quae fratres Christianos de summa religionis eadem et recte sentientes tam acriter committunt, et quae salva religione et animarum salute, modo absit superstitio vel hypocrisis, possint vel observari vel omitti.

LG38   Verum demus zelotis, et omnia quae | sua non sunt damnantibus, ex his circumstantiis diversas et in diversa tendentes nasci vias; quid tandem proficiemus? Unica ex his re vera salutis sit via. Verum inter mille, quas homines ingrediuntur, de recta ambigitur: nec cura rei publicae, nec legum condendarum jus, illam quae ducit ad caelum viam, magistratui certius detegit, quam suum privato studium. Debile traho corpus et gravi morbo languidum, cujus unicam eamque ignotam ponamus esse medelam. Ideone magistratus est praescribere

the other way. For if there were several ways that led thither, there would not be so much as a pretence left for compulsion. But now if I be marching on with my utmost vigour in that way which, according to the sacred geography, leads straight to *Jerusalem*, why am I beaten and ill-used by others because, perhaps, I wear not buskins; because my hair is not of the right cut; because, perhaps, I have not been dipped in the right fashion; | because I eat flesh upon the road, or some other food SE31 which agrees with my stomach; because I avoid certain by-ways, which seem unto me to lead into briars or precipices; because, amongst the several paths that are in the same road, I choose that to walk in which seems to be the straightest and cleanest; because I avoid to keep company with some travellers that are less grave, and others that are more sour than they ought to be; or, in fine, because I follow a guide that either is, or is not, clothed in white, or crowned with a mitre? Certainly, if we consider right, we shall find that, for the most part, they are such frivolous things as these that (without any prejudice to religion or the salvation of souls, if not accompanied with superstition or hypocrisy) might either be observed or omitted. I say, they are such-like things as these which breed implacable enmities | amongst Christian brethren, who PE23 are all agreed in the substantial and truly fundamental part of religion.

But let us grant unto these zealots, who condemn all things that are not of their mode, that from these circumstances are different ends. What shall we conclude from thence? There is only one of these which is the true way to eternal happiness: but in this great variety of ways that men follow, it is still doubted which is the right one. Now, neither the care of the commonwealth, | nor the right enacting of laws, does discover this way SE32 that leads to heaven more certainly to the magistrate than every private man's search and study discovers it unto himself. I have a weak body, sunk under a languishing disease, for which (I suppose) there is one only remedy, but that unknown. Does it therefore belong unto the magistrate to prescribe me a

remedium, quia unicum tantum est, idque inter tot
variâ ignotum? Ideone quia unicum quo mortem evi-
tem mihi agendum restat, id quod jubet fieri magistratus erit tutum? Quae a singulis studio, consilio, judicio,
cogitatione, et sincera mente indaganda, ea non uni
alicui hominum sorti, tamquam ipsi propria, tribuenda
sunt. Nascuntur principes potestate superiores, natura
LG39 vero aequales reliquis mortalibus, | nec regnandi jus vel
peritia secum trahit aliarum rerum certam cognitionem
nedum religionis verae. Si enim ita esset, qui fit quod de
rebus religionis tam in diversum abeunt terrarum domi-
ni? Sed demus verisimile esse, viam ad vitam aeternam
principi esse quam subditis notiorem; vel saltem tutius
commodiusve esse in hac rerum incertitudine illius
mandatis obtemperare. Dices igitur: An si te juberet
mercatura victum quaerere, recusares, quia dubitares
an hac arte quaestum faceres? Respondeo: Mercator
fierem jubente principe: quia si male succederet, ille
oleum et operam mercatura perditam potens est alio
modo abunde resarcire; et si famen pauperiemque (uti
prae se fert) a me amotam velit, id facile praestare potest,
si mea omnia absumpserit infelicis mercaturae mala
sors. Verum hoc non fit in rebus vitae futurae. Si illic
male operam locavero; si illic semel spe excidi, magistra-
LG40 tus nequaquam | potest resarcire damnum, levare ma-
lum, nec me in aliquam partem, multo minus in integrum restituere. Qua sponsione de regno caelorum
cavebitur? Dices forte, magistratui civili de rebus sacris
ML13 certum, quod sequi omnes debent, | non tribuimus ju-
dicium, sed ecclesiae. Quod definivit ecclesia id magistratus civilis ab omnibus observari jubet,

remedy, because there is but one, and because it is unknown? Because there is but one way for me to escape death, will it therefore be safe for me | to do whatsoever the magistrate HL46 ordains? Those things that every man ought sincerely to inquire into himself, and by meditation, study, search, and his own endeavours, attain the knowledge of, cannot be looked upon as the peculiar possession [39] of any sort of men. Princes, indeed, are born superior unto other men in power, but in nature equal. Neither the right nor the art of ruling does necessarily carry along with it the certain knowledge of other things, and least of all of true religion. For if it were so, how could it come to pass that the lords of the earth should differ so vastly as they do in religious matters? But let us grant that it is probable the way to eternal life may be better known by a prince than by his subjects, or at least that in this incertitude of things the safest and most commodious way for private persons is to follow his dictates. You will say, what | then? If SE33 he should bid you follow merchandise for your | livelihood, PE24 would you decline that course for fear it should not succeed? I answer: I would turn merchant upon the prince's command, because in case I should have ill-success in trade, he is a-bundantly able to make up my loss some other way. If it be true, as he pretends, that he desires I should thrive and grow rich, he can set me up again when unsuccessful voyages have broken me. But this is not the case in the things that regard the life to come; if there I take a wrong course, if in that respect I am once undone, it is not in the magistrate's power to repair my loss, to ease my suffering, nor [40] to restore me in any measure, much less entirely to a good estate. What security can be given for the kingdom of heaven?

Perhaps some will say that they do not suppose this *infallible judgment*, that all men are bound to follow in the affairs of religion, to be in the civil magistrate, but *in the church*. What the church has determined, that the civil magistrate orders to be

[39] LW: profession   [40] SE, HL, LW: or

49

et nequis aliud in sacris vel agat vel credat quam quod docet ecclesia, auctoritate sua cavet: adeo ut judicium sit penes ecclesiam; obsequium magistratus ipse praestat, et ab aliis exigit. Respondeo: Venerandum illud Apostolorum tempore ecclesiae nomen, sequioribus saeculis ad fucum faciendum non raro usurpatum fuisse, quis non videt? Praesenti saltem in re nihil opis nobis affert. Ego unicam illam angustam quae ad caelum ducit semitam, magistratui non magis notam esse dico quam privatis; ideoque tuto eum non possum sequi LG41 ducem, qui cum viae potest esse aeque ignarus, | de mea certe salute non potest non esse minus sollicitus quam ego ipse. Inter tot gentis Hebraeae reges quotusquisque fuit, quem secutus aliquis Israelita, non a vero cultu Dei deflexisset in idololatriam, in certam perniciem caeca hujusmodi obedientia ruiturus? Tu contra bono me esse animo jubes, in tuto dicis res est; jam enim magistratus non sua sed ecclesiae de rebus religionis decreta populo observanda proponit, et sanctione civili stabilit. Sed rogo cujus demum ecclesiae? Illius scilicet quae principi placet. Quasi vero ille de religione suum non interponit judicium, qui me in hanc vel illam ecclesiam lege, supplicio, vi cogit? Quid interest sive ipse me ducat, sive aliis ducendum tradat? Ex illius pariter pendeo voluntate, et de mea salute utrimque aeque statuit. Quanto securior Judaeus, qui ex edicto regis Baali se adjunxit, quod ipsi dictum sit, regem suo arbitrio nihil in religione statuere, nihil subditis in cultu LG42 divino | injungere, nisi quod sacerdotum concilio et illius religionis mystis comprobatum et pro divino habitum? Si ideo vera, ideo salutifera sit alicujus ecclesiae religio,

observed; and he provides by his authority that nobody shall either act or believe in the business of religion otherwise than the church teaches. So that the judgment of those things is in the church; the magistrate himself yields obedience thereunto, and requires the like obedience from others. I answer: Who sees not how frequently the | name of the church, which was vener- SE34 able in time of the apostles, has been made use of to throw dust in the people's eyes, in the following ages? But, however, in the present case it helps us not. The one only narrow way which leads to heaven is not better known to the magistrate than to private persons, and therefore I cannot safely take him for my guide, who may probably be as ignorant of the way as myself, and who certainly is less concerned for my salvation than I myself am. Amongst so many kings of the *Jews*, how many of them were there whom any *Israelite*, | thus blindly following, PE25 had not fallen into idolatry, and thereby into destruction? Yet nevertheless, you bid me be of good courage, and tell me that all is now safe and secure, because the magistrate does not now enjoin the observance of his own decrees in matters of religion, but only the decrees of the church. Of what church, I beseech you? Of that, certainly, which [41] likes him best. As if he that compels me by laws and penalties to enter into this or the other church, did not interpose his own judgment in the matter. What difference is there whether | he lead me HL47 himself, or deliver me over to be led by others? I depend both ways upon his will, and it is he that determines both ways of my eternal state. Would an *Israelite*, that had worshipped *Baal* upon the command of his king, have | been in any better SE35 condition, because somebody had told him that the king ordered nothing in religion upon his own head, nor comman- ded anything to be done by his subjects in divine worship but what was approved by the counsel of priests, and declared to be of divine right by the doctors of their [42] church? If the religion of any church become therefore true and saving,

[41] LW: which certainly   [42] CM: that LW: the

quia sectae illius antistites, sacerdotes, asseclae eam laudant, praedicant, et quantum possunt suffragiis suis commendant: quae tandem erit erronea, falsa, perniciosa? De Socinianorum fide dubito; Pontificiorum vel Lutheranorum cultus mihi suspectus est; an igitur tutior mihi ingressus est in hanc vel illam ecclesiam, jubente magistratu, quod ille nihil imperat, nihil de religione sancit, nisi ex auctoritate et consilio doctorum istius ecclesiae?

Quamquam si verum dicere volumus, facilius plerumque se aulae accommodat ecclesia (si ita dicendus sit ecclesiasticorum decreta facientium conventus) quam aula ecclesiae. Sub principe orthodoxo vel Ariano qualis fuit ecclesia satis notum. Sed si haec nimis remota, recentiora nobis offert Anglorum historia, quam belle, | quam prompte, ecclesiastici decreta, fidei articulos, cultum, omnia ad nutum principis componebant sub Henrico, Eduardo, Maria, Elizabetha: qui principes tam diversa de religione et sentiebant et jubebant, ut nemo nisi amens (paene dixeram atheus) asserere audeat, quemvis virum probum et veri Dei cultorem posse salva conscientia, salva erga Deum veneratione, eorum de religione decretis obtemperare. Sed quid multa? Si rex, sive ex proprio judicio, sive auctoritate ecclesiastica et ex aliorum opinione, leges alienae religioni ponere velit, perinde est. Ecclesiasticorum, quorum dissensiones et dimicationes plus satis notae, nec magis sanum nec magis tutum judicium: neque aliquam vim potestati civili eorum undecumque collecta addere possunt suffragia. Quamquam hoc notatu dignum, quod Principes ecclesiasticorum, suae fidei | et cultui non faventium opiniones et suffragia non solent aliquo in loco habere. |

LG43

ML14

because the head of that sect, the prelates and priests, and those of that tribe, do all of them, with all their might, extol and praise it, what religion can ever be accounted erroneous, false, and destructive? I am doubtful concerning the doctrine of the *Socinians*, I am suspicious of the way of worship practised by the *Papists*, or *Lutherans*? Will it be ever a jot safer for me to join either unto the one or the other of those churches, upon the magistrate's command, because he commands nothing in religion but by the authority and counsel of the doctors of that church?

But, to speak the truth, we must acknowledge that the church (if a convention of clergymen, making canons, must be called by that name) is for the most part more apt | to be PE26 influenced by the court than the court by the church. How the church was under the vicissitude of orthodox and Arian emperors is very well known. Or if those things be too remote, our modern *English* history affords us fresh examples in | the SE36 reigns of *Henry* the 8th, *Edward* the 6th, *Mary*, and *Elizabeth*, how easily and smoothly the clergy changed their decrees, their articles of faith, their form of worship, everything according to the inclination of those kings and queens. Yet were those kings and queens of such different minds *in point* of religion, and enjoined thereupon such different things, that no man in his wits (I had almost said none but an atheist) will presume to say that any sincere and upright worshipper of God could, with a safe conscience, obey their several decrees. To conclude, it is the same thing whether a king that prescribes laws to another man's religion, pretend to do it by his own judgment, or by the ecclesiastical authority and advice of others. The decisions of churchmen, whose differences and disputes are sufficiently known, cannot be any sounder or safer than his; nor can all their suffrages joined together add a new strength to the civil power. Though this also must be taken notice of, that princes seldom have any regard to the suffrages of ecclesiastics that are not favourers of their own faith and way of worship.

LG44   Sed quod caput rei est, et rem penitus conficit; etiamsi magistratus de religione potior sit sententia, et via quam inire jubet vere Evangelica; si hoc mihi ex animo non persuasum sit, mihi non erit salutaris. Nulla, quam reclamante conscientia ingredior viam, me ad beatorum sedes umquam deducet. Arte quam aversor ditescere possum, medicamentis de quibus dubito sanus fieri; religione vero de qua dubito, cultu quem aversor, salvus fieri non possum. Incredulus externos frustra induit mores, cum fide et interna sinceritate opus sit ut Deo placeat. Medicina utcumque speciosa, utcumque aliis probata, frustra propinatur, si statim sumptam rejiciet stomachus; nec invito infundi debet remedium, quod idiosyncrasiae vitio mutabitur in venenum. Quicquid de religione in dubium vocari potest, hoc demum certum est, quod nulla religio, quam ego non

LG45 credo esse veram, mihi vera aut | utilis esse potest. Nequicquam igitur salvandae animae praetextu subditos ad sacra sua cogit magistratus, si credant, sponte venturos, si non credant, quamvis venerint, nihilominus perituros. Quantumvis igitur prae te fers alteri bene velle; quantumvis de salute ejus labores, homo ad salutem cogi non potest: post omnia, sibi et conscientiae suae relinquendus.

   Sic tandem homines habemus in rebus religionis ab alieno dominio liberos: quid jam facient? Deum publice colendum et sciunt et agnoscunt omnes, quorsum alias ad coetus publicos cogimur? Hominibus itaque in ea libertate constitutis ineunda est societas ecclesiastica, ut coetus celebrent, non solum ad mutuam aedificationem, sed

But, after all, the *principal consideration*, and which absolutely determines this controversy, is this: Although the magistrate's opinion in religion be sound, and the way that he appoints be truly evangelical, yet, if I be not thoroughly persuaded thereof | in my own mind, there will be no safety for me in following SE37 it. No way whatsoever that I shall walk in against the dictates of my conscience will ever bring me to the mansions of the blessed. I may grow rich by an art that I take not delight in, I may be cured of some disease by remedies that I have not faith | in; but I cannot be saved by a religion that I distrust, and PE27 by a worship that I abhor. It is in vain for an | unbeliever to take HL48 up the outward show of another man's profession. Faith only, and inward sincerity, are the things that procure acceptance with God. The most likely and most approved remedy can have no effect upon the patient if his stomach reject it as soon as taken; and you will in vain cram a medicine down a sick man's throat, which his particular constitution will be sure to turn into poison. In a word, whatsoever may be doubtful in religion, yet this at least is certain, that no religion which I believe not to be true can be either true or profitable unto me. In vain, therefore, do princes compel their subjects to come into their church communion, under pretence of saving their souls. If they believe, they will come of their own accord; if they believe not, their coming will nothing avail them. How great soever, in fine, may be the pretence of good-will and charity, and concern for the salvation of men's souls, men cannot be | forced to be saved whether they will or no. And SE38 therefore, when all is done, they must be left to their own consciences.

Having thus at length freed men from all dominion over one another in matters of religion, let us now consider *what they are to do*. All men know and acknowledge that God ought to be publicly worshipped; why otherwise do they compel one another unto the public assemblies? Men, therefore, constituted in this liberty are to enter into some religious society, that they meet together, not only for mutual edification, but

etiam ut se coram populo testentur cultores esse Dei, eumque se divino numini cultum offerre, cujus ipsos non pudet, nec Deo credunt aut indignum aut ingra-

LG46 tum; ut doctrinae puritate, | vitae sanctimonia et rituum modesto decore, alios ad religionis veritatisque amorem pelliceant, aliaque praestent quae a singulis privatim fieri non possunt.

Has societates religiosas ecclesias voco, quas magistratus tolerare debet; quia a populo ita in coetus collecto non aliud agitur, quam quod singulis hominibus seorsum [9] integrum est et licitum, scilicet de salute animarum: nec hac in re discrimen aliquod est inter ecclesiam aulicam, reliquasque ab ea diversas.

Sed cum in omni ecclesia duo praecipue consideranda sunt, cultus scilicet externus, sive ritus, et dogmata; de utrisque separatim agendum est, ut clarius de universa tolerantiae ratione constet.

[Primo.] Magistratus nec in sua, nec (quod multo minus licet) in aliena ecclesia potest ritus aliquos ecclesiasticos, vel caerimonias in cultu Dei usurpandas, lege |

LG47 civili sancire; non solum quia liberae sunt societates, sed quicquid in cultu divino Deo offertur, id ea solum ratione probandum est, quod a colentibus Deo acceptum fore creditur. Quicquid ea fiducia non agitur, nec licitum est, nec Deo acceptum. Repugnat enim, ut, cui libertas permittitur religionis, cujus finis est Deo placere, eum in ipso cultu jubeas Deo displicere. Dices: Anne igitur negabis, quae ab omnibus conceditur, magistratui in res adiaphoras potestatem, quae si auferatur, nulla

ML15 restabit legum ferendarum | materia? Respondeo: Concedo res indifferentes

[9] LG, ML: seorsim

56

to own to the world that they worship God, and offer unto his Divine Majesty such service as they themselves are not a-shamed of, and such as they think not unworthy of him, nor unacceptable to him; and finally, that by the purity of doctrine, holiness of life, and decent form of worship, they may draw others unto the love of the true religion, and | perform such PE28 other things in religion as cannot be done by each private man apart.

These religious societies I call churches: and these, I say, the magistrate ought to tolerate. For the business of these assemblies of the people is nothing but what is lawful for every man in particular to take care of; I mean the salvation of their souls. Nor in this case is there any difference between the national church and other separated congregations. But as in every church | there SE39 are two things especially to be considered, *the outward form and rites of worship, and the doctrines and articles of faith*, these things must be handled each distinctly, that so the whole matter of toler-ation may the more clearly be understood.

Concerning outward worship, I say (in the first place), that the magistrate has no power to enforce by law, either in his own church, or much less in another, the use of any rites or ceremonies whatsoever in the worship of God. And this, not only because these churches are free societies, but because whatsoever is practised in the worship of God is only so far justifiable as it is believed by those that practise it to be ac-ceptable unto him. Whatsoever is not done with that assur-ance of faith is neither well in itself, nor can it be acceptable to God. To impose such things, therefore, upon any people, contrary to their own judgment, is in effect to command them to offend God, which, considering that the end of all religion is to please him, and | that liberty is essentially necessary to that HL49 end, appears to be absurd beyond expression.

But perhaps it may be concluded from hence that I deny unto the magistrate all manner of power about *indifferent things*, which, if it be not granted, the whole subject-matter of law-making is taken away. No, I readily grant that indifferent

easque forsan solas, potestati legislativae subjici.

1. Non inde tamen sequitur, quod licitum sit magistratui de quavis re indifferente quodcumque placuerit statuere. Legum ferendarum modus et mensura est publicum commodum. Si quid ex usu rei publicae non fuerit, utcumque sit res indifferens, non potest ilico lege sanciri. |

LG48 2. Res utcumque sua natura indifferentes extra magistratus jurisdictionem positae sunt, cum in ecclesiam et cultum divinum transferuntur; quia illo in usu nullam habent cum rebus civilibus conexionem: ubi solum agitur de salute animarum, nec vicini nec rei publicae interest sive hic sive ille ritus usurpetur. Caeremoniarum in coetibus ecclesiasticis sive observatio, sive omissio, aliorum vitae, libertati, opibus, ne obest quidem nec obesse potest. Exempli gratia, infantem nuper natum aqua lavare, res sit sua natura indifferens. Detur etiam magistratui licitum esse id lege statuere, modo sciat utilem esse hujusmodi lotionem ad morbum aliquem, cui obnoxii sunt infantes, vel sanandum vel praecavendum, credatque etiam tanti esse ut de ea edicto caveatur. An igitur dicet aliquis, eodem jure licere magistratui lege etiam jubere, ut infantes a sacerdote sacro fonte abluantur ad purgationem animarum? Vel LG49 ut | sacris aliquibus initientur? Quis non primo aspectu videt res hasce toto caelo differre? Supponas Judaei esse filium, et [10] res ipsa per se loquitur. Quid enim vetat, magistratum Christianum Judaeos habere subditos? Quam injuriam, in re sua natura indifferenti, Judaeo non faciendam agnoscis, scilicet ut in cultu religioso contra quam ipse sentiat aliquid agere cogatur, eam Christiano homini faciendam asseris?

[10] HE: ut

things, | and perhaps none but | such, are subjected to the SE40/PE29
legislative power. But it does not therefore follow that the
magistrate may ordain whatsoever he pleases concerning
anything that is indifferent. The public good is the rule and
measure of all law-making. If a thing be not useful to the
commonwealth, though it be never [43] so indifferent, it may
not presently be established by law.

But [44] *further*, things never [45] so indifferent in their own
nature, when they are brought into the church and worship
of God, are removed out of the reach of the magistrate's
jurisdiction, because in that use they have no connection at
all with civil affairs. The only business of the church is the
salvation of souls, and it no ways [46] concerns the commonwealth, or any member of it, that this or the other ceremony
be there made use of. Neither the use nor the omission of any
ceremonies in those religious assemblies does either advantage
or prejudice the life, liberty, or estate of any man. For example,
let it be granted that the washing of an infant with water is in
itself an indifferent thing, let it be granted also that the magistrate understand such washing to be profitable to the curing or
preventing of any disease the children are subject unto, and
esteem the matter weighty enough to be taken care of by a law.
In that case he may order it to be done. But will any one there-
fore say that a [47] magistrate | has the same right to ordain by SE41
law that all children shall be baptized by priests in the sacred
font in order to the purification of their souls? The extreme
difference of these two cases is visible to every one at first sight.
Or let us apply the last case to the child of a *Jew*, and the thing
will speak [48] itself. For what hinders but a Christian magistrate may have subjects that are *Jews*? Now, if we acknowledge
that such an injury may not be done unto a *Jew* as to compel
him, against his own opinion, to practise in his religion a thing
that is in its nature indifferent, | how can we maintain that PE30
anything of this kind may be done to a Christian?

[43] LW: ever   [44] PE, CM, GH: *And*   [45] LW: ever   [46] GH: way
[47] HL, LW: the   [48] PE, CM, GH: thing speaks

3. Res sua natura indifferentes non possunt fieri pars cultus divini auctoritate et arbitrio humano, et hanc ipsam ob rationem, quia sunt indifferentes. Nam cum res indifferentes nulla virtute sua propria aptae natae sunt ad Numen propitiandum, nulla humana potestas vel auctoritas eam illis conciliare valet dignitatem et excellentiam, ut Deum possint demereri. In communi vita rerum sua natura indifferentium liber is [11] et licitus est usus quem Deus non prohibuerit, adeoque in iis LG50 locum habere potest arbitrium | vel auctoritas humana: sed eadem non est in religione et sacris libertas. In cultu divino res adiaphorae non alia ratione sunt licitae, nisi quatenus a Deo institutae, eamque illis certo mandato tribuerit Deus dignitatem ut fiant pars cultus, quam approbare et ab homunculis et peccatoribus accipere dignabitur supremi Numinis majestas. Nec Deo indignabunde roganti: *Quis requisivit*? satis erit respondere, jussisse magistratum. Si jurisdictio civilis eo usque extendatur, quid non licebit in religione? Quae rituum farrago, quae superstitionis inventa, modo magistratus auctoritate innixa, etiam reclamante et condemnante conscientia, non erunt Dei cultoribus amplectenda,[11b] cum horum pars maxima in religioso rerum sua natura indifferentium usu consistat, nec in alio peccat, quam quod Deum non habeat auctorem? Aquae aspersio, panis et vini usus, res sunt sua natura et in communi vita maxime indifferentes: an igitur haec in usus sacros LG51 introduci, | et divini cultus pars fieri poterant sine instituto divino? Hoc si potuit humana aliqua, vel civilis ML16 potestas, quidni | etiam et jubere possit tamquam partem cultus divini, in sacra synaxi piscibus et cerevisia epulari; jugulatarum bestiarum sanguinem

[11] LG: liberis   [11b] LG, ML, HE: amplectanda

Again: Things in their own nature indifferent cannot, by any human authority, be made any part of the worship of God, for this very reason: because they are indifferent. For, since indifferent things are not capable, by any virtue of their own, to propitiate the Deity, no human power or authority can confer on them so much dignity and excellency as to enable them to do it. In the common affairs of life that use of indifferent things which God has not forbidden is free and lawful, and therefore in those things human authority has place. But it is not so in matters of religion. Things indifferent are not otherwise lawful in the worship of God than as they are instituted by God himself, and as he, by some positive command, has ordained them | to be made a part of that SE42 worship which he will vouchsafe to accept of at [49] the hands of poor sinful men. Nor, when an incensed Deity | shall ask us: HL50 *Who has required these, or such-like things at your* [50] *hands?* will it be enough to answer him that the magistrate commanded them. If civil jurisdiction extended [51] thus far, what might not lawfully be introduced into religion? What hodgepodge of ceremonies, what superstitious inventions, built upon the magistrate's authority, might not (against conscience) be imposed upon the worshippers of God? For the greatest part of these ceremonies and superstitions consists in the religious use of such things as are in their own nature indifferent; nor are they sinful upon any other account than because God is not the author of them. The sprinkling of water, and the use of bread and wine, are both in their own nature and in the ordinary occasions of life altogether indifferent. Will any man therefore say that these things could have been introduced into religion, and made a part of divine worship, if not by divine institution? If any human authority or civil | power PE31 could have done this, why might it not also enjoin the eating of fish and drinking of ale in the holy banquet as a part of divine worship? Why not the sprinkling of the blood of beasts

[49] GH: accept at   [50] PE: our   [51] GH: extend

in templo aspergere; aqua vel igne lustrare; et hujusmodi alia infinita, quae quamvis extra religionem indif-
ferentia sint, cum in sacros ritus sine auctoritate divina
adsciscantur, aeque Deo exosa sunt ac canis immolatio[?]
Quid enim catulum inter et hircum interest respectu
divinae naturae, ab omni materiae affinitate aequaliter
et infinitum distantis, nisi quod hoc animalium genus
vellet, illud nollet Deus in sacris cultuque suo adhiberi?
Vides igitur, quod res in medio positae, utcumque sub-
jaceant potestati civili, non possunt tamen eo nomine in
sacros ritus introduci, et coetibus religiosis injungi: quia
in sacro cultu desinunt protinus esse indifferentes. Qui
Deum colit, eo colit animo, ut placeat, propitiumque
LG52 reddat; | quod tamen facere non potest is, qui jubente
alio illud Deo offert, quod credit Numini, quia non jus-
sit, displiciturum. Hoc non est Deum placare, sed mani-
festa contumelia, quae cum cultus ratione consistere
non potest, sciens prudensque lacessere.

Dices: Si nihil in cultu divino permittatur humano
arbitrio, quomodo tribuitur ecclesiis ipsis potestas
aliquid de tempore locoque etc. statuendi? Respondeo:
In cultu religioso aliud est pars, aliud circumstantia.
Illud pars est, quod creditur a Deo requiri et ipsi placere;
unde fit necessarium. Circumstantiae sunt, quae etsi in
genere a cultu abesse non possunt, tamen earum certa
species non definitur, adeoque sunt indifferentes: cujus-
modi sunt locus et tempus, cultoris habitus et corporis
situs; cum de iis nihil mandaverit voluntas divina;
v[erbi] g[ratia] tempus [12] locusque

---

[12] LG: v: g: Tempus ML: v. g. Tempus

in churches, and expiations by water or fire, and abundance more of this kind? | But these things, how indifferent soever SE43 they be in common uses, when they come to be annexed unto divine worship, without divine authority, they are as abominable to God as the sacrifice of a dog. And why is a dog so abominable? What difference is there between a dog and a goat, in respect of the divine nature, equally and infinitely distant from all affinity with matter, unless it be that God required the use of one in his worship, and not of the other? We see, therefore, that indifferent things, how much soever they be under the power of the civil magistrate, yet cannot, upon that pretence, be introduced into religion, and imposed upon religious assemblies, because, in the worship of God, they wholly cease to be indifferent. He that worships God does it with design to please him and procure his favour. But that cannot be done by him who, upon the command of another, offers unto God that which he knows will be displeasing to him, because not commanded by himself. This is not to please God, or appease his wrath, but willingly and knowingly to provoke him by a manifest contempt, which is a thing absolutely repugnant to the nature and end of worship.

But it will here be asked: *If nothing belonging to divine worship be left to human discretion, how is it then that churches themselves have the power of ordering* | *anything about the time and place of worship, and the like?* To SE44 this I answer, that in religious worship we must distinguish between what is part of the worship itself and what is but a circumstance. That is a part of the worship which is believed to be appointed by God, and to be well-pleasing to him, and therefore that is necessary. | Circumstances are such things PE32 which, though in general they cannot be separated from worship, yet the particular instances or modifications of them are not determined, and therefore they are indifferent. Of this sort are the time and place of worship, habit, and posture of him that worships. These are circumstances, and perfectly indifferent, where God has not given any express command about them. For example: amongst the *Jews* the time and

et sacra facientium habitus apud Judaeos non erant merae circumstantiae, sed pars cultus, in quibus si quid LG53 mancum aut immutatum, | sperare non poterant sacra sua Deo fore grata et accepta. Quae tamen Christianis, quibus constat libertas Evangelica, purae sunt cultus circumstantiae, quas prudentia cujusque ecclesiae potest in morem trahere, prout eas credit hoc vel illo modo cum ordine et decore aedificationi maxime inservire. Iis vero quibus sub Evangelio persuasum est diem dominicum suo cultui a Deo segregatum esse, illis tempus hoc non est circumstantia, sed pars cultus divini, quae nec mutari nec negligi potest.

[Secundo.] Magistratus ecclesiae cujusvis ritus sacros et cultum in ea receptum prohibere non potest in coetibus religiosis: quoniam eo modo ipsam tolleret ecclesiam, cujus finis est ut Deum suo more libere colat. Dices: An igitur si infantem immolare; si (quod Christianis olim falso affictum) in promiscua stupra ruere velint, an et haec et hujusmodi, quia in coetu ecclesiastico fiunt, a magistratu sint toleranda? Respondeo: LG54 Haec domi et in civili vita | non licita, itaque nec in coetu aut cultu religioso. Si vero vitulum immolare vellent, id lege prohibendum esse nego. Meliboeus, cujum pecus est, domi vitulum suum mactare potest partemque quam velit igne cremare: nulli facta est injuria, alienae possessioni nihil detrahitur.

place | of their worship, and the habits of those that officiated HL51
in it, were not mere circumstances, but a part of the worship
itself, in which if anything were defective, or different from the
institution, they could not hope that it would be accepted by
God. But these, to Christians under the liberty of the Gospel,
are mere circumstances of worship, which the prudence of
every church may bring into such use as shall be judged most
subservient to the end of order, decency, and edification.
Though [52] even under the Gospel, also those [53] who believe
the first or the seventh day to be set apart by | God, and SE45
consecrated still to his worship, to them that portion of time
is not a simple circumstance, but a real part of divine worship,
which can neither be changed nor neglected.

In the next place: As the magistrate has no power to *impose* by
his laws the use of any rites and ceremonies in any church, so
neither has he any power to *forbid* the use of such rites and
ceremonies as are already received, approved, and practised by
any church; because, if he did so, he would destroy the church
itself: the end of whose institution is only to worship God with
freedom after its own manner.

You will say, by this rule, if some congregations should have
a mind to *sacrifice infants*, or (as the primitive Christians were
falsely accused) *lustfully pollute themselves in promiscuous uncleanness*, or
practise any other such heinous enormities, is the magistrate
obliged to tolerate them, | because they are committed in a PE33
religious assembly? I answer: No. These things are not lawful
in the ordinary course of life, nor in any private house; and
therefore neither are they so in the worship of God, or in any
religious meeting. But, indeed, if any people congregated upon
account of religion should be desirous to sacrifice a calf, I deny
that that ought to be prohibited by a law. *Melibœus*, whose calf
it is, may lawfully kill his [54] calf at home, and | burn any part SE46
of it that he thinks fit. For no injury is thereby done to any
one, no prejudice to another man's goods. And for the same

[52] PE, CM, GH: But   [53] PE, CM, GH: Gospel, those
[54] SE: his own calf

In cultu igitur divino vitulum jugulare itidem licet: an
Deo placeat, ipsorum est videre. Magistratus solum,
prospicere nequid detrimenti res publica capiat, ne
alterius vel vitae vel bonis fiat damnum; adeoque quod
convivio poterat, potest et sacrificio impendi. Quod si
is sit rerum status, ut e re publica foret, parcere omni
ML17 boum sanguini | in subsidium armentorum lue aliqua
absumptorum, quis non videt, licere magistratui,
quamcumque vitulorum in quosvis usus caedem omnibus subditis interdicere [?] Sed eo in casu non de re
religionis, sed politica fit lex, nec prohibetur vituli immolatio, sed caedes. Jam vides ecclesiam inter et rem
publicam quae sit differentia. Id quod in re publica li-
LG55 citum | est, in ecclesia non potest a magistratu pro-
hiberi; quodque aliis subditis permissum in quotidiano
usu, id ne fiat in coetu ecclesiastico et ab hujus vel illius
sectae mystis ad sacros usus, nullo modo lege caveri
potest aut debet. Si domi panem vel vinum discumbens
vel flexis genibus sumere quis licite potest; lex civilis ve-
tare non debet, quo minus idem in sacris faciat, etiamsi
illic vini et panis longe diversus sit usus, et in ecclesia ad cultum divinum et mysticos sensus transfe-
ratur. Quae per se civitati noxia in vita communi, legibus in commune bonum latis prohibentur, ea in
ecclesia sacro usu licita esse non possunt, nec impunita-
tem mereri. Sed maxime cavere debent magistratus,
ne civilis utilitatis praetextu ad opprimendam alicujus
ecclesiae libertatem abutantur; e contra vero quae in vita
communi et extra cultum Dei licita sunt, ea in cultu
divino locisve sacris quo minus fiant lege civili prohiberi
non possunt. |
LG56   Dices: Quid si ecclesia aliqua sit idololatrica, anne illa
etiam a magistratu toleranda? Respondeo: Ecquod jus
dari potest

66

reason he may kill his calf also in a religious meeting. Whether the doing so be well-pleasing to God or no, it is their part to consider that do it. The part of the magistrate is only to take care that the commonwealth receive no prejudice, and that there be no injury done to any man, either in life or estate. And thus what may be spent on a feast may be spent on a sacrifice. But if peradventure such were the state of things that the interest of the commonwealth required all slaughter of beasts should be forborne for some while, in order to the increasing of the stock of cattle that had been destroyed by some extraordinary murrain, who sees not that the magistrate, in such a case, may forbid all his subjects to kill any calves for any use whatsoever? Only it is to be [55] observed that, in this case, the law is not made about a religious, but a political matter; nor is the sacrifice, but the slaughter of calves, thereby prohibited.

By this we see what difference there is between the church and the commonwealth. Whatsoever is lawful in the commonwealth cannot be prohibited by the magistrate in the church. Whatsoever is permitted unto any [56] of his subjects | for their SE47 ordinary use, neither can nor ought to be forbidden | by him HL52 to any sect of people for their religious uses. If any man may lawfully take bread or wine, either sitting or kneeling in his own house, the law ought | not to abridge him of the same PE34 liberty in his religious worship; though in the church the use of bread and wine be very different, and be there applied to the mysteries of faith and rites of divine worship. But those things that are prejudicial to the commonweal of a people in their ordinary use, and are therefore forbidden by laws, those things ought not to be permitted to churches in their sacred rites. Only the magistrate ought always to be very careful that he do not misuse his authority to the oppression of any church, under pretence of public good.

It may be said: *what if a church be idolatrous, is that also to be tolerated by the magistrate?* In answer, I ask: [57] What power can be given

[55] LW: to observed   [56] SE: any one of
[57] PE, CM, GH: magistrate? I answer, what

magistratui, ad supprimendam ecclesiam idololatricam,
quod etiam suo tempore et loco non pessumdabit orthodoxam? Nam memineris oportet, quod eadem est ubique civilis potestas et sua cuique principi orthodoxa
religio. Ideoque si in rebus religionis magistratui civili
concessa sit potestas quae Genevae vi et sanguine extir-
pare debet religionem, quae pro falsa vel idololatrica
habetur; in vicinia eodem jure orthodoxam opprimet,
et in Indiis Christianam. Potestas civilis vel omnia potest
in religione ad opinionem principis mutare, vel nihil.
Si aliquid liceat in rebus sacris lege, vi, poenis introducere, frustra quaeritur modus: omnia licebit ad normam
veritatis, quam sibi magistratus finxerit, iisdem armis
exigere. Nemo hominum religionis causa bonis suis
terrestribus evertendus, nec Americani principi Chris-
LG57 tiano subjecti ideo | vita aut bonis exuendi, quia Chris-
tianam religionem non amplectuntur. Si patriis ritibus
se Deo placere et salvos fieri credant, sibi et Deo relin-
quendi. Rem ab origine retexam. Venit in Ethnicorum
ditionem Christianorum parva et debilis turba, omnium
rerum egena: postulant extranei ab indigenis, homines
ab hominibus, uti par est, subsidia vitae: dantur necessaria, conceduntur sedes, coalescit in unum populum
utraque gens. Christiana religio radices agit, dissemina-
tur, sed nondum fortior; colitur adhuc pax, amicitia,
fides; et aequa servantur jura: tandem magistratu in
eorum partes transeunte fortiores facti sunt Christiani.
Tum demum pacta

to the magistrate for the suppression of an idolatrous church, which may not in time and place be made use of to the ruin of an orthodox one? For it must be remembered that the civil power is the same everywhere, and the religion of every prince is orthodox to himself. If, therefore, such a power be granted unto the civil magistrate in spirituals, as that at *Geneva* (for example) he may extirpate, by violence | and blood, the re- SE48 ligion which is there reputed idolatrous, by the same rule another magistrate, in some neighbouring country, may oppress the reformed religion, and, in *India*, the Christian. The civil power can either change everything in religion, according to the prince's pleasure, or it can change nothing. If it be once permitted to introduce anything into religion, by the means of laws and penalties, there can be no bounds put to it; but it will in the same manner be lawful to alter everything, accor- ding to that rule of truth which the magistrate has framed unto himself. No man whatsoever ought therefore to be deprived of his terrestrial enjoyments upon account of his religion. Not even *Americans*, subjected unto a Christian prince, are to be punished either in body or goods for not embracing our faith and worship. If they are | persuaded that they please God in PE35 observing the rites of their own country, and that they shall obtain happiness by that means, they are to be left unto God and themselves. Let us trace this matter to the bottom. Thus it is: an inconsiderable and weak number of Christians, destitute of everything, arrive in a Pagan country; these foreign- ers beseech the inhabitants, by the bowels of humanity, that they would succour them with the necessaries of life; those necessaries are given them, habitations are granted, and | they SE49 all join together, and grow up into one body of people. The Christian religion by this means takes root in that country, and spreads itself, but does not suddenly grow the strongest. While things are in this condition peace, friendship, faith, and equal justice are preserved amongst them. At length the magistrate becomes a Christian, and by that means their party becomes the most powerful. Then immediately all compacts

proculcanda, violanda jura, ut amoveatur idololatria,
et ni ritus suos antiquos relinquere, et in alienos novos-
que transire velint, vita, bonis terrisque avitis exuendi
innocui et juris observantissimi ethnici, utpote contra
bonos mores et legem civilem non peccantes; et tum
demum, quid zelus pro ecclesia, scilicet cum amore |
LG58 dominandi conjunctus, suadet aperte constat: et quam
commode rapinae et ambitioni praetexitur religio et
salus animarum palam demonstratur. [13] |

ML18   Si legibus, poenis, ferro et igne alicubi extirpandam
credis esse idololatriam, mutato nomine de te fabula
narratur. Quandoquidem non meliore jure res suas in
America amittunt ethnici, quam in regno aliquo Euro-
paeo ab ecclesia aulica quovis modo discrepantes Christiani; nec magis hic quam illic propter religionem civilia
vel violanda vel mutanda jura.

   Dices: Idololatria peccatum est, ideoque non toleranda. Respondeo: Si dicas, idololatria peccatum est, ideoque studiose vitanda, recte admodum infers; si vero peccatum est, ideoque a magistratu punienda, non item.
Non enim magistratus est, in omnia, quae apud Deum
credit peccata esse, vel legibus animadvertere, vel gladium suum stringere. Avaritia, non subvenire aliorum
indigentiae, otium et alia hujusmodi multa, omnium
LG59 consensu peccata | sunt; quis autem unquam a magis-
tratu castiganda censuit? Quia alienis possessionibus
nullum fit detrimentum, quia pacem publicam haec
non perturbant, iis ipsis in locis ubi pro peccatis agnos-
cuntur legum censura non coercentur: de mendacibus,
immo perjuriis, ubique silent leges, nisi certis quibusdam
in casibus, in quibus non respicitur Numinis provocatio
vel criminis turpitudo, sed intentata vel rei publicae
vel vicino injuria. Et quid si principi ethnico vel Mahumedano videatur religio Christiana falsa et

[13] HE: demonstratu

are to be broken, all civil rights to be violated, that idolatry may be extirpated; and unless these innocent Pagans, strict observers of the rules of equity and the law of nature, and no ways offending against the laws of the society, I say, unless they will forsake their ancient religion, and embrace a new and strange one, they are | to be turned out of the lands and pos- HL53 sessions of their forefathers, and perhaps deprived of life itself. Then, at last, it appears what zeal for the church, joined with the desire of dominion, is capable to produce, and how easily the pretence of religion, and of the care of souls, serves for a cloak to covetousness, rapine, and ambition.

Now whosoever maintains that idolatry is to be rooted out of any place by laws, punishments, fire, and sword, may apply this story to himself. For the reason of the thing is equal, both in *America* and *Europe*. And neither Pagans there, nor any dissenting Christians here, can, with | any right, be deprived | PE36 of their worldly goods by the predominating faction of a court- SE50 church; nor are any civil rights to be either changed or violated upon account of religion in one place more than another.

But *idolatry*, (say some) *is a sin*, and therefore not to be tolerated. If they said it were therefore to be avoided, the inference were good. But it does not follow, that because it is a sin it ought therefore to be punished by the magistrate. For it does not belong unto the magistrate to make use of his sword in punishing everything, indifferently, that he takes to be a sin against God. Covetousness, uncharitableness, idleness, and many other things are sins, by the consent of men, which yet no man ever said were to be punished by the magistrate. The reason is, because they are not prejudicial to other men's rights, nor do they break the public peace of societies. Nay, even the sins of lying and perjury are nowhere punishable by laws; unless, in certain cases, in which the real turpitude of the thing and the offence against God are not considered, but only the injury done unto men's neighbours and to the commonwealth. And what if in another country, to a Mahometan or a Pagan prince, the Christian religion seem false and

Deo displicere, nonne eodem jure et eodem modo extir-
pandi etiam et Christiani?

Dices: Lege Mosaica idololatras exterminandos.
Respondeo: Recte quidem Mosaica, quae nullo modo
Christianos obligat. Nec tu quidem totum illud, quod
lege positum est Judaeis, in exemplum trahes; nec usui
tibi erit proferre tritam illam, sed hac in re futilem, legis
Moralis, Judicialis et Ritualis distinctionem. Lex enim
quaecumque positiva nullos obligat, nisi eos quibus |
LG60 ponitur. *Audi Israel,* satis coercet ad eam gentem Mosai-
cae legis obligationem. Hoc unicum sufficeret contra
illos, qui idololatris capitale supplicium ex lege Mosaica
statuere volunt. Libet tamen hoc argumentum paulo
fusius expendere.

Idololatrarum respectu rei publicae Judaicae duplex
erat ratio: Primo, eorum, qui sacris Mosaicis initiati et
istius rei publicae cives facti a cultu Dei Israelis descive-
rint. Hi tamquam proditores et rebelles laesae majestatis rei agebantur. Res publica enim Judaeorum ab aliis
longe diversa, quippe quae in Theocratia fundabatur;
nec, uti post Christum natum, ulla fuit aut esse potuit
inter ecclesiam et rem publicam distinctio; leges de
unius invisibilisque Numinis cultu in ea gente fuere
civiles et politici regiminis pars, in quo ipse Deus legislator. Si rem publicam eo jure constitutam uspiam
ostendere potes, in ea fatebor leges ecclesiasticas in civiles
transire, omnesque subditos etiam a cultu extraneo et
LG61 sacris alienis magistratus gladio | cohiberi et posse et
debere. Sed sub Evangelio nulla prorsus est res publica
Christiana. Multa fateor sunt regna et civitates

offensive to God; may not the Christians for the same reason, and after the same manner, be extirpated there? |

But it may be urged farther, that, by the law of *Moses*, SE51 idolaters were to be rooted out. True, indeed, by the law of *Moses;* but that is not obligatory to us Christians. Nobody pretends that everything generally enjoined by the law of *Moses* ought to be practised by Christians, but there is nothing more frivolous than that common distinction of moral, judicial, and ceremonial law, which men ordinarily make use of. For no positive law whatsoever can oblige any people but those to whom it is given. *Hear, O Israel,* sufficiently restrains | the obligations of the law of Moses only to that people. And PE37 this consideration alone is answer enough unto those that urge the authority of the law of *Moses* for the inflicting of capital punishment upon idolaters. But, however, I will examine this argument a little more particularly.

The case of idolaters, in respect of the *Jewish* commonwealth, falls under a double consideration. The first is of those who, being initiated in the *Mosaical* rites, and made citizens of that commonwealth, did afterwards apostatize from the worship of the God of *Israel.* These were proceeded against as traitors and rebels, guilty of no less than high treason. For the commonwealth of the *Jews,* different in that from all others, was an absolute | *theocracy*; nor was there, or could there | be, any HL54/SE52 difference between that commonwealth and the church. The laws established there concerning the worship of one invisible Deity were the civil laws of that people, and a part of their political government, in which God himself was the legislator. Now, if any one can show me where there is a commonwealth at this time, constituted upon that foundation, I will acknowledge that the ecclesiastical laws do there unavoidably become a part of the civil, and that the subjects of that government both may, and ought to be kept in strict conformity with that church by the civil power. But there is absolutely no such thing under the Gospel as a Christian commonwealth. There are, indeed, many cities and kingdoms

quae in fidem transierunt Christianam, retenta et
conservata veteris rei publicae et regiminis forma, de
qua Christus nihil sua lege statuit. Qua fide, quibus
moribus vita aeterna singulis obtinenda sit, docuit:
verumtamen nullam rem publicam instituit, novam
civitatis formam et suo populo peculiarem nullam
introduxit, nullos magistratus gladio armavit, quo
homines ad fidem vel cultum eum, quem suis propo-
suit, cogerentur, vel ab alienae religionis institutis arce-
rentur. |

ML19   Secundo, extranei et a re publica Israelis alieni non vi
cogebantur ad ritus Mosaicos transire; verum eo ipso
paragrapho quo mors Israelitis idololatris intentatur,
Exod. xxii, 20, 21, nequis peregrinum vexet [14] vel opprimat
lege cautum est. Exscindendae penitus fateor erant
LG62 septem gentes quae terram | Israelitis promissam possi-
debant, quod factum non quod idololatrae fuerint, hoc
enim si esset, cur Moabitis et aliis nationibus etiam idololatris parcendum? Sed cum Deus populi Hebraei
peculiari modo rex erat, venerationem alterius Numinis (quod erat proprie crimen laesae majestatis) suo
illo in regno, terra nempe Cananaea, pati non poterat:
hujusmodi aperta defectio cum Jehovae imperio istis
in terris plane politico, nullo modo potuit consistere.
Expellenda erat igitur a limitibus regni omnis idololatria, qua rex alius, alius scilicet Deus contra jus imperii
agnoscebatur. Expellendi etiam incolae, ut vacua et
integra Israelitis daretur possessio; qua plane ratione
populi Emmim et Horim exterminati sunt ab Esavi et
Lothi posteris, eorum territoria eodem plane jure a Deo
concessa invadentibus: quod facile patebit caput secundum Deuteronomii legenti. Expulsa igitur licet e finibus
terrae Cananaeae omnis idololatria, non tamen in |
LG63 omnes idololatras animadversum. Rahabae toti familiae,
Gibeonitarum universo populo pepercit Josuah ex
pacto.

[14] HE: vexat

that have embraced the faith of Christ, but they have retained their ancient form of government, with which the law of Christ hath not at all meddled. He, indeed, hath taught men how, by faith and good works, they may obtain eternal life; but he instituted no commonwealth. He prescribed unto his followers no new and peculiar form of government, nor put he the sword | into any magistrate's hand, with commission PE38 to make use of it in forcing men to forsake their former religion and receive his.

Secondly, foreigners, and such as were strangers to the *commonwealth* of *Israel*, | were not compelled by force to observe SE53 the rites of the *Mosaical* law; but, on the contrary, in the very same place where it is ordered that *an Israelite that was an idolater should be put to death*, there it is provided that *strangers should not be vexed nor oppressed, Exod.* XXII. 20, 21. I confess that the seven nations that possessed the land which was promised to the Israelites were utterly to be cut off; but this was not singly because they were idolaters. For if that had been the reason, why were the *Moabites* and other nations to be spared? No: the reason is this. God being in a peculiar manner the King of the *Jews*, he could not suffer the adoration of any other deity (which was properly an act of high treason against himself) in the land of *Canaan*, which was his kingdom. For such a manifest revolt could no ways consist with his dominion, which was perfectly political in that country. All idolatry was therefore to be rooted out of the bounds of his kingdom, because it was an acknowledgment of another god, that is to say, another king, against the laws of empire. The inhabitants were also to be driven out, that the entire possession of the land might be given to the *Israelites*. And for the like reason the *Emims* and the *Horims* were driven out of their countries | by the children of *Esau* SE54 and *Lot;* and their lands, upon the same grounds, given by God to the invaders, *Deut.* II. But, though all idolatry was thus rooted out of the land of *Canaan*, yet every idolater was not brought to execution. The whole family of *Rahab*, the whole nation of the *Gibeonites*, articled with *Josuah*, and were allowed by treaty; and

Captivi idololatrae passim inter Hebraeos. Regiones etiam ultra limites terrae promissae a Davide et Salomone ad Euphraten usque subjugatae et in provincias redactae. Ex his tot mancipiis, tot populis potestati Hebraeae subjectis, nemo unquam (quod legimus) ob idololatriam, cujus certe omnes rei erant, castigatus: nemo vi et poenis ad religionem Mosaicam et veri Dei cultum coactus. Si quis proselyta civitate donari cupierat, civitatis Israeliticae etiam leges, hoc est religionem simul amplexus est: sed id sponte sua pronus, non imperantis vi coactus, tamquam privilegium cupidus ambivit, non invitus in obsequii testimonium accepit. Simul atque civis factus est legibus rei publicae obnoxius erat, quibus intra pomeria et limites terrae Cananaeae prohibebatur idololatria. De exteris regionibus populis- LG64 que ultra eos terminos | sitis nihil ea lege statutum.

Hactenus de cultu externo: sequitur ut de fide agamus.

Ecclesiarum dogmata alia practica, alia speculativa; et quamvis utraque in veritatis cognitione consistunt, haec tamen opinione et intellectu terminantur, illa aliquo modo ad voluntatem et mores spectant. Speculativa igitur dogmata, et, (uti vocantur) articulos fidei, quod attinet, qui nihil aliud exigunt nisi solum ut credantur, illos lex civilis nullo modo in ecclesiam aliquam potest introducere; quorsum enim attinet id lege sancire, quod qui vellet maxime, non potest agere? Ut hoc vel illud verum esse credamus in nostra voluntate situm non est. Sed de hoc satis jam dictum. Verum profiteatur se credere. Nimirum ut pro salute animae suae Deo et hominibus mentiatur. Bella sane religio. Si magistratus ita servari homines velit, quae sit via salutis videtur parum intelligere; si id non agit ut

76

there were many captives amongst the *Jews* who were idolaters. *David* and *Solomon* subdued | many countries without the PE39 confines of the land of promise, and carried their conquests as far as Euphrates. Amongst so many captives taken, so many nations reduced under their obedience, we find not one man forced into the Jewish religion and the worship of the true God, | and punished for idolatry, though all of them were HL55 certainly guilty of it. If any one indeed, becoming a proselyte, desired to be made a denizen of their commonwealth, he was obliged to submit to their laws; that is, to embrace their religion. But this he did willingly, on his own accord, not by constraint. He did not unwillingly submit, to show his obedience, but he sought and solicited for it as a privilege. And, as soon as he was admitted, he became subject to the laws of the commonwealth, by which all idolatry was forbidden within the borders of the land of *Canaan*. But that law (as I have said) | did not reach to any of those regions, however subjected unto SE55 the *Jews*, that were situated without those bounds.

Thus far concerning outward worship. Let us now consider *articles of faith*.

The *articles* of religion are some of them *practical* and some *speculative*. Now, though both sorts consist in the knowledge of truth, yet these terminate simply in the understanding, those influence the will and manners. Speculative opinions, therefore, and *articles of faith* (as they are called) which are required only to be believed, cannot be imposed on any church by the law of the land. For it is absurd that things should be enjoined by laws which are not in men's power to perform. And to believe this or that to be true, does not depend upon our will. But of this enough has been said already. But (will some say) let men at least profess that they believe. A sweet religion, indeed, that obliges men to dissemble and tell lies, both to God and man, for the salvation of their souls! If the | magistrate thinks to save men thus, he seems to under- PE40 stand little of the way of salvation. And if he does it not in

LG65 serventur, quare de | articulis religionis tam sollicitus,
ut lege jubeat?

Deinde, opiniones quasvis speculativas quo minus in
ecclesia quavis teneantur doceanturve prohibere non
debet magistratus; quia hae ad civilia subditorum jura
nequaquam attinent. Si quis Pontificius credat id cor-
ML20 pus | Christi re vera esse, quod alius panem vocaret, nul-
lam injuriam facit vicino. Si Judaeus non credat novum
testamentum esse verbum Dei, nulla mutat jura civilia.
Si ethnicus de utroque dubitat testamento, non igitur
puniendus tamquam improbus civis. Haec si quis credat,
sive non, sarta tecta esse possunt magistratus potestas
et civium bona. Falsas has esse et absurdas opiniones libenter concedo; ceterum de opinionum veritate non
cavent leges, sed de bonorum cujusque et rei publicae
tutela et incolumitate. Nec hoc plane dolendum est.
Bene profecto cum veritate actum esset, si sibi aliquando
permitteretur. Parum opis illi attulit vel afferet um-
LG66 quam potentiorum | dominatus, quibus nec cognita
semper nec semper grata veritas; vi opus non habet, ut
ad hominum mentes aditum inveniat; nec legum voce
docetur. Mutuatitiis et extraneis auxiliis regnant errores.
Veritas si sua luce sibi non arripiat intellectum, alieno
robore non potest. Sed de his hactenus. Ad opiniones
practicas jam pergendum.

Morum rectitudo, in qua consistit non minima religionis et sincerae pietatis pars, etiam ad vitam civilem spec-
tat et in ea versatur animarum simul et rei publicae
salus; ideoque utriusque sunt fori, tam externi quam
interni, actiones morales, et utrique subjiciuntur imperio, tam moderatoris civilis quam domestici, scilicet
magistratus et conscientiae. Hic igitur metuendum est,
ne alter

order to save them, why is he so solicitous about the articles of
faith as to enact them by a law?

Further, the magistrate ought not to forbid the preaching or
professing of any speculative opinions in any church, because |
they have no manner of relation to the civil rights of the sub- SE56
jects. If a *Roman Catholic* believe that to be really the body of
Christ, which another man calls bread, he does no injury
thereby to his neighbour. If a Jew do not believe the New
Testament to be the word of God, he does not thereby alter
anything in men's civil rights. If a heathen doubt of both
Testaments, he is not therefore to be punished as a pernicious
citizen. The power of the magistrate and the estates of the
people may be equally secure whether any man believe these
things or no. I readily grant that these opinions are false and
absurd. But the business of laws is not to provide for the truth
of opinions, but for the safety and security of the commonwealth, and of every particular man's goods and person.
And so it ought to be. For the truth certainly would do well
enough if she were once left to shift for herself. She seldom has
received, and I fear never will receive, much assistance from
the power of great men, to whom she is but rarely known, and
more rarely welcome. She is not taught by laws, nor has she
any need of force to procure her entrance into the minds of
men. Errors indeed prevail by the assistance of foreign and
borrowed succours. But if truth makes not her way into the
understanding by her own light, she will be but the weaker
for any | borrowed | force violence can add to her. Thus much SE57/HL56
for speculative opinions. Let us now proceed to *practical* ones.

A good life, in which consists not the least part of religion and
true piety, concerns also the civil government; | and in it lies PE41
the safety both of men's souls and of the commonwealth.
Moral actions belong therefore to the jurisdiction both of the
outward and inward court; both of the civil and domestic
governor; I mean both of the magistrate and conscience.
Here, therefore, is great danger, lest [58] one of these jurisdic-

[58] PE, SE: least

alterius jus violet et inter pacis et animae custodem lis
oriatur. Sed si ea, quae supra de utriusque limitibus dicta
sunt, recte perpendantur, rem hanc totam facile expedient.

Quivis mortalium animam habet immortalem, |
LG67 aeternae beatitudinis aut miseriae capacem, cujus salus
cum ex eo pendeat, quod homo in hac vita egerit ea
quae agenda, et ea crediderit quae credenda, ad Numinis
conciliationem sunt necessaria et a Deo praescripta.
Inde sequitur, 1) [15] quod ad haec observanda ante
omnia obligatur homo et in his praecipue investigandis
peragendisque omnem suam curam studium et dili-
gentiam ponere debet; quandoquidem nihil habet haec
mortalis conditio quo cum illa aeterna ullo modo sit
aequiparanda. Sequitur, 2) [16] quod cum homo aliorum
hominum jus suo erroneo cultu nequaquam violet,
cum alteri injuriam non faciat quod cum eo recte de
rebus divinis non sentiat, nec illius perditio aliorum
rebus prosperis fraudi sit; ad singulos solum salutis suae
curam pertinere. Hoc autem non ita dictum velim, ac
si omnia caritatis monita, et studium errores redar-
guentium, (quae maxima sunt Christiani officia) exclu-
dere vellem. Hortationum et argumentorum quantum |
LG68 velit cuivis licet alterius saluti impendere; sed vis
omnis et coactio abesse debet, nihil illic faciendum pro
imperio. Nemo alterius monitis vel auctoritati hac in re
ultra quam ipsi visum fuerit obtemperare tenetur: suum
cuique de sua salute supremum et ultimum judicium
est; quia ipsius solum res agitur, aliena inde nihil detrimenti capere potest.

Praeter animam immortalem vita insuper homini est
in hoc saeculo, labilis quidem et incertae durationis, ad
quam sustentandam terrenis commodis opus est, labore
et industria conquirendis, aut jam conquisitis.

[15] LG, ML: praescripta; inde 1. Sequitur,
[16] LG, ML: 2. Sequitur,

tions intrench upon the other, and discord arise between the keeper of the public peace and the overseers of souls. But if what has been already said concerning the limits of both these governments be rightly considered, it will easily remove all difficulty in this matter.

Every man has an immortal soul, capable of eternal happiness or misery; whose happiness depending upon his believing and doing those things in this life which are necessary to the obtaining of God's favour, and are prescribed by God to that end. It follows from thence, *first*, that the observance of these things is the highest obligation that lies upon mankind, and that our utmost care, application, and diligence ought to be exercised in the search and performance of them; because there | is nothing in this world that is of any consideration in SE58 comparison with eternity. *Secondly*, that seeing one man does not violate the right of another by his erroneous opinions and undue manner of worship, nor is his perdition any prejudice to another man's affairs, therefore, the care of each man's salvation belongs only to himself. But I would not have this understood as if I meant hereby to condemn all charitable admonitions, and affectionate endeavours to reduce men from errors, which are indeed the greatest duty of a Christian. Any one may employ as many exhortations and arguments as he pleases, towards the promoting of another man's salvation. But all force and compulsion are to be forborne. Nothing is to be done imperiously. Nobody is obliged in that matter to yield obedience unto the admonitions or injunctions of another, further than he himself | is persuaded. Every man in that has PE42 the supreme and absolute authority of judging for himself. And the reason is because nobody else is concerned in it, nor can receive any prejudice from his conduct therein.

But besides their souls, which are immortal, men have also their temporal lives here upon earth; the state whereof being frail and fleeting, and the duration uncertain, they have need of several | outward conveniencies to the support thereof, SE59 which are to be procured or preserved by pains and industry.

Quae enim ad bene beateque vivendum necessaria sunt, non sponte nascuntur. Hinc homini de his rebus altera ML21 cura. Cum vero ea sit hominum improbitas, ut | plerique mallent alieno labore partis frui, quam suo quaerere; ideo homini parta, ut opes et facultates; vel ea quibus parantur, ut corporis libertatem et robur, tuendi gratia, ineunda est cum aliis societas, ut mutuo auxilio et LG69 junctis viribus harum | rerum ad vitam utilium sua cuique privata et secura sit possessio, relicta interim unicuique salutis suae aeternae cura; cum illius acquisitio nec alterius juvari poterit industria, nec amissio alterius cedere in damnum, nec spes ulla vi abripi. Cum vero homines in civitatem coeuntes, pacta ad rerum hujus vitae defensionem mutua ope, possint nihilominus rebus suis everti, vel civium rapina et fraude; vel exterorum hostili impetu; huic malo, armis, opibus et multitudine civium; illi, legibus quaesitum est remedium; quarum omnium rerum cura et potestas a societate magistratibus demandata est. Hanc originem habuit; ad hos usus constituebatur; et his cancellis circumscribitur legislativa quae suprema est rei publicae cujusvis potestas: ut scilicet prospiciat singulorum privatis possessionibus, adeoque universo populo ejusque publicis commodis, ut pace opibusque floreat ac augeatur: et contra aliorum invasionem quantum fieri possit suo robore tutus sit. |

LG70   His positis, intellectu facile est quibus regitur finibus magistratus in legibus ferendis praerogativa

For those things that are necessary to the comfortable support of our lives are not the spontaneous products of nature, nor do offer themselves fit and prepared for our use. This part therefore draws on another care, and necessarily gives another employment. But the pravity of mankind being such that they had rather injuriously prey upon the fruits of other men's labours than take pains to provide for themselves, the necessity of preserving men in the possession of what honest industry has already acquired, and also of preserving their liberty and strength, whereby they may acquire what they | farther want, obliges men to enter into society with one an- HL57 other, that by mutual assistance and joint force they may secure unto each other their properties, in the things that contribute to the comfort and happiness of this life, leaving in the meanwhile to every man the care of his own eternal happiness, the attainment whereof can neither be facilitated by another man's industry, nor can the loss of it turn to another man's prejudice, nor the hope of it be forced from him by any external violence. But, forasmuch as men thus entering into societies, grounded upon their mutual compacts of assistance for the defence of their temporal goods, may, | nevertheless, be deprived of them, either by the rapine and SE60 fraud of their fellow citizens, or by the hostile violence of foreigners, the remedy of this evil consists in arms, riches, and multitudes of | citizens; the remedy of the other in laws; PE43 and the care of all things relating both to one and the other is committed by the society to the civil magistrate. This is the original, this is the use, and these are the bounds of the legislative (which is the supreme) power in every commonwealth. I mean, that provision may be made for the security of each man's private possessions; for the peace, riches, and public commodities of the whole people; and, as much as possible, for the increase of their inward strength against foreign invasions.

These things being thus explained, it is easy to understand to what end the legislative power ought to be directed, and by

(bono scilicet publico terrestri sive mundano, quod idem unicum ineundae societatis argumentum, unicusque constitutae rei publicae finis), quaeque ex altera parte privatis restat in rebus ad futuram vitam spectantantibus libertas; nempe ut quod credit placere Deo, ex cujus beneplacito pendet hominum salus, id quisque agat. Primum enim debetur Deo obsequium, deinde legibus. Sed dices: Quid si edicto jusserit magistratus quod privatae conscientiae videatur illicitum? Respondeo: Si bona fide administretur res publica et ad bonum commune civium re vera dirigantur magistratus consilia, hoc raro eventurum; quod si forte eveniat, dico abstinendum privato ab actione quae ipsi dictante conscientia est illicita; sed poena quae ferenti non est illicita subeunda. Privatum enim cujusque judicium legis in bonum publicum et de rebus politicis latae, non LG71 tollit obligationem, nec meretur | tolerantiam. Quod si lex sit de rebus extra magistratus provinciam positis, scilicet ut populus, ejusve pars aliqua, ad alienam religionem amplectendam, et ad alios ritus transire cogatur; ea lege non tenentur aliter sentientes: quandoquidem ad rerum hujus vitae solummodo conservandam privato cuique possessionem, nec alium in finem, inita est societas politica. Animae suae et rerum caelestium cura (quae ad civitatem non pertinet nec ei subjici potuit) privato cuique reservata atque retenta. Vitae inde et rerum ad hanc vitam spectantium tutela civitatis est negotium, et earum possessoribus suis conservatio officium magistratus. Non possunt igitur

what measures regulated; and that is the temporal good and outward prosperity of the society; which is the sole reason of men's entering into society, and the only thing they seek and aim at in it. And it is also evident what liberty remains to men in reference to their eternal salvation, and that is, that every one should do what he in his conscience is persuaded to be acceptable to the Almighty, on whose good pleasure and acceptance depends his [59] eternal | happiness. For obedience SE61 is due, in the first place, to God, and afterwards to the laws.

But some may ask: *What if the magistrate should enjoin anything by his authority that appears unlawful to the conscience of a private person?* I answer, that if government be faithfully administered, and the counsels of the magistrates be indeed directed to the public good, this will seldom happen. But if, perhaps, it do so fall out, I say, that such a private person is to abstain from the action that he judges unlawful, and he is to undergo the punishment which it is not unlawful for him to bear. For the private judgment of any person concerning a law enacted in political matters, for the public good, does not take away the obligation of that law, nor deserve a dispensation. But | if the law indeed PE44 be concerning things that lie not within the verge of the magistrate's authority (as for example, that the people, or any party amongst them, should be compelled to embrace a strange religion, and join in the worship and ceremonies of another church), men are not in these cases obliged by that law, against their consciences. For the political society is instituted for no other end, but only to secure every man's possession of the things of this life. The care of each man's soul, and of the things of heaven, which neither does belong to the commonwealth nor | can be subjected to it, is left SE62 entirely to every man's self. Thus the safeguard of men's lives, and of the things that belong unto this life, is the business of the commonwealth; | and the preserving of those things HL58 unto their owners is the duty of the magistrate. And therefore

[59] PE, CM, GH: their

res hae mundanae ad magistratus libitum his auferri,
illis tradi; nec earum (ne quidem lege) mutari inter
concives privata possessio propter causam, quae ad
concives nullo modo pertinet, nempe religionem, quae
sive vera sive falsa, nullam facit reliquis civibus in rebus
mundanis (quae solae reipublicae subjiciuntur) inju-
riam. |

LG72   Sed dices: Quid si magistratus credat hoc in bonum
publicum fieri? Respondeo: Quemadmodum privatum
cujusque judicium, si falsum sit, illum a legum obliga-
tione nequaquam eximit, sic privatum (ut ita dicam)
magistratus judicium novum illi in subditos legum
ML22 ferendarum jus non acquirit, quod | ipsa rei publicae
constitutione illi non concessum fuit, nec concedi
quidem potuit; multo minus, si id agat magistratus, ut
suos asseclas, suae sectae addictos, aliorum spoliis
augeat et ornet. Quaeris: Quid si magistratus id quod
jubet in sua potestate esse situm et ad rem publicam
utile credat, subditi vero contrarium credant [?] Quis
erit inter eos judex? Respondeo: Solus Deus: quia inter
legislatorem et populum nullus in terris est judex. Deus
inquam hoc in casu solus est arbiter, qui in ultimo
judicio pro cujusque meritis, prout bono publico paci-
que et pietati sincere et secundum jus fasque consuluit,
rependet. Dices: Quid interim fiet? Respondeo: Prima
LG73 animae cura habenda, et paci quam maxime | studen-
dum; quamquam pauci sint qui ubi solitudinem factam
vident pacem credant. [17] Eorum quae inter homines
disceptantur duplex est ratio, una jure, alia vi agentium;
quorum ea est natura, ut ubi alterum desinit, alterum
incipiat. Quousque jura magistratus

[17] LG, ML: credent

the magistrate cannot take away these worldly things from this
man or party, and give them to that; nor change propriety
amongst fellow-subjects (no not even by a law), for a cause
that has no relation to the end of civil government, I mean for
their religion, which whether it be true or false does no prejudice to the worldly concerns of their fellow-subjects, which
are the things that only belong unto the care of the commonwealth.

*But what if the magistrate believe such a law as this to be for the public
good?* I answer: As the private judgment of any particular
person, if erroneous, does not exempt him from the obligation
of law, so the private judgment (as I may call it) of the magistrate does not give him any new right of imposing laws upon
his subjects, which neither was in the constitution of the
government granted him, nor ever was in the power of the
people to grant: and least of all [60] if he make it his business to
enrich and advance his followers and fellow-sectaries with the
spoils of others. *But what if the magistrate | believe that he | has a right* PE45/SE63
*to make such laws, and that they are for the public good? and his subjects
believe the contrary? Who shall be judge between them?* I answer: God
alone. For there is no judge upon earth between the supreme
magistrate and the people. God, I say, is the only judge in this
case, who will retribute unto every one at the last day according to his deserts; that is, according to his sincerity and
uprightness in endeavouring to promote piety, and the public
weal and peace of mankind. *But what shall be done in the meanwhile?*
I answer: The principal and chief care of every one ought to
be of his own soul first, and, in the next place, of the public
peace; though yet there are very few will think it is peace there,
where they see all laid waste.

There are two sorts of contests amongst men, the one
managed by law, the other by force; and these are of that
nature that where the one ends, the other always begins. But
it is not my business to inquire into the power of the magis-

[60] PE, CM, GH: much less

apud singulas gentes extendantur, non meum est in-
quirere: hoc solum scio quid fieri solet ubi ambigitur
absente judice. Dices: Igitur magistratus quod e re sua
fore crediderit viribus potior efficiet. Respondeo:
Rem dicis; ceterum hic de recte faciendorum norma,
non de dubiorum successu quaeritur.

Sed ut ad magis particularia descendamus, dico primo: Nulla dogmata, humanae societati vel bonis moribus ad societatem civilem conservandam necessariis
adversa et contraria, a magistratu sunt toleranda.
Sed horum rara sunt in quavis ecclesia exempla: quae
enim societatis fundamenta manifesto subruunt, adeo-
LG74 que universi humani generis judicio damnata | sunt,
nulla secta eo vesaniae progredi solet, ut ea pro religionis dogmatibus docenda judicet, quibus suae ipsorum
res, quies, fama in tuto esse non possunt.

[Secundo] [18]. Tectius sane, sed et periculosius rei
publicae malum est eorum, qui sibi suaeque sectae hominibus peculiare aliquod praerogativum contra jus
civile arrogant, verborum involucris ad fucum faciendum aptis occultum. Nusquam fere invenies qui crude
et aperte doceant,[19] nullam fidem esse servandam; prin-
cipem a quavis secta e solio suo deturbari posse: dominium omnium rerum ad se solos pertinere. Haec enim ita
nude et aperte proposita excitarent statim magistratus
animos, et rei publicae oculos curamque ad malum
hoc in sinu suo latens ne ultra serperet, ilico conver-
terent. Inveniuntur tamen qui aliis verbis idem dicunt.
Quid enim aliud sibi volunt, qui docent, nullam fidem
servandam esse cum haereticis? Illud scilicet volunt, sibi
concessum esse fidei fallendae privilegium, quandoqui-
LG75 dem omnes | ab ipsorum communione alieni haeretici
pronuntiantur, vel data occasione possunt pronuntiari.
Reges excommunicatos regno excidere, quo tendit

[18] LG, ML: 2 and so on: 3, 4
[19] LG, ML: docent

88

trate in the different constitutions of nations. I only know what usually happens where controversies arise without a judge to determine them. You will say, then, the magistrate being the stronger will have his will, and carry his point. Without doubt; but the question is not here concerning the doubtfulness of the event, but the rule of right. |

But to come to particulars. I say, *first*, no opinions contrary SE64 to human society, or to those moral rules which are necessary to the preservation of civil society, are to be tolerated by the magistrate. But of these, indeed, examples in any church are rare. For no sect can easily arrive to such a degree of madness as that it should think fit to teach, for doctrines of religion, such things as manifestly undermine the foundations of society, and are, therefore, condemned by the judgment of all mankind; because their own interest, peace, reputation, everything would be thereby endangered. |

Another more secret evil, but more dangerous to the PE46 commonwealth, is when men arrogate to themselves, and to those of their own sect, some peculiar prerogative covered over with a specious show of deceitful words, but in effect opposite to the civil right of the community. For example: we cannot | find any sect that teaches, expressly and openly, that HL59 men are not obliged to keep their promise; that princes may be dethroned by those that differ from them in religion; or that the dominion of all things belongs only to themselves. For these things, proposed thus nakedly and plainly, would soon draw on them the eye and hand of the magistrate, and awaken all the care of the commonwealth to a watchfulness against the spreading of | so dangerous an evil. But, nevertheless, SE65 we find those that say the same things in other words. What else do they mean, who teach *that faith is not to be kept with heretics?* Their meaning, forsooth, is that the privilege of breaking faith belongs unto themselves; for they declare all that are not of their communion to be heretics, or at least may declare them so whensoever they think fit. What can be the meaning of their asserting that *kings excommunicated forfeit their crowns and*

nisi ut reges regno suo exuendi potestatem sibi arroga-
rent, cum excommunicationis jus suae soli hierarchiae
vindicent? Dominium fundari in gratia, tribuet tandem
omnium rerum possessionem hujus sententiae pro-
pugnatoribus, qui usque adeo sibi non deerunt, ut
credere vel profiteri nolint se vere pios esse et fideles. Hi
igitur et hujusmodi, qui fidelibus, religiosis, orthodoxis,
id est sibi, aliquod prae reliquis mortalibus privilegium
vel potestatem in rebus civilibus tribuunt; quive potestatem aliquam in homines a communione sua ecclesiastica alienos, vel quocumque modo separatos, praetextu
religionis sibi vindicant, ut a magistratu tolerentur jus
nullum habere possunt: uti nec ii, qui alios etiam a se de
ML23 religione | dissentientes tolerandos esse docere nolunt.
LG76 Quid enim aliud docent hi et hujusmodi omnes, | quam
se quacumque data occasione rei publicae jura et civium
libertatem ac bona invasuros; idque solum a magistratu petunt, ut sibi detur venia et libertas, usque dum
ad id audendum ipsis copiarum et virium satis sit? [20]

[Tertio.] Ea ecclesia ut a magistratu toleretur jus habere
non potest, in quam quicumque initiantur ipso facto
in alterius principis clientelam et obedientiam transeunt.
Hoc enim pacto extraneae jurisdictioni, suis in finibus
urbibusque, locum praeberet magistratus; et ex suis
civibus contra suam rem publicam milites conscribi
pateretur. Nec huic malo remedium aliquod affert
futilis illa et fallax inter aulam et ecclesiam distinctio;
cum utraque absoluto ejusdem hominis imperio aeque
subjicitur, qui quicquid libet, potest, vel quatenus
spirituale vel in ordine ad spiritualia, suadere,

[20] ML: fit

kingdoms? It is evident that they thereby arrogate unto themselves the power of deposing kings, because they challenge the power of excommunication, as the peculiar right of their hierarchy. That *dominion is founded in grace* is also an assertion by which those that maintain it do plainly lay claim to the possession of all things. For they are not so wanting to themselves as not to believe, or at least as not to profess themselves to be the truly pious and faithful. These therefore, and the like, who attribute unto the faithful, religious, and orthodox, that is, in plain terms, unto themselves, any peculiar privilege or power above other mortals, in civil concernments; | or who upon PE47 pretence of religion do challenge any manner of authority over such as are not associated with them in their ecclesiastical communion, I say these have no right to be tolerated by the magistrate; as | neither those that will not own and SE66 teach the duty of tolerating all men in matters of mere religion. For what do all these and the like doctrines signify, but that they may,[61] and are ready upon any occasion to seize the government, and possess themselves of the estates and fortunes of their fellow-subjects; and that they only ask leave to be tolerated by the magistrate so long until they find themselves strong enough to effect it?

Again: That church can have no right to be tolerated by the magistrate which is constituted upon such a bottom that all those who enter into it do thereby *ipso facto* deliver themselves up to the protection and service of another prince. For by this means the magistrate would give way to the settling of a foreign jurisdiction in his own country, and suffer his own people to be listed, as it were, for soldiers against his own government. Nor does the frivolous and fallacious distinction between the court and the church afford any remedy to this inconvenience; especially when both the one and the other are equally subject to the absolute authority of the same person, who has not only power to persuade the members of

[61] SE: those men may

immo injungere suae ecclesiae hominibus sub poena ignis
aeterni. Frustra aliquis se religione solum Mahume-
danum esse, cetera magistratus Christiani fidelem sub-
LG77 ditum dicet, si fateatur se caecam | obedientiam Mufti
Constantinopolitano debere, qui et ipse Imperatori
Ottomano obsequentissimus, ad illius voluntatem con-
ficta promit religionis suae oracula. Quamquam aliquanto apertius rei publicae Christianae renuntiaret ille
inter Christianos Turca, si eundem agnosceret esse
ecclesiae suae qui et imperii caput.

[Quarto.] Ultimo, qui Numen esse negant nullo modo
tolerandi sunt. Athei enim nec fides, nec pactum, nec
jus jurandum aliquod stabile et sanctum esse potest,
quae sunt societatis humanae vincula; adeo ut Deo vel
ipsa opinione sublato haec omnia corruant. Praeterea,
nullum sibi religionis nomine vindicare potest tolerantiae privilegium, qui omnem funditus tollit per atheis-
mum religionem. Reliquas opiniones practicas quod
attinet, etiamsi non omni errore vacuas, si iis nulla
dominatio nec impunitas civilis quaeratur ecclesiae, in
quibus docentur, cur tolerari non debeant nulla dari
potest ratio.

LG78   Restat ut pauca de coetibus dicam, qui | maximam
doctrinae de tolerantia afferre creduntur difficultatem,
cum seditionum fomenta et factionum conciliabula
vulgo audiant; et forte aliquando fuerunt; sed non suo
peculiari aliquo genio, sed oppressae vel male stabilitae
libertatis infortunio. Cessarent ilico hae criminationes,
si concessae quibus debetur tolerantiae ea esset lex, ut
omnes ecclesiae tenerentur docere et pro libertatis suae
fundamento [21] ponere,

[21] ML: fundamenta

his church to whatsoever he lists, (either as purely religious, or as [62] in order thereunto) but can also enjoin it them on pain of eternal fire. It is ridiculous for any one to profess himself to | be a *Mahometan* only in his religion, but in every- SE67 thing else a faithful subject to a Christian magistrate, whilst at the same time he acknowledges himself bound to yield blind obedience to the *Mufti* of *Constantinople*, who himself is entirely obedient to the *Ottoman* Emperor, and frames the feigned oracles of that religion according to his pleasure. | But PE48 this Mahometan living amongst | Christians would yet more H60 apparently renounce their government if he acknowledged the same person to be head of his church who is the supreme magistrate in the state.

Lastly, those are not at all to be tolerated who *deny the being of a God.* Promises, covenants, and oaths, which are the bonds of human society, can have no hold upon an atheist. The taking away of God, though but even in thought, dissolves all; besides also, those that by their atheism undermine and destroy all religion, can have no pretence of religion whereupon to challenge the privilege of a toleration. As for other practical opinions, though not absolutely free from all error, yet if [63] they do not tend to establish domination over others, or civil impunity to the church in which they are taught, there can be no reason why they should not be tolerated.

It remains that I say something concerning those assemblies which being vulgarly | called, and perhaps having sometimes SE68 been *conventicles* and nurseries of factions and seditions, are thought to afford the strongest matter of objection against this doctrine of toleration. But this has not happened by anything peculiar unto the genius of such assemblies, but by the unhappy circumstances of an oppressed or ill-settled liberty. These accusations would soon cease if the law of toleration were once so settled that all churches were obliged to lay down toleration as the foundation of their own liberty, and

[62] PE, CM, GH: or in   [63] PE, CM, GH: error, if

scilicet quod alii etiam a se in sacris dissentientes essent tolerandi, et quod nemo vel lege vel vi ulla in rebus religionis deberet coerceri; quo uno stabilito, omnis querelarum tumultuumque conscientiae nomine adimeretur praetextus. His autem sublatis motuum vel irarum causis, nihil restat quod in his quam in aliis coetibus non esset magis pacificum, et a rebus politicis turbandis alienum. Verum percurramus accusationum capita.

Dices: Coetus et hominum concursus rei publicae sunt periculosi, et paci minantur. Respondeo: Hoc si LG79 ita sit, quare in foro quotidie | coitio, quare in judiciis contiones, quare in collegiis conventus et in urbibus frequentia? Dices: Hi sunt coetus civiles, illi vero de quibus agitur ecclesiastici. Respondeo: Quasi vero illi coetus, qui a rebus civilibus tractandis inter ceteros longissime absunt, rebus civilibus turbandis maxime essent ML24 accommodi. Dices: Coetus | civiles sunt hominum de rebus religionis diversa sentientium; ecclesiastici vero hominum qui in eadem sunt opinione. Respondeo: Quasi vero de rebus sacris et salute animae eadem sentire esset contra rem publicam conspirare: nec minus, immo vero acrius consentiunt, quo minor publice coeundi libertas. Dices: In coetus civiles cuivis liber ingressus, in religiosorum conciliabulis commodior tectis et clandestinis consiliis locus. Respondeo: Nego omnes coetus civiles, ut sunt collegia, etc. omnibus patere: si vero clandestinae sunt quorundam ad rem sacram coitiones, quinam quaeso hac in re criminandi, qui cupiunt, an qui prohibent publicos coetus? Dices: Sacrorum communionem maxime |

teach that liberty of conscience is every man's natural right, equally belonging to dissenters as to themselves; and that nobody ought to be compelled in matters of religion either by law or force. The establishment of this one thing would take away all ground of complaints and tumults upon account of conscience; and these causes of discontents and animosities being once removed, there would remain nothing in these assemblies that were not | more peaceable and less apt to PE49 produce disturbance of state than in any other meetings whatsoever. But let us examine particularly the heads of these accusations.

You will say that *assemblies and meetings endanger the public peace, and threaten the commonwealth*. I answer: If this be so, why are there daily such numerous | meetings in markets and courts of SE69 judicature? Why are crowds upon the exchange, and a concourse of people in cities suffered? You will reply: These [64] are civil assemblies, but those we object against are ecclesiastical. I answer: It is a likely thing indeed, that such assemblies as are altogether remote from civil affairs should be most apt to embroil them. Oh, but civil assemblies are composed of men that differ from one another in matters of religion, but these ecclesiastical meetings are of persons that are all of one opinion. As if an agreement in matters of religion were in effect a conspiracy against the commonwealth; or as if men would not be so much the more warmly unanimous in religion the less liberty they had of assembling. But it will be urged still, that civil assemblies are open and free for any one to enter into, whereas religious conventicles are more private, and thereby give opportunity to clandestine machinations. I answer, that this is not strictly true, for many civil assemblies are not open to every one. And if some religious meetings be private, who are they (I beseech you) that are to be blamed for it? Those that desire, or those that forbid their being public? Again, you will say that religious communion does exceedingly

[64] PE, CM, GH: those ... these

95

LG80 hominum inter se devincire animos, ideoque maxime
metuendam. Respondeo: Si ita se res habet, quare
magistratus a sua sibi non metuit ecclesia, eosque coetus
tamquam sibi minitantes non prohibet? Dices: Quia
ipse illorum pars est et caput. Respondeo: Quasi vero
et ipsius rei publicae non sit pars, totiusque populi caput. Dicamus igitur quod res est; metuit ab aliis ecclesiis,
a sua vero non metuit, quia his favet et benignus est, aliis
severus et immitis; his liberorum conditio est, quibus
indulgetur usque ad lasciviam; illis servorum, quibus
ergastulum, carcer, capitis imminutio, bonorum sectio,
frequentiores sunt vitae inculpatae mercedes: hi foven-
tur, illi quavis de causa vapulant. Mutentur vices, vel
aequo cum reliquis civibus in rebus civilibus utantur jure,
senties ilico non amplius a coetibus religiosis metuendum esse: si quid enim factiose meditentur homines, id
non congregatis suadet religio, sed oppressis miseria.
Justa et temperata imperia ubique quieta, ubique tuta
LG81 sunt; injustis et tyrannicis | gravati semper reluctabun-
tur. Scio seditiones saepe fieri, easque plerumque religionis nomine: verum et religionis causa subditi
plerumque male mulctantur, et iniqua sorte vivunt;
sed crede mihi, non sunt ii quarundam ecclesiarum vel
religiosarum societatum peculiares, sed communes
ubique hominum mores, sub iniquo onere gementium
et jugum quod gravius cervicibus suis insidet succutien-
tium. Quid credis, si neglecta religione et facta a corporis habitu discriminatione, iis qui nigro sunt capillo

unite men's minds and affections to one another, | and is SE70
therefore | the more dangerous. But if this be so, why is not HL61
the magistrate afraid of his own church; and why does he not
forbid their assemblies as things dangerous to his government?
You will say because he himself is a part, and even the | head of PE50
them. As if he were not also a part of the commonwealth, and
the head of the whole people.

Let us therefore deal plainly. The magistrate is afraid of
other churches, but not of his own; because he is kind and
favourable to the one, but severe and cruel to the other. These
he treats like children, and indulges them even to wantonness.
Those he uses as slaves, and how blamelessly soever they
demean themselves, recompenses them no otherwise then by
galleys, prisons, confiscations, and death. These he cherishes
and defends; those he continually scourges and oppresses.
Let him turn the tables. Or let those dissenters enjoy but the
same privileges in civils as his other subjects, and he will
quickly find that these religious meetings will be no longer
dangerous. For if men enter into seditious conspiracies, it is not
religion inspires them to it in their meetings, but their suffer-
ings and oppressions that make them willing to ease themsel-
ves. Just and moderate governments are everywhere | quiet, SE71
everywhere safe; but oppression raises ferments and makes
men struggle to cast off an uneasy and tyrannical yoke. I know
that seditions are very frequently raised upon pretence of
religion, but it is as true that for religion subjects are frequently ill treated, and live miserably. Believe me, the stirs that are
made proceed not from any peculiar temper of this or that
church or religious society, but from the common disposition
of all mankind, who when they groan under any heavy
burthen endeavour naturally to shake off the yoke that galls
their necks. Suppose this business of religion were let alone,
and that there were some other distinction made between
men and men upon account of their different complexions,
shapes, and features, so that those who have black hair (for

97

aut caesiis oculis iniqua esset inter reliquos cives conditio, ut non libera illis esset emptio et venditio, artis
exercitium prohibitum, liberorum educatio et tutela
parentibus adempta, fora aut clausa, aut tribunalia
iniqua, quid, nonne existimas ab his, qui solum crinium
vel oculorum colore conjunguntur adjecta persecutione, aeque metuendum esse magistratui, quam ab aliis
inter quos societatem conciliaverit religio? Alios in
LG82 societatem redigit ad negotia sumptus lucrique | com-
munitas, alios ad hilaritatem otium; hos conjungit urbs
eadem, tectorumque vicinitas ad convictum, illos religio ad cultum divinum; sed una est quae populum ad
seditionem congregat: oppressio. Dices: Quid igitur vis,
ad sacra celebranda coetus fieri invito magistratu? Respondeo: Quid invito? Res enim est licita et necessaria.
Invito, dicis, magistratu: hoc est quod queror, hoc mali
fons, et fundi nostri calamitas. Cur magis displicet
in templo quam in theatro aut circo hominum con-
cursus? Non vitiosior hic nec turbulentior multitudo.
Nempe huc tandem tota res redit, quod male ha-
biti, ideo minus ferendi. Tolle juris iniquam distinctionem, mutatis legibus tolle supplicii poenam, et omnia
tuta, omnia secura erunt; tantoque magis a magistratus religione alieni rei publicae paci studendum exis-
ML25 timabunt, | quantum in ea melior eorum sit conditio
quam alibi plerumque inveniatur: omnesque particu-
lares et inter se dissidentes ecclesiae, tamquam publi-
cae quietis custodes, acrius in aliarum mores invicem |
LG83 invigilabunt, nequid

example) or grey eyes should not enjoy the same privileges as |
other citizens; that they should not be permitted either to buy PE51
or sell, or live by their callings; that parents should not have
the government and education of their own children; that
they [65] should either be excluded from the benefit of the laws,
or meet with partial judges; can it be doubted but these persons,
thus distinguished from others by the colour of their hair and
eyes, and united together by one common persecution, |
would be as dangerous to the magistrate as any others that had SE72
associated themselves merely upon the account of religion?
Some enter into company for trade and profit, others for want
of business have their clubs for claret. Neighbourhood joins
some, and religion others. But there is only one thing [66]
which gathers people into seditious commotions, and that is
oppression.

You will say: What, will you have people to meet at divine
service *against the magistrate's will?* I answer: Why, I pray, against
his will? Is it not both lawful and necessary that they should
meet? Against his will, do you say? That is what I complain of;
that is the very root of all the mischief. Why are assemblies less
sufferable in a church than in a theatre or market? Those that
meet there are not either more vicious or more turbulent
than those that meet elsewhere. The business in that is that
they are ill used, and therefore they are not to be suffered.
Take away the partiality that is used towards | them in matters HL62
of common right; change the laws, take away the penalties
unto which they are subjected, and all things will immediately
become safe and peaceable; nay, those that are averse to the
religion of the magistrate will think themselves so much the |
more bound to maintain the peace of the commonwealth as SE73
their condition is better in that | place than elsewhere; and all PE52
the several separate congregations, like so many guardians
of the public peace, will watch one another, that nothing may

[65] PE, CM, GH: all
[66] PE, SE, CM, HL: one only thing LW: one thing only

novarum rerum moliantur, nequid in regiminis forma
mutetur, cum meliora sperare non possint, quam quae
jam possident, scilicet sub justo et moderato imperio
aequam cum reliquis civibus sortem. Quod si maximum
habetur regiminis civilis columen ea ecclesia, quae cum
principe de religione consentit, idque eam solam ob
causam (uti jam probavi) quod magistratum habet
propitium legesque faventes; quanto magis aucto sa-
tellitio securior erit res publica cum omnes boni cives
ex quacumque demum ecclesia, eadem principis benignitate, eademque legum aequitate fruantur, nulla habita ob religionem distinctione; solisque facinorosis et
contra pacem civilem peccantibus metuenda sit legum
severitas?

Ut finem aliquando faciamus, concessa aliis civibus
jura petimus. Licetne more Romano Deum colere?
Liceat et Genevensi. Permissumne est latine loqui in
foro? Permittatur etiam quibus libet in templo. Fas est
LG84 domi suae genua flectere, ⸶ stare, sedere, gesticulationi-
bus his vel illis uti, vestibus albis vel nigris, brevibus vel
talaribus indui? In ecclesia nefas ne sit panem comedere,
vinum bibere, aqua se abluere; reliquaque quae in communi vita lege libera sunt, in sacro cultu libera cuique
ecclesiae permaneant. Nullius ob haec labefactetur vita,
aut corpus; nullius domus aut res familiaris evertatur.
Presbyterorum apud te ecclesia permittitur disciplinae;
cur non itidem quibus placet etiam et episcoporum?
Ecclesiastica potestas, sive unius sive plurium manibus
administretur, ubique eadem est, nec in res civiles jus,
nec vim cogendi habet ullam; nec divitiae aut reditus
annui ad regimen ecclesiasticum pertinent.

be innovated or changed in the form of the government, because they can hope for nothing better than what they already enjoy; that is, an equal condition with their fellow-subjects under a just and moderate government. Now if that church which agrees in religion with the prince be esteemed the chief support of any civil government, and that for no other reason (as has already been shewn) than because the prince is kind and the laws are favourable to it, how much greater will be the security of government where all good subjects, of whatsoever church they be, without any distinction upon account of religion, enjoying the same favour of the prince and the same benefit of the laws, shall become the common support and guard of it, and where none will have any occasion to fear the severity of the laws but those that do injuries to their neighbours and offend against the civil peace?

That we may draw towards a conclusion. *The sum of all* we drive at is | *that every man may enjoy the same rights that are granted to* SE74 *others.* Is it permitted to worship God in the *Roman* manner? Let it be permitted to do it in the *Geneva* form also. Is it permitted to speak *Latin* in the market-place? Let those that have a mind to it be permitted to do it also in the church. Is it lawful for any man in his own house to kneel, stand, sit, or use any other posture; and to clothe himself in white or black, in short or in long garments? Let it not be made unlawful to eat bread, drink wine, or wash with water in the church. In a word: Whatsoever things are | left free by law in the common occasions of life, PE53 let them remain free unto every church in divine worship. Let no man's life, or body, or house, or estate, suffer any manner of prejudice upon these accounts. Can you allow of the *Presbyterian* discipline? Why should not the *Episcopal* also have what they like? Ecclesiastical authority, whether it be administered by the hands of a single person or many, is everywhere the same; and neither has any jurisdiction in things civil, nor any manner of power of compulsion, nor anything at all to do with riches and revenues.

Licitos esse coetus ecclesiasticos et contiones usu publico comprobatur: hos unius ecclesiae vel sectae civibus conceditis, quare non omnibus? Si quid in coetu religioso contra pacem publicam agitatum, reprimendum est eodem nec diverso modo quam si in nundinis acciderit. LG85 Si quid in contione ecclesiastica seditiose | vel dictum vel factum, eodem modo puniendum ac si in foro delictum esset. Haec non debent esse nec factiosorum nec flagitiosorum perfugia; nec e contra concursus hominum in templo quam in curia magis illicitus, nec in his quam in illis civibus magis culpandus; quisque suo solum crimine, non aliorum vitio, in odium vel suspicionem vocandus. Seditiosi, homicidae, sicarii, latrones, rapaces, adulteri, injusti, conviciatores etc. ex quacumque demum ecclesia, sive aulica sive non, castigentur reprimanturque. Quorum vero doctrina pacifica, quorum mores casti et inculpati, eodem sint cum reliquis civibus loco. Atque si aliis coetus, sollemnes conventus, festorum dierum celebrationes, contiones et sacra publica permittantur; haec omnia Remonstranti, Antiremonstranti, Lutherano, Anabaptistae, Sociniano pari jure permittenda. Immo si, quod verum est, et quod hominem erga homines decet, aperte loqui liceat, ne Ethnicus quidem, vel Mahumedanus, vel Judaeus religionis causa LG86 a re publica | arcendus; nihil simile jubet Evangelium; id non desiderat ecclesia quae *I. Cor.* v. 12, 13 extraneos non judicat, non poscit res publica quae homines [22] modo probos, pacificos, industrios, recipit et amplectitur. An Ethnicum apud te mercaturam exercere ML26 permittes, Deum | vero precari vel colere prohibebis? Judaeis habitatio et tecta privata conceduntur, Synagoga cur negatur? An eorum doctrina falsior, cultus turpior, vel concordia periculosior, in coetu publico quam in privatis aedibus? Si haec Judaeis et Ethnicis concedenda,

[22] LG, ML: quae homines qua homines, modo

Ecclesiastical assemblies and sermons are justified by daily experience and | public allowance. These are allowed to people SE75 of some one persuasion, why not to all? If anything pass in a religious meeting seditiously and contrary to the public peace, it is to be punished in the same manner, and no otherwise than as if it had happened in a fair or market. These meetings ought not to be sanctuaries for factious and flagitious fellows. Nor ought it to be less lawful for men to meet in churches than in halls; nor are one part of the subjects to be esteemed more blameable for their meeting together than others. Every one is to be accountable for his own actions, and no man is to be laid under a suspicion or odium for the fault of another. Those that are seditious, murderers, thieves, robbers, adulterers, slanderers, etc., of whatsoever church, whether national or not, ought to be punished and sup-pressed. | But those whose doctrine is peaceable, and whose HL63 manners are pure and blameless, ought to be upon equal terms with their fellow-subjects. Thus if solemn assemblies, obser-vations of festivals, public worship be | permitted to any one PE54 sort of professors, all these things ought to be permitted to the *Presbyterians, Independents, Anabaptists, Arminians, Quakers,* and others, with the same liberty. Nay, if we may openly speak the truth, and as becomes one man to another, | neither *Pagan* nor SE76 *Mahometan,* nor *Jew,* ought to be excluded from the civil rights of the commonwealth because of his religion. The Gospel commands no such thing. The church which *judgeth not those that are without,* I *Cor.* v. 12, 13 wants it not. And the commonwealth, which embraces indifferently all men that are honest, peacea-ble, and industrious, requires it not. Shall we suffer a *Pagan* to deal and trade with us, and shall we not suffer him to pray unto and worship God? If we allow the *Jews* to have private houses and dwellings amongst us, why should we not allow them to have synagogues? Is their doctrine more false, their worship more abominable, or is the civil peace more endanger-ed by their meeting in public than in their private houses? But if these things may be granted to *Jews* and *Pagans,* surely

pejorne erit in re publica Christiana Christianorun conditio? Dices: Immo vero, quia ad factiones, tumultus et
bella civilia magis proclives. Respondeo: Anne religionis
Christianae hoc vitium? Si ita, pessima certe omnium
est religio Christiana, et digna quam nec tu profitearis,
nec res publica omnino toleret. Nam si hic sit genius,
haec natura ipsius religionis Christianae, ut turbulenta
sit et paci civili inimica; ipsa illa quam fovet magistra-
LG87 tus ecclesia aliquando non | erit innocens. Sed absit ut
hoc dicatur de religione, avaritiae, ambitioni, dissidiis,
jurgiis, terrenisque cupiditatibus contraria et omnium quae unquam fuerunt maxime modesta et
pacifica. Alia igitur malorum quae religioni imputantur
quaerenda causa; quae si recte rem reputemus, in ea de
qua nunc agitur quaestione tota consistere apparebit.
Non opinionum diversitas, quae vitari non potest, sed
negata diversa opinantibus tolerantia, quae concedi
poterat, pleraque quae in orbe Christiano nata sunt
de religione jurgia et bella produxit: dum primores
ecclesiae avaritia et dominandi libidine acti, magistratum saepe ambitione impotentem et populum super-
stitione semper vanum, adversus heterodoxos omni-
modo excitarent et acuerent; et contra leges Evangelii,
contra caritatis monita, schismaticos haereticosque
spoliandos exterminandosque praedicarent; et duas res
diversissimas miscerent, ecclesiam et rem publicam.
Quod si, uti fit, homines rebus suis honesto labore partis
LG88 se exui haud patienter | ferunt, et contra jus humanum

the condition of any Christians ought not to be worse than theirs in a Christian commonwealth.

You will say, perhaps: Yes, it ought to be; because they are more inclinable to factions, tumults, and civil wars. I answer: Is this the fault of the Christian religion? If it be so, truly the Christian religion is the worst of all religions, and ought neither to be embraced by any particular | person, nor toler- SE77 ated by any commonwealth. For if this be the genius, this the nature of the Christian religion, to be turbulent, and destructive to the civil peace, that church itself which the magistrate indulges will not always be innocent. But far be it from us to say any such | thing of that religion which carries the PE55 greatest opposition to covetousness, ambition, discord, contention, and all manner of inordinate desires; and is the most modest and peaceable religion that ever was. We must therefore seek another cause of those evils that are charged upon religion. And if we consider right, we shall find it to consist wholly in the subject that I am treating of. It is not the diversity of opinions (which cannot be avoided), but the refusal of toleration to those that are of different opinions (which might have been granted), that has produced all the bustles and wars that have been in the Christian world upon account of religion. The heads and leaders of the church, moved by avarice and insatiable desire of dominion, making use of the immoderate ambition of magistrates and the credulous superstition of the giddy multitude, have incensed and animated them against those that dissent from themselves, by preaching unto them, contrary to the laws of the Gospel | and SE78 to the precepts of charity, that schismatics and heretics are to be outed of their possessions and destroyed. And thus have they mixed together and confounded two things that are in themselves most different, the church and the commonwealth. Now as it is very difficult for men patiently to suffer themselves to be stripped of the goods which they have got by their honest industry, and, contrary to all the laws of equity, both human

divinumque alienae violentiae et rapinae praedam fieri; praesertim cum alias omnino inculpati sint, et ea res agitur quae ad jus civile minime pertinet, sed ad suam cujusque conscientiam et animae salutem, cujus ratio soli Deo reddenda est: quid aliud paene expectari potest, quam ut homines malorum, quibus opprimuntur, pertaesi, sibi tandem persuadeant licere vim vi repellere, et jura sibi a Deo et natura concessa, nec propter religionem sed flagitia solum amittenda, armis [23] quibus poterunt defendere? Haec nimirum ita hactenus fuisse plus satis testatur historia, et ita in posterum fore demonstrat ratio, quam diu illa de persecutione propter religionem valebit sive apud magistratum sive apud populum opinio, et ita ad arma clament et bella totis lateribus ebuccinent illi, qui debent esse pacis et concordiae praecones. Quod magistratus hujusmodi incendiarios et publicae quietis perturbatores passi fuerint mirandum esset, nisi pateret et eos in praedae | societatem vocatos, aliena libidine et fastu ad suam augendam potentiam saepe usos fuisse. Quis enim non videt, hos bonos viros non tam Evangelii quam imperii fuisse ministros, et principum ambitioni potentiorumque dominationi adulatos: idque omni studio et opera allaborasse, ut in re publica promoverent, quam alias frustra affectarent in ecclesia, tyrannidem. Haec fuit plerumque ecclesiae et rei publicae concordia, inter quas, si utraque suis se contineret finibus, discordia quidem esse non potuit, dum haec mundanis civitatis bonis, illa animarum saluti unice studeret.

LG89

[23] ML: arma

and divine, to be delivered up for a prey to other men's
violence and rapine; especially when they are otherwise
altogether | blameless; and that the occasion for which HL64
they are thus treated does not at all belong to the
jurisdiction of the magistrate, but entirely to the conscience of
every particular man, for the conduct | of which he is ac- PE56
countable to God only; what else can be expected but that
these men, growing weary of the evils under which they
labour, should in the end think it lawful for them to resist
force with force, and to defend their natural rights (which
are not forfeitable upon account of religion) with arms as well
as they can? That this has been hitherto the ordinary course of
things is abundantly evident in history, and that it will continue to be so hereafter is but too apparent in reason. It cannot,
indeed, be otherwise so long as the principle of persecution
for religion shall prevail, as | it has done hitherto, with magis- SE79
trate and people, and so long as those that ought to be the
preachers of peace and concord shall continue with all their
art and strength to excite men to arms and sound the trumpet
of war. But that magistrates should thus suffer these in-
cendiaries and disturbers of the public peace might justly be
wondered at if it did not appear that they have been invited by
them unto a participation of the spoil, and have therefore
thought fit to make use of their covetousness and pride as
means whereby to increase their own power. For who does not
see that *these good men* are indeed more ministers of the government than ministers of the Gospel, and that by flattering the
ambition and favouring the dominion of princes and men in
authority, they endeavour with all their might to promote
that tyranny in the commonwealth which otherwise they
should not be able to establish in the church? This is the
unhappy agreement that we see between the church and
state. Whereas if each of them would contain itself within its
own bounds, the one attending to the worldly welfare of the
commonwealth, | the other to the salvation of souls, it is PE57
impossible that any discord should ever have happened be-

Sed pudet haec opprobria. Faxit Deus O.M. ut aliquando Evangelium pacis praedicetur, magistratusque civilis de sua ad legem Dei conformanda multum; de aliena conscientia legibus humanis alliganda minus solliciti, tamquam patres patriae ad communem liberorum suorum |

ML27 (quotquot non protervi non aliis iniqui nec maligni) felicitatem civilem promovendam omnia sua studia

LG90 et consilio dirigant. Virique ecclesiastici, | qui se Apostolorum successores praedicant, Apostolorum vestigiis insistentes, omissis rebus politicis, saluti animarum cum pace et modestia unice incumbant! Vale. [*]

[*] In LG, ML the *Postcriptum*, that here is reproduced in the next page, follows in this same page.

tween them. *Sed pudet hæc opprobria, etc.* God Almighty grant, I beseech him, that the Gospel of Peace may at length be | preached, and that civil magistrates, growing more careful to SE80 conform their own consciences to the law of God and less solicitous about the binding of other men's consciences by human laws, may, like fathers of their country, direct all their counsels and endeavours to promote universally the civil welfare of all their children, except only of such as are arrogant, ungovernable, and injurious to their brethren; and that all ecclesiastical men, who boast themselves to be the successors of the apostles, walking peaceably and modestly in the apostles' steps, without intermeddling with state affairs, may apply themselves wholly to promote the salvation of souls.

Farewell

Forsan abs re non fuerit pauca de haeresi et schismate hic subjungere. Mahumedanus Christiano haereticus vel schismaticus non est, nec esse potest: et si aliquis a fide Christiana ad Islamismum deficiat, non eo haereticus vel schismaticus factus est, sed apostata et infidelis. De his nemo est qui dubitat. Unde constat homines diversae religionis hominibus haereticos vel schismaticos esse non posse.

Inquirendum est igitur quinam sint ejusdem religionis. Qua in re manifestum est eos esse ejusdem religionis, qui unam eamdemque habent fidei et cultus divini regulam: illi vero religionis sunt diversae, qui eamdem non habent fidei et cultus regulam. Quia cum omnia quae ad istam religionem pertinent in ea regula contineantur, | necesse est eos qui in eadem regula conveniunt, in eadem etiam religione convenire, et vice versa. Sic Turci et Christiani diversae sunt religionis; quia hi S. Scripturam, illi Alcoranum pro regula religionis suae agnoscunt. Eadem plane ratione sub nomine Christiano diversae possunt esse religiones; Pontificii et Lutherani, quamvis utrique plane Christiani, utpote in nomine Christi fidem professi, non sunt ejusdem religionis; quia hi solum S. Scripturam agnoscunt pro religionis suae regula et fundamento; illi vero S. Scripturae adjiciunt traditiones et Pontificis decreta; et inde sibi conficiunt religionis suae regulam. Christiani S. Johannis (uti vocantur) et Christiani

LG91

POSTSCRIPTUM

Perhaps it may not be amiss to add a few things concerning SE81
heresy and *schism*. A Turk is not, nor can be, either heretic or
schismatic to a *Christian;* and if any man fall off from the
Christian faith to *Mahometism,* he does not thereby become a
heretic or schismatic, but an apostate and an infidel. This
nobody doubts of; and by this it appears that men of different
religions cannot be heretics or schismatics to one another.

We are to inquire therefore what men are of the same religion. Concerning which it is manifest that those who have
one and the same rule of faith | and worship are of the same PE58
religion; and those who | have not the same rule of faith and HL65
worship are of different religions. For since all things that
belong unto that religion are contained in that rule, it follows
necessarily that those who agree in one rule are of one and the
same religion, and *vice versa.* Thus *Turks* and *Christians* are of
different religions, because these take the *Holy Scriptures* | to be SE82
the rule of their religion, and those the *Alcoran.* And for the
same reason there may be different religions also even amongst
Christians. The *Papists* and *Lutherans,* though both of them profess
faith in Christ, and are therefore called *Christians,* yet are not both
of the same religion, because these acknowledge nothing but
the *Holy Scriptures* to be the rule and foundation of their religion,
those take in also traditions and the decrees of popes, and of
all [67] these together make the rule of their religion; and thus
the Christians of St. *John* (as they are called) and the Christians

[67] PE, CM, GH: of these

III

Genevenses diversae sunt religionis (quamquam utrique Christiani nuncupentur) quod hi S. Scripturam,
illi traditiones nescio quas pro regula religionis suae
habent. His positis sequitur:

  1. Quod haeresis sit separatio facta in communione
ecclesiastica inter homines ejusdem religionis ob dog-
mata quae in ipsa regula non continentur. |

LG92 2. Quod apud illos, qui solam S. Scripturam pro
regula fidei agnoscunt, haeresis sit separatio facta in
communione Christiana ob dogmata disertis S. Scripturae verbis non contenta.

Haec separatio duplici modo fieri potest:

  1. Quando major, vel patrocinante magistratu fortior
pars ecclesiae separat se ab aliis, eos e communione
ejiciendo excludendoque, quia certa dogmata verbis
Scripturae non concepta se credere profiteri nolunt.
Non enim separatorum paucitas, nec magistratus auctoritas, haereseos reum potest aliquem reddere; sed ille
solus haereticus est, qui ob hujusmodi dogmata ecclesiam in partes scindit, distinctionum nomina et notas
introducit, et sponte sua separationem efficit.

  2. Quando aliquis se separat ab ecclesiae communione,
quia in ea publica non sit professio quorumdam dog-
matum quae disertis verbis non exhibet S. Scriptura.

  Horum utrique haeretici sunt: quia in fundamentali-
LG93 bus errant, et prudentes scientesque | obstinate errant.
Cum enim pro unico fundamento fidei posuerint S.
Scripturam, aliud nihilominus ponunt fundamentum,
propositiones scilicet quae in S. Scriptura nusquam
ML28 reperiuntur; et quia alii | adscititias hasce ipsorum opinio-
nes S. Scripturae assutas tamquam necessarias et funda-
mentales agnoscere et iis inniti nolunt, eos a se abigen-
do, vel

of *Geneva* are of different religions, because these also take only the Scriptures, and those I know not what traditions, for the rule of their religion.

This being settled, it follows, *first*, that heresy is a separation made in ecclesiastical communion between men of the same religion for some opinions no way contained in the rule itself; and, *secondly*, that amongst those who acknowledge nothing but the Holy Scriptures to be their rule of faith, heresy is a separation made in their Christian communion for opinions not contained in the express words of Scripture. Now this separation may be made in a twofold manner. |

1 . When the greater part, or (by the magistrate's patronage) SE83 the stronger part, of the church separates itself from others by excluding them out of her communion because they will not profess their belief of | certain opinions which are not to be PE59 found in the express [68] words of the Scripture. For it is not the paucity of those that are separated, nor the authority of the magistrate, that can make any man guilty of heresy, but he only is a heretic who divides the church into parts, introduces names and marks of distinction, and voluntarily makes a separation because of such opinions.

2. When any one separates himself from the communion of a church because that church does not publicly profess some certain opinions which the Holy Scriptures do not expressly teach.

Both these are *heretics, because they err in fundamentals, and they err obstinately against knowledge.* For when they have determined the Holy Scriptures to be the only foundation of faith, they nevertheless lay down certain propositions as fundamental which are not in the Scripture, and because others will not acknowledge these additional opinions of theirs, nor build upon them as if they were necessary | and fundamental, they SE84 therefore make a separation in the church, either by with-

[68] PE, CM, GH: are not the express words

se ab iis subtrahendo, secessionem faciunt. Nec attinet
dicere, suas confessiones et articulos fidei S. Scripturae et
analogiae fidei esse consonos; si enim S. Scripturae
verbis concipiantur, nulla potest esse quaestio, quia
omnium consensu fundamentalia ea sunt, et ejusmodi
omnia, quia theopneusta. Quod si dicas, articulos illos
tuos, quorum professionem exigis, esse S. Scripturae
porismata; recte quidem facis, si ipse ea credas et profitearis quae tibi videntur cum regula fidei, scilicet S. Scriptura, consentire; pessime vero, si ea velis aliis obtrudere,
quibus non videntur indubia S. Scripturae dogmata; et
LG94 haereticus es, si ob haec quae nec fundamentalia | sunt,
nec esse possunt, separationem introducas. Non enim
credo aliquem eo insaniae provectum esse, ut audeat
sua consectaria, suaque S. Scripturae interpretamenta,
pro theopneustis venditare, et articulos fidei ad modu-
lum mentemque suam concinnatos auctoritati S. Scripturae aequare. Scio aliquas esse propositiones tam
evidenter S. Scripturae consonas, ut nemo dubitare
possit eas inde sequi: de his igitur nullum fieri potest
dissidium. Quod autem tibi videtur legitima deductione
e S. Scriptura sequi, id tamquam necessarium fidei arti-
culum alteri obtrudere non debes, quia tu ipse regulae
fidei consonum credis; nisi tu ipse aequum judicas, ut
tibi pari jure aliorum obtrudantur opiniones, et tu coga-
ris admittere et profiteri diversa et inter se pugnantia,
Lutheranorum, Calvinistarum, Remonstrantium, Ana-
baptistarum, aliarumque sectarum dogmata, quae tamquam necessaria et genuina S. Scripturae consectaria
asseclis suis ingerere et depredicare solent Symbolorum,
LG95 Systematum | et Confessionum artifices.

drawing themselves from others, or expelling the others from them. Nor does it signify anything for them to say that their confessions and symbols are agreeable to Scripture and to the analogy of faith; for if they be conceived in the express words of Scripture, there can be no question about them, because those [69] are acknowledged by all Christians to be of divine inspiration, and therefore fundamental. | But if they say that HL66 the articles which they require to be professed are consequences deduced from the Scripture, it is undoubtedly well done of them to [70] believe and profess such things as seem unto them so agreeable to the rule of faith. But it would be very ill done to obtrude those things upon others unto whom they do not seem to be the indubitable doctrines | of the Scripture; PE60 and to make a separation for such things as these, which neither are nor can be fundamental, is to become heretics; for I do not think there is any man arrived to that degree of madness as that he dare give out his consequences and interpretations of Scripture as divine inspirations, and compare the articles of faith that he has framed according to his own fancy with the authority of Scripture. | I know there are some SE85 propositions so evidently agreeable to Scripture that nobody can deny them to be drawn from thence, but about those, therefore, there can be no difference. This only I say, that however clearly we may think this or the other doctrine to be deduced from Scripture, we ought not therefore to impose it upon others as a necessary article of faith because we believe it to be agreeable to the rule of faith, unless we would be content also that other doctrines should be imposed upon us in the same manner, and that we should be compelled to receive and profess all the different and contradictory opinions of *Lutherans, Calvinists, Remonstrants, Anabaptists,* and other sects which the contrivers of symbols, systems, and confessions are accustomed to deliver unto [71] their followers as genuine and necessary deductions from the Holy Scripture. I cannot but wonder at

[69] PE, CM, GH: those things are   [70] PE, CM, GH: who
[71] GH: to

Non possum non mirari inauspicatam illorum arrogan-
tiam, qui ea, quae ad salutem sunt necessaria, putant se
clarius et dilucidius posse tradere, quam Spiritus Sanc-
tus, infinita illa et aeterna sapientia, tradere possit.

Hactenus de haeresi, quae vox secundum communem
usum solis dogmatibus tribuitur. Jam de schismate videndum, quod cognatum haeresi vitium est: utraque
enim vox mihi videtur significare separationem in
communione ecclesiastica temere et de rebus non necessariis factam. Sed cum usus, quem penes arbitrium et
jus et norma loquendi, obtinuerit, ut haeresis erroribus
in fide, schisma in cultu vel disciplina tribueretur, de iis
sub ea distinctione hic agendum est.

Schisma igitur ob rationes supra memoratas nihil
aliud est, quam separatio in ecclesiae communione
facta ob aliquod in cultu divino vel disciplina ecclesiastica non necessarium. Nihil in cultu divino vel disciplina
LG96 ecclesiastica ad communionem | Christiano esse potest
necessarium, nisi quod disertis verbis jusserit legislator
Christus, vel instinctu Spiritus Sancti Apostoli.

Verbo dicam: Qui non negat aliquid quod disertis
verbis enunciant eloquia divina, nec separationem facit
ob aliquod quod in sacro textu expresse non continetur,
haereticus vel schismaticus esse non potest, quantumvis male audiat apud quasvis Christiani nominis sectas,
et ab iis, vel aliquibus vel omnibus, tamquam vera
religione Christiana destitutus pronuncietur.

Haec ornatius et fusius deduci potuissent, sed tibi
adeo perspicaci indicasse sufficiat.

FINIS

the extravagant arrogance of those men who think that they themselves can explain things necessary to salvation more clearly than the Holy Ghost, the eternal and infinite wisdom of God.

Thus much concerning *heresy*, which word in common use is applied only to the doctrinal part of religion. Let us now consider *schism*, which is a crime near akin to it; for both those [72] words seem | unto me to signify an *ill-grounded* SE86 *separation in ecclesiastical communion made about things not necessary.* But | since use, which is the supreme law in matter of language, has PE61 determined that heresy relates to errors in faith, and schism to those in worship or discipline, we must consider them under that distinction.

Schism, then, for the same reasons that have already been alleged, is nothing else but a separation made in the communion of the church upon account of something in divine worship or ecclesiastical discipline that is not any necessary part of it. Now, nothing in worship or discipline can be necessary to Christian communion but what Christ our legislator, or the apostles by inspiration of the Holy Spirit, have commanded in express words.

In a word: he that denies not anything that the Holy Scriptures teach in express words, nor makes a separation upon occasion of anything that is not manifestly contained in the sacred text; however he may be nicknamed by any sect of Christians, and declared by some or all of them to be utterly void of true Christianity, yet in deed and in truth this man cannot be either a heretic or schismatic. |

These things might have been explained more largely and SE87 more advantageously, but it is enough to have hinted at them thus briefly to a person of your parts.

FINIS

[72] CM, GH: these

117

THE SOCINIANISM OF LOCKE AND THE ENGLISH
EDITION OF THE LETTER CONCERNING
TOLERATION

1. Exactly two centuries have had to pass before the Latin text of the famous *Epistola* on toleration, published in Gouda in 1689[1] and never again re-printed after Hollis's edition of 1768,[2] was re-discovered and put into circulation once again. This has coincided with a rich flowering of studies and research on the work and personality of Locke.[3]

But in re-discovering the Latin text of the *Epistola* and in contrasting and comparing it with Popple's contemporary translation[4] some modern editors have been tempted to devalue, sometimes radically, the reliability of the English text[5] through which, it is certain, the *Epistola*

---

1. The *Epistola de Tolerantia* appeared anonymously at Gouda in Holland in the Spring of 1689 some months after Locke's return to England.

For all that regards the composition and publication of the *Epistola* see *Introduction*, p. XV-XXX, reprinted in this volume.

2. HOLLIS first supervised an edition of the *Epistola* in *Letters concerning Toleration* by J. LOCKE, London, 1765 (*Epistola* pp. 3-28) and then re-published the same edition of the *Epistola* in the *Works of J. Locke*, 4 vols, 7th ed., London 1768 (*Epistola*, vol. II, pp. 317-343).

3. For these studies we refer to the critical review of them made by N. BOBBIO, *Studi Lockiani*, in the Riv. Storica Italiana LXXVII, I, 1965, pp. 96-130, reprinted in *Da Hobbes a Marx*, Naples, 1965, pp. 75-128, with the declared aim of "informing the Italian reader on the questions discussed and of raising certain doubts about the solutions proposed." Also by BOBBIO one should bear in mind: *Locke e il Diritto naturale*, Turin, 1963. To be noted too is the brief review by C. SCURATI, *Orientamenti e problemi della critica pedagogica Lockiana* in Cultura e Scuola, I, 17, 1966, pp. 126-137.

4. WILLIAM POPPLE, Socinian merchant associated with the philanthropic circle of Firmin, recognised head of the English Unitarians. Popple translated Locke's *Epistola* into English the very same year that the Latin original appeared in Holland.

On Popple and the events that accompanied the English translation of the *Epistola*, see my ed. *Introduction*, p. XXX et seq. and what else will be said in the course of this study.

5. This devaluation began 20 years ago with J. EBBINGHAUS who opened

---

itself has always been known. Thus it has happened that, just when a happy revival of Locke's major writing on toleration has taken place, a revival of which the impact in contemporary culture is shown by the fact that no less than 12 editions have followed each other in the decade from 1956 to 1966,[6] on the one hand the Latin edition of

the sequence of editions on Locke's writing for the series *"La Philosophie et la Communauté mondiale,"* J. LOCKE, *Ein Brief über Toleranz, Englisch-deutsch. Übersetzt, eingeleitet und in Anmerkungen erläutert von* J. EBBINGHAUS, Hamburg, 1957. He showed that Popple's translation contained a number of variants and errors (p. VIII) which were noted and discussed on p. 126 et seq. These variants, in Ebbinghaus' view, made it impossible to grant the English text any sort of authenticity vis-a-vis the Latin text (cf. p. 138 of the 2nd edition, Hamburg, 1966).

A. WAISMANN, though he adds nothing new to Ebbinghaus' notes, expresses himself more sharply in the Spanish edition of the *Letter* published in the same series: J. LOCKE, *Carta sobre la Tolerancia, Latín-Castellano, Traducción, Introducción y Notas de* A. WAISMANN. *Prologo de* R. KLIBANSKY, Montreal, 1962, p. 107: "Creemos firmamente que la famosa traducción inglesa de Popple no merece, ni desde el punto de vista filológico, ni desde el punto de vista filosófico, que concierne al contenido mismo del pensamiento lockiano, la fama de que ha gozado y goza. Está muy lejos de ser una traducción fiel: está llena de interpretaciones arbitrarias, es exageradamente perifrastica y adornata, allí donde el estilo de Locke es simple y llano. Con rara frecuencia el traductor quiere llevar agua para su molino."

6. In 1956 J.W. GOUGH published a new edition "corrected and revised" (I, 1946; II, 1948) of the English translation of the *Epistola* in *The Second Treatise of Government* [...] *and a Letter concerning Toleration* by J. LOCKE, Oxford, 1956.

In 1957 J. EBBINGHAUS started, as has been said above, the series of editions of the *Epistola* in the Series *"La Philosophie et la Communauté mondiale,"* directed by Klibansky, in which he produced the English text of the 1823 edition of *Locke's Works* suppressing Popple's preface. Ebbinghaus' second edition came out, also in Hamburg in 1966 with the addition of 4 variants not recorded in the first edition and with a *Nachwort zum Englischen Text*, pp. 136-138, in which he rejects a comment of mine (cf. my ed. *Introd.* p. XXXI and p. L) and reaffirms the unreliability of the English text.

After Ebbinghaus' notes the English text was never re-issued by those who supervised the series *"La Philosophie et la Communauté mondiale."*

In 1961 there appeared an Italian edition of the *Epistola* which for the first time reproduced the Latin text of Hollis' 1768 edition of *Locke's Works*: J. LOCKE, *Lettera sulla Tolleranza. Testo latino e versione italiana. Premessa di* R. KLIBANSKY, *Introduzione di* E. DE MARCHI, *Trad. di* L. FORMIGARI, Florence, 1961. The same translation and the same *Premessa* by Klibansky were used by SABETTI for his edition, with comments, of the *Lettera* (Florence, 1963). Mention has already been made of Waismann's Spanish edition in the

Gouda has been dragged from the oblivion of two centuries to which it had been condemned, on the other the reputation that the most famous London edition had long enjoyed was impugned.

It is certainly undeniable that if Locke's Latin is not always impeccable, Popple's translation often seems defective in comparison.[7] But can one, for this reason, demand that the English text be expunged from *Locke's Works*?[8] A demand in this sense might be considered

preceding note. A Polish edition came out in Warsaw in 1963 in JOACHIMO-WICZ's translation with a *Preface* by KLIBANSKY and an *Introduction* by DE MARCHI. Finally in 1964 the French edition: *Lettre sur la Tolérance. Texte Latin et Traduction Française. Edition critique et Préface* par R. KLIBAN-SKY. *Trad. et Introd.* par R. POLIN, Montreal, 1964. Meanwhile an anthology of Locke's works with long extracts from the *Letter* appeared in 1960. This was under the care of M. SALVADORI, *Locke and Liberty, Selection from the works of J. Locke*, London, 1960. At the same time as the Italian edition of the *Letter* appeared, C.A. VIANO produced his own translation of the Latin text of the *Epistola* to which he added Popple's *Preface* to the English version in J. LOCKE, *Scritti editi ed inediti sulla Tolleranza*, Turin, 1961. In the *Antologia* of Locke's political writing, supervised by F. BATTAGLIA, Bologna, 1962 a new translation appeared, made by A. DE CAPRARIIS from Popple's English text, without, however, Popple's own *Preface*. My own edition of the Latin and English texts with the variants found in the major editions appeared in 1963 and was followed in 1964 by the French edition of KLIBANSKY-POLIN and in 1966 by EBBING-HAUS' 2nd German edition.

7. Cf. EBBINGHAUS, I ed., p. VII and the remarks on the variants introduced by Popple, p. 127; but on this topic see my ed. p. XXXI and p. L and Ebbinghaus' reply (II ed., p. 136 et seq.). WAISMANN (Spanish ed., op. cit. p. 107) takes over Ebbinghaus' remarks and restates them more dogmatically and intransigently. In contrast Klibansky, who had noted in the Italian ed. of 1961 (p. VIII) that "Popple, though trying to remain faithful to Locke's text, here and there introduced variants which in some cases distort the original meaning," repeated the same opinion in the subsequent editions of the series he supervised until that of SABETTI in 1963; in the French edition of 1964, which appeared with a fuller and more carefully considered *Preface*, he watered down his judgement distinctly, writing (p. XIX) that Popple's variants "finissent par altérer un peu le sens original." In reality POLIN has assessed Popple's work more soundly; in the *Introduction* to the French edition, p. XXXVIII, he writes: "si William Popple a été fidèle au sens général de l'oeuvre, il a suivi de façon peu stricte le détail du texte." Polin's assessment agrees in substance with that earlier expressed by FOX BOURNE, *The Life of J. Locke*, 2 vols., London, 1876, II, p. 54 and more recently by VIANO, *Scritti*, op. cit. p. 12 and by me, my ed. *Introd.*, p. XXXI.

8. Which in point of fact is what WAISMANN demands (Spanish ed., p. 107) when he writes that neither from the point of view of philology nor from that of fidelity to Locke's thought does Popple's translation merit the prestige that it

121

legitimate if it were a matter of an untrustworthy and spurious translation,[9] but this is not the case. On the contrary, a good deal of incontrovertible evidence, unknown or overlooked until now, refutes the erroneous belief given currency by Coste, who must be held responsible for having first declared that the *Epistola* had been translated "à l'insu de M. Locke."[10] Hence the suspicion that during the course of time has

has enjoyed and still enjoys, and he replaces Popple's translation with one "as faithful as possible to the Latin text" (lo mas fiel posible del texto latino).

9. Such in fact has been the opinion of various editors both past and present, beginning with COSTE, *Eloge de M. Locke* in *Nouvelles de la Republique des Lettres*, Mois de Fevrier, 1705, p. 154 et seq. reprinted in J. LOCKE, *Essay Philosophique concernant l'Entendement Humain*, Traduit de l'Anglois par M. COSTE, Amsterdam, 1700, 1735[3], pp. XXI-XXIX, from which we quote, continuing with CHRISTOPHERSEN, *A Bibliographical Introduction to the Study of J. Locke*, Oslo, 1930-31, p. 15, and coming to KLIBANSKY, Italian ed. 1961, *Premessa*, p. VIII; Spanish ed. 1962, *Prologo*, p. VII; ed. SABETTI, 1963, *Premessa*, p. V, which rejects "the affirmation that Locke had endorsed Popple's translation with his authority" because, according to Klibansky, this affirmation is based "*solely* on the fact that in leaving the Bodleian Library of Oxford his works, he mentions the English translation in the codicil to his will, rendered in the following terms: "I further leave to the public library of Oxford University the following books, that is to say three letters on toleration, the first of which was written by me in Latin and published at Tergouw (that is Gouda) in Holland in 1689 under the title *Epistola de Tolerantia* and then translated into English *without my having knowledge of it.*" In the *Préface* to the French ed. 1964 (p. VII) KLIBANSKY corrects his judgement, admitting that with that codicil "Locke reconnut être l'auteur de l'*Epistola* et avalisa en même temps de son autorité la traduction de Popple." In consequence even Locke's phrase, which occurs in that codicil with reference to the English translation of the *Epistola* "without my privity" is no longer understood by Klibansky to mean "without my having knowledge of it." "Cette expression un peu ambigue," Klibansky now writes, "ne signifie pas nécessairement, comme les biographes récents de Locke l'ont voulu (!), que Locke prétend avoir ignoré que l'on préparait une traduction mais – en ce contexte – qu'elle se faisait sans la participation active du philosophe, très soucieux de maintenir l'anonimat." Hence the modified assessment of Popple's translation which alters the original sense only "un peu" as it now seems to Klibansky (op. cit. n. 7).

I hope that in the interest of truth I may be allowed to bring to mind the fact that I had refused the accepted meaning of the phrase "without my privity" as being "without my knowledge" and had proposed instead the philologically and accurate "without my consent" in the legal sense of an agreement between two parties, in this case between the author and the translator. Locke was not called upon to give his consent having kept silent about, or denied to Popple that he was the author of the *Epistola*. For the whole matter see my ed. *Introd.* p. XXXIII et seq. and what more will be said during the course of this study.

10. COSTE, *Eloge*, op. cit. p. XXVIII.

accompanied the English edition of the *Epistola,* even through its innumerable reprintings, and hence, too, the severity of certain recent assessments; unjust nevertheless given that Locke himself guarantees, as we shall see, the authenticity and fidelity of that translation, which, not without reason, he wished to have preserved for posterity alongside the original Latin in the Bodleian Library in Oxford. If therefore Locke, when leaving to the famous Oxford Library those of his works that had appeared anonymously or under a pseudonym, wrote in a codicil to his will that the *Epistola* had been translated into English "without my privity"[11] he clearly did not mean "without my knowledge" as has generally been thought from the time of Coste on, since we know that Locke himself not only knew very well that Popple had started and carried through to the end, the translation of the *Epistola,*[12] but also that he followed the work of translation very closely. We have, further, many reasons for believing that the second London edition of the *Letter concerning Toleration* was personally supervised by Locke.

The assessment, therefore, of the reliability of the English text does not so much depend on a textual comparison between the Latin original with the London version as on an exact reconstruction of the events surrounding the English translation, together with an evocation of the historical climate in which the translation was made and in which, in contrast to the Latin text, the translation became a potent influence and, for that very reason, indispensable.

It may therefore be worthwhile going over those events once again, if by so doing one can succeed in confirming not only the reliability of the English version of the *Epistola* but also the undeniable historical influence on the struggle for religious liberty that developed between the English Unitarians and the Latitudinarians against the limitations of the Act of Toleration of May, 1689 and in general in the shaping and development of the modern liberal conscience.

11. The codicil to the will, dated 15th Sept. 1704, is in the Bodleian Library of Oxford, Mss Locke, b. 5/14, reproduced in my ed. *Introd.* p. XXXII n. 2.
12. It has not escaped CRANSTON, *John Locke, A Biography*, London, 1957, p. 320, that Locke knew about the translation begun, and carried through by Popple, but, interpreting the phrase "without my privity" to mean "without my knowledge" in the sense given it by Coste, he accuses Locke of mendacity. Cf. my ed. *Introd.* p. XXXIII.

2. Locke's relations with the English Unitarians and with the Dutch Remonstrants are well known chapters in Locke's biography[13] and recent studies have shown perfectly clearly the basic acceptance by the Latitudinarian philosopher of the essential anti-trinitarianism of the two groups[14] on account of which the author of *Reasonableness of Christianity* has been accused, not without reason, of Socinianism.[15]

But it must be added that if the *Reasonableness* revealed the Socinian mould of the dilemma of the justification that lay at the centre of Locke's tract, Locke himself will privately and with his habitual secrecy furnish the rational proofs of the Unity of God which for the sake of prudence he omitted from the Essay and which transparently form the premises of the *Reasonableness* itself.[16] "Je croy que quiconque re-

13. Relations amply reconstructed by FOX BOURNE, op. cit., I, p. 310 et seq.; II, p. 6 seq. and by CRANSTON, op. cit. p. 124 seq.; 233 seq.

14. Cf. CRANSTON, op. cit. p. 390; VIANO, *John Locke, Dal razionalismo all'illuminismo*, Turin, 1960, p. 369 seq.; R. CRIPPA, *Studi sulla coscienza etica e religiosa del Seicento. Esperienza e Libertà in J. Locke*, Milan, 1960, p. 154 et seq.

15. On the argument with Edwards, who accused Locke of Socinianism see FOX BOURNE, op. cit. II, pp. 282-293; 408-415; CRANSTON, op. cit. p. 390; CRIPPA, op. cit. p. 158: "However much Locke may react to the criticisms of Edwards [...] the accusation remains valid." VIANO, op. cit. p. 376: "Socinian ideas are widely found in the *Reasonableness of Christianity*."

16. The rational proofs of the Unity of God are furnished in three of Locke's letters to Limborch, respectively dated 29th Oct. 1697, 2nd April 1698 and 21st May 1698. All three letters are written in French due to the lack of practice in Latin which, as Locke regrets, made it difficult for him to write it readily. Cf. *Postscriptum* to the letter of 29th Oct. 1697. These letters are published in *Some Familiar Letters between Mr Locke and several of his Friends*, appended by the editor to the first edition of *Locke's Works*, London, 1714, Vol. III, respectively pp. 624-25; 628-30; and 632. On the 29th Oct. 1697 Locke wrote to Limborch: "J'avois résolu de faire quelques additions (to the *Essay on Human Understanding*) dont j'ai deja composé quelques unes qui sont assez amples et qui auraient pû paroitre en leur place dans la quatrieme edition que le libraire se dispose à faire. Et j'aurois volontiers satisfait à votre désir, ou au désir d'aucun de vos amis en y insérant les preuves que l'unité de Dieu peut être établie sur des preuves qui ne laisseront aucun sujet d'en douter. Mais j'aime la paix, et il y a des gens dans le monde qui aiment si fort les crailleries et les vaines contestations, que je doute si je dois leur fornir de nouveaux sujets de dispute." Asked by Limborch to give at long last his thoughts on an argument of such deep interest, Locke asked his theologian friend: "vous ne donnerez aucune copie de ce que je vous écris à qui que soit (...), vous me promettez de jetter cette lettre au feu quand je vous prierai de la faire," in the letter of 2nd April 1698 he asked himself "How can the Unity of God be proved?" or in other words "How can

flechira sur soymême" Locke wrote to Limborch,[17] "connaitra evidement, sans en pouvoir douter le moins du monde, qu'il y a eû de toute éternité un Etre intelligent. Je croy encore qu'il est évident à tout homme qui pense, qu'il y a aussi un Etre infini. Or je dis qu'il ne peut y avoir qu'un Etre infini, et que cet Etre infini doit avoir été infini de toute éternité, car aucunes additions faites dans le temps, ne sauraient rendre une chose infinie, si elle ne l'est pas en elle même, et par elle même, de toute éternité. Telle étant la nature de l'infini qu'on n'en peut rien ôter, et qu'on n'y peut rien ajouter. D'où il ensuit que l'infini ne saurait être separé en plus d'un, ni être qu'un.

C'est là, selon moy, une preuve *à priori* que l'Etre éternel independent n'est qu'un; et si nous y joignons l'idée de toutes les perfections possibles, nous avons alors l'idée d'un Dieu éternel, infini, omniscient et tout-puissant etc."

Locke's acceptance of the Socinian thesis that excludes the nature of the Word in Christ, come out much more intimately and pungently from this explicit confession to the Arminian theologian than it does from the arguments of the *Reasonableness*. We could, rather, say that the rational demonstration of the Unity of God, finally reveals a Locke who is without any doubt Unitarian and Socinian, in spite of his obstinate denial and of his honest rejection of the sectarianism and dogmatism of the Socianians. It is true that if assent to the doctrine of the Trinity was obligatory by law, Locke did not want to be taken for Unitarian or Socinian, preferring to remain, as he had always been, an Anglican, but it is from now on quite clear that in his heart of hearts he

one prove that there is only one God?" to which he replied with the arguments which he summarised in the third letter, dated 21st May 1698 and given below.

Nevertheless, in order to determine more precisely Locke's thought on the impossibility of the existence of two Beings having divine attributes, I transcribe the following passage from the letter of 2nd April 1698: "Si pour anéantir les raisonements que je viens de faire, on dit que les deux Dieux qu'on suppose; ou les deux cent mille (car par la même raison qu'il peut y avoir deux il y en peut avoir deux millions, parce qu'on n'a plus aucun moyen d'en limiter le nombre), si l'on suppose, la même, qu'ils ont aussi la meme connoissance, la même volonté et qu'ils existent également dans le même lieu, c'est seulement multiplier le même être, mais dans le fonds et dans la verité de la chose on ne sait que reduire une pluralité supposée à une veritable unité. Car supposer deux êtres intelligens, qui connoissent, veulent et sont incessament la même chose et qui n'ont pas une existence separée, c'est supposer en paroles une pluralité, mais poser effectivement une simple unité."

17. Letter dated 21st May 1698, op. cit. p. 632.

was closer to the Unitarians and the Socinians than he was to the Latitudinarian wing of the Anglican church.

This clarification of Locke's doctrinal position will help us to a better understanding of the nature of his relationships with the Arminians of Holland and the Socinians of England, and at the same time to grasp the extent of the influence these same relationships had on the spirit and fortune of the *Letter on Toleration*, whether in the original Latin of Gouda or in the English translation of London.

For this reason it is worth remembering that if the *Epistola* was first conceived and written in Holland[18] in an Arminian circle[19] in the autumn of 1685, immediately after the revocation of the Edict of Nantes and under the sense of horror aroused by the tragic stories of the Huguenots who had escaped from the brutalities of the dragonnades;[20] in contrast the *Letter* came out in November 1689 in England and in a socinian circle, and it became a cry of protest by the Unitarians disappointed and offended at being excluded from the Act of Toleration.[21] And, just as the Arminian influence was made clear by that

18. For the time and place of the composition of the *Epistola* cf. my ed. *Introd.* p. XV.

19. On the Arminians of Holland it is worth remembering the entry *Remonstrants ou Arminiens* written or elaborated by Le Clerc for *Le Grand Dictionnaire Historique* of MORERI, Amsterdam, ed. 1740 in Vol. 7 of which one reads the following judgement of Stoupp: "Les mêmes Arminiens d'aujourd'hui croient que la doctrine de la Trinité n'est point nécessaire à salut, et qu'il n'y a dans l'Ecriture aucun précepte qui nous commande d'adorer le Saint Esprit." Bayle, who showed little tenderness towards the Arminians of Holland (cf. E. LABROUSSE, *P. Bayle*, I, The Hague, 1963, pp. 262-263; BRUSH, *Montaigne and Bayle*, The Hague, 1966, p. 237) wrote: "tous les Arminiens savans sont sociniens pour le moins" (*Oeuvres Diverses*, La Haye, 1737[2], IV, p. 619, ed. LABROUSSE) and added: "nos Calvinistes se font un honneur et un mérite de s'eloigner d'un secte qui est l'égout de tous les Athées, Déistes et Sociniens de l'Europe." The Socinian conditioning of Limborch's *Theologia Christiana* has been well shown by VIANO (op. cit. p. 378) and Limborch was the spiritual head of the Arminians of Holland.

20. Cf. my ed. of the *Letter, Introd.*, p. XV-XX.

21. The *Bill of Indulgence*, wrongly called the *Act of Toleration* was tabled in the House of Lords by Nottingham, the recognised parliamentary representative of the Anglican Church; it was passed in May 1689. Catholics and Unitarians were excluded from the benefits of toleration: the former because it was thought they would be hostile to the new regime for extraneous political reasons, and so not doctrinal ones; the latter, by contrast, because they were considered absolute heretics (cf. G.M. TREVELYAN, *The English Revolution 1688-89*, London, 1938, p. 151 ss.; *England under the Stuarts*, Penguin Books, 1960[2], p. 432.

Post-scriptum which recapitulated the reasons in defence of the Remonstrants against the insistent attacks and severe persecutions suffered at the hands of the Gomarists, who seriously threatened to renew the tragic events of 1685;[22] so Popple's *Introduction* to the English translation confers a quality of protest to the *Letter* which is not to be found in the *Epistola*.

Produced by two quite different historical situations and two different spiritual environments, the *Post-scriptum* to the *Epistola* and the *Introduction* to the *Letter* conferred profoundly different meanings to the same order of thoughts. For this reason the *Letter* became substantially different from the *Epistola*. But while the latter quickly exhausted its function in the small circle of learned Arminians in Holland,[23]

22. For the Arminian influence in the *Epistola*, which was demonstrated even by contemporaries, one should remember that when the *Epistola* appeared in Gouda, it was supposed that its author was Limborch himself, theologian and spiritual head of the Arminians, so much did the *Epistola* seem to be "selon ses principes" as was noted by BAYLE, *Oeuvres Diverses*, op. cit. II, p. 729, anast. ed. by E. LABROUSSE, Hildesheim, 1965. For the whole problem see my ed. *Introd.*, p. XXVII et seq.

Furthermore, in my view the *Post-scriptum* to the *Epistola* was added later and at Limborch's request (cf. my ed. *Introd.* p. XXIV) in defence of the Arminians who had been accused at the Synod of Dordrecht by the Gomarists of schism and heresy and in consequence condemned and banned. Further, the danger of seeing the persecutions renewed was not lacking, if among the refugees in Holland BAYLE, who wrote in the *Dictionnaire Historique et Critique* under the heading *Socin. Faust*: "Le schisme des Arminiens a favorisé l'entrée des Sociniens dans la Hollande; car ils ne refusent pas la Communion Ecclésiastique aux Sociniens. De sorte que ceux-ci ont pu séjourner dans plusieurs villes des Provénces Unies sans y être reconnus," showed, in the very year 1685, "sans ménagement aucun, combien catégoriquement [...] réprouvait l'arminianisme et le socinianisme," (LABROUSSE, op. cit. I, p. 262 seq.; II, p. 328; BRUSH, op. cit. p. 236) so much so that Le Clerc, writing to Locke on 1st November, 1690, still had reason to say: "J'ai aussi quelques livres anglois de la Tolérance que je ferai valoir comme il faut contre nos Persecuteurs" in BONNO, *Lettres inédites de Le Clerc à Locke*, Berkeley and Los Angeles, 1959, p. 44.

23. The *Epistola*, as has already been mentioned, was not re-printed again till 1765 nor did it ever appear on its own. Le Clerc, himself an Arminian, when he decided to translate the *Epistola* into French, made use of Popple's English text even though Limborch, who claimed to be the addressee of that letter, was still alive (cf. my ed. *Introd.* p. XL et seq.). Now, even POLIN has admitted that the *Lettre* is translated from the English (French ed. *Introd.* n. 3). It is also from the English that the *Epistola* was translated into Dutch, at least so it seems to me from the examples that I have found in the libraries of Amsterdam and The Hague (cf. my ed. *Introd.* p. XXXVI et seq.).

127

the *Letter*, on the contrary, precisely because it had been converted by Popple into the manifesto of the Socinian community[24] calling for absolute religious liberty,[25] turned out to be of burning actuality and

24. It is at least surprising that none of the modern editors, commentators or scholars who have worked on Locke's *Letter on Toleration* should have disclosed the circumstance, extremely important for the evaluation of the character and the historical function conferred on the *Letter* by Popple's *Preface*, namely that Popple was a Socinian and as such was excluded from the benefits of the *Act of Toleration* (cf. my ed. *Introd.* pp. XXIV-XXXV and n. 1).

In the prefaces to the successive editions of the series directed by him, up to the most recent one in French, KLIBANSKY finds (p. XX) an explanation of the contents and tone of Popple's *Preface* in the fact that Popple was a "friend of William Penn's" and therefore "much more radical than Locke, both in his interpretation of Christianity as moral guidance and in his attitude to politico-religious questions" (Italian ed. p. IX). SABETTI (ed. 1963, p. 88 n. 1) and POLIN (French ed. 1964, *Introd.* p. XXXVIII) follow Klibansky along the road, and the latter aggravates the judgement writing: "sa *Preface* [Popple's] *to the Reader*, a longtemps passé pour être de la main de Locke, bien qu'elle en présente les idées d'une façon déformante parce que trop radicale."

Worse still EBBINGHAUS (II German ed. 1966, p. 137) charges the Popple of the *Introduction* of being quite simply a "tribune" (die Stimme eines Volksredners) and a demagogue (*demagogen*), and he concludes, without a shadow of doubt, that the English translation is made by "a man moved much less by the difficulty of the problem than by the need to indicate his readers to take action (zur Tat werden zu lassen) to solve the problem, a solution he assumes as given" (p. 138). Who? Popple? Come now! How can Ebbinghaus believe that, when Popple wrote in the Preface *To the Reader* "it is neither *Declaration of Indulgence* nor *Acts of Comprehension*, such as have yet been practised or published amongst us, that can do the work. The first will but palliate, the second increase our evil. Absolute liberty, just and true liberty, is the thing that we stand in need of," that when he wrote these words Popple believed the solution to the problem was given? Evidently Ebbinghaus has not to taken account of what I noted in my ed. *Introd.* p. XXXV and n. 1, that is to say that Popple, like all the Unitarians and Socinians, had been excluded from the *Act of Toleration*; hence his disappointment which can be sensed in the tone of the *Preface*. The question of religious toleration, or rather of religious liberty, was, as far as Popple was concerned, still to be posed, let alone solved. The fact that he did not take this circumstance into account explains why, in the eyes of Ebbinghaus, Popple appears as a demagogue or tribune, but it also explains that his opinion of Popple's *Preface*, the elimination of this same *Preface* from his editions, and finally the rejection of my arguments, clearly derive from a mistake into which he was led by a failure to study the problem deeply.

25. It is, in fact, against the discriminatory provisions adopted by Parliament with the *Declaration of Indulgence* and the *Act of Comprehension* that the Unitarian Popple entreats with the celebrated sentence "Absolute liberty, just and true liberty, equal and impartial liberty, is the thing that we stand in need of."

took on such energy and power of penetration that it contributed in large measure to the abrogation of the limitations of the Act of Toleration within a short time.[26] In this way the *Letter* caused the *Epistola* to be forgotten, and out-lived it. To claim now to expunge the text of the *Letter* from *Locke's Works,* treating Popple's introduction as a curious appendix, when not actually excluded from modern editions, is in reality not to know that if Locke's major tract on toleration had a real impact on history, it is only by reason of Popple's English transla-

KLIBANSKY's remark (Ital. ed. 1961, p. IX and repeated in the successive editions) that Locke did not believe in absolute liberty is totally irrelevant. To Popple's entreaty he opposes the passage in the *Essay* (IV, 3, 18) in which Locke affirms that the proposition that "no government concedes an absolute liberty" is evident like any "mathematical proposition" but this is irrelevant because while Popple is talking of religious liberty, in the passage quoted Locke is talking of civil liberty. This only, in fact, is regulated by the political society, which limits it in conformity with its own aims, while religious liberty is removed from the competence of the civil powers: "cura salutis animorum nullo modo pertinere potest ad magistratum civilem" (cf. my ed. p. 20) in so far as it is an incontestable right of every man and therefore absolute in its enjoyment. In contrast the English Parliament had set itself up as judge in matters of religion when it had defined the Unitarians as absolute heretics and excluded them from the benefits of the *Act of Toleration.* Hence the protest of Popple and of the Unitarians, who rejected the *Declaration of Indulgence* and demanded an "absolute [religious] liberty," against any imposition or discrimination of the civil power as far as religious matters were concerned. In that they found that Locke was of the same mind, when he wrote in the *Letter* "potestas civilis non debet articulos fidei, sive dogmata, vel modo colendi Deum lege civili prescribere" (cf. my ed. p. 19). As a consequence, even the exclusion of the catholics from the Toleration, an exclusion Locke himself desired, is justified, not on religious grounds, because Locke denied no one the widest possible religious liberty, but rather on political ones, since the Catholics, in so far as they obeyed a foreign prince, would have created a state within a state, and would therefore have endangered the very existence of the state of which they were citizens. The exclusion of the Catholics from the Toleration, demanded by Locke, and exclusion of the Unitarians, decreed by the *Act of Toleration* are therefore quite differently motivated and arise from two totally different principles: the first from one of political expediency and so legitimate; the second from one of religious orthodoxy and so illegitimate. That also applies to what CRANSTON wrote (op. cit. p. 260) "Locke did not believe in absolute liberty."

26. Cf. TREVELYAN, *The English Revolution,* op. cit. p. 158-9. As proof, it is enough to remember for the rest, that already in 1696, the Unitarian Popple was nominated Secretary of the Board of Trade of which Locke was Commissioner and that at a time when assent to the doctrine of the Trinity had not been abrogated by law.

tion and by virtue of the character that Popple himself was able to set upon it.[27]

It remains to be known, of course, whether Popple, when he adapted the *Epistola* to a situation that could not have been foreseen at the time it was written and inserted it in the heart of a politico-religious quarrel for which it had not originally been intended, did so without Locke's knowledge and so betrayed his thought and spirit or whether, on the contrary, he did perfectly interpret Locke's feelings about the situation created in England by injustices that arose from the Act of Toleration. It is a matter therefore of reconstructing the relations between Locke and Popple and the circumstances of the English translation in the light of the relations in order to see first of all whether Popple really translated the *Epistola* "à l'insû de M. Locke;" and then whether or not he was a faithful interpreter of Locke's thought; and on the basis of the results obtained, to decide on the authenticity and reliability of the English text which is today under attack.

3. The story of relations between Locke and Popple is still to be written and remains more or less unexplored in the copious correspondence between the broad-minded philosopher and the Socinian merchant.[28]

27. That did not escape WAISMANN who writes (Spanish ed. p. 106) that "La traducción inglesa de Popple es la que dio a la carta lockiana su universal, su prodigiosa difusión: con el titulo de *A Letter concerning Toleration* gano influjo y eficacia en todo el viejo mundo y al otro lado del Atlántico." But when he adds (ibid. p. 107) that Popple's translation "esta muy lejos de ser una traduccion fiel" and for that reason is unworthy of the reputation which is enjoyed and still enjoys, he clearly shows that he has not realised that the "prodigious diffusion" of the *Letter* became possible precisely for the reason that Popple changed Locke's "estilo [...] simple y llano" into a tone of burning polemic, and thus made the *Letter*, which out-lived the *Epistola*, into an indestructible document of the struggle for religious liberty. Now, to make "todo nuestro esfuerzo, nuestro honrado esfuerzo" as WAISMANN writes (op. cit. p. 107) in order to offer a translation "lo más fiel posible del texto latino" means, by definition, if one aims to replace Popple's translation, to present instead a cold copy of the *Epistola*, and so to strip Locke's writing of those features of tone and style which assured it that acknowledged "eficacia en todo el viejo mundo y al otro lado del Atlántico."

28. Of the correspondence between Popple and Locke 32 letters written between 1692 and 1702 exist in the *Lovelace Collection* of the Bodleian Library in Oxford (BL Mss. Locke c. 17 fol. 201-266). I am indebted to the courtesy of Mr. Martin of the Department of Western Manuscripts of the Bodleian Library for this information and take this opportunity to thank him publicly.

However some of the evidence is not unknown and more will be adduced here, which allows one to reconstruct with sufficient exactness the state of those relations, at least during the period in which the *Epistola* was translated and which is the only period that interests us here.

As for the first point under discussion, Locke himself provides us with incontrovertible evidence which is anything but unpublished and yet is neglected and ignored by the modern editors of the *Letter*. When, after having prepared the *Epistola* for the press, the Arminian theologian Limborch wrote from Amsterdam to announce that it had just appeared: "prodiit hic hisce diebus libellus elegantissimus de Tolerantia per modum epistolae scriptus non expresso authoris nomine,"[29] and sent him at the same time some copies, Locke replied on the 6th of June thanking him: "gratias tibi ago pro exemplaribus tractatus de Tolerantia (...) quae mihi misisti,"[30] and adding the following unexpected revelation immediately afterwards: "in vertendo de tolerantia libello aliquem anglum jam jam occupatum intelligo."[31] On the 10th September Locke wrote again to Limborch: "*Epistola de Tolerantia* jam in anglicanum sermonem versa est."[32]

Locke therefore knew very well that someone had started and finished the job of translating the *Epistola* between the months of June and September, and he also knew very well that that *anglum* was none other than his friend William Popple, merchant of Unitarian faith who belonged like he did to the circle round Firmin, recognised spiritual leader of the English Unitarians.[33]

Besides we have a good witness in Le Clerc for the friendship between Locke and Popple which was already established at the time when the *Epistola* was being translated.[34] In the preface to the French edition of the *Epistola*, which first appeared in the *Oeuvres Diverses de Mr.*

29. Limborch to Locke, 6 May 1689 (Mss R.L. III D 16 f. 195) (cf. my ed. *Introd.* p. XXI).
In my ed. *Introd.* p. XXII et seq. I proved that the *Epistola* was not a "personal letter" to Limborch, as Limborch himself claimed, but a "*tractatus*" or "*libellus de Tolerantia per modum epistolae scriptus.*"
30. Locke to Limborch, 6 June 1689 (MSS R.L. B.a. 256 I); my ed. *Introd.* p. XXII.
31. Ibid. my ed. *Introd.* p. XXXIII.
32. Locke to Limborch (MSS. R.L. B.a. 256); my ed. *Introd.* p. XXXIII.
33. On the circle round Firmin cf. FOX BOURNE (op. cit. vol. I, p. 310 seq.; CRANSTON, op. cit. p. 127. For the influence on Locke's religious thinking cf. VIANO, op. cit. p. 370 seq.
34. A different view is taken by FOX BOURNE (op. cit. II, p. 154) who

Locke, edited at Rotterdam in 1710, Le Clerc wrote in fact: "Elle (the *Epistola*) n'eut pas plutôt vu le jour qu'un de ses amis la traduisit en Anglais".[35] One can, it is true, object that Le Clerc wrote that *Avertissement* to the *Oeuvres Diverses* 20 years after the event mentioned and, as the relations between Locke and Popple after 1696[36] were well known, might well have mistakenly moved the start of that friendship forward in time. But with regard to this question one should note that when Le Clerc was collecting material for his *Eloge Historique de feu Mr Locke*,[37] there appeared in the *Nouvelles de la Republique des Lettres*[38] of the month of February, 1705, the *Eloge de M. Locke* by Coste, in which he stated that the "Lettre Latine sur la Tolerance, imprimée à Tergou (Gouda)" had been translated "quelque temps après en Anglois à l'insû de M. Locke."[39] Le Clerc was very friendly with Coste, whom Le Clerc himself had introduced to Locke as "extremement de mes amis."[40] Coste was with Locke when the philosopher dictated that codicil to his will in which he admitted paternity of the works that had appeared anonymously or under a pseudonym and of which Coste himself first gave news in the *Republique des Lettres,* mentioning among other works the *Epistola* and the translation that was said to have been done "à l'insû de M. Locke." The *Eloge* of Coste must have been a precious source of information for Le Clerc who learned from it the works of which "M. Locke se reconnoit l'Auteur." Yet Le Clerc did not pick up another piece of information

holds that Locke sought out Popple only after the translation of the *Epistola* and so won his friendship: cf. my ed. *Introd.* p. XLII.

35. I quote from the 1732 ed. which appeared with the title *Oeuvres Diverses de Mr Locke. Nouvelle Ed. considerablement augmentée*, 2 vols, Amsterdam, 1732, *Avertissement*, p. V: cf. my ed. *Introd.* p. XXXVI seq.

36. It has already been stated that when Locke was named Commissioner of the Board of Trade in 1696, Popple was named secretary (cf. CRANSTON, op. cit. p. 399 seq.).

37. *Eloge Historique de feu Mr Locke* par J. LE CLERC in *Bibliothèque Choisie*, Vol. VI, 1705, p. 342 seq., first reprinted in *Oeuvres Diverses de Mr Locke*, Rotterdam, 1710, and then in *Oeuvres Diverses de Mr Locke. Nouvelle Ed. considérablement augmentée*, 2 vols., Amsterdam, 1732, vol. I, pp. I-CXIX. On Le Clerc's sources of information cf. my ed. *Introd.* p. XV n. 1.

38. On this publication of Bayle see now the pages dedicated to it by LABROUSSE in *Pierre Bayle*, op. cit. I, p. 190 et seq.

39. COSTE, *Eloge*, cit. p. XXVIII and n. 9 above.

40. Le Clerc to Locke dated 8 July 1695 in BONNO, cit. p. 86. The relations between Locke and Coste and Le Clerc's good offices, ibid. *Introduction*, p. 22 seq.

provided by Coste nor did he repeat it later in the *Avertissement* to his translation of the *Epistola,* where he related on his own account that the *Epistola* "n'eut pas plutôt vu le jour qu'un de ses amis la traduisit." Clearly Le Clerc should have been better informed on this point, especially as he himself chose to base his French translation of the *Letter* not on the Latin original but rather on Popple's English text.[41] And since Le Clerc well knew how carefully Locke followed the translation of his works,[42] the preference for the English text must have been suggested to him not only by the fact that Popple's translation restored the *Epistola* from an acquired language which only a few years later Locke regretted he no longer knew well[43] into Locke's mother tongue, but also from the certainty which came to him from his own experience in translating Locke's works, that Locke himself must have followed and revised the work of his friend.[44]

The preference shown by Le Clerc for the English translation confirms, then, even if only indirectly, the fact that Le Clerc must have been well informed about the state of the relationship between Locke and Popple in 1689, if, in spite of Coste's opinion to the contrary he was able to write that the *Epistola* had been immediately translated into English by a friend of Locke's.

4. Besides we know that in 1692, three years that is to say after the publication of the translation of the *Epistola*, Locke and Popple were on

41. I have given the proof and discussed the motives in my ed. *Introd.* p. XL et seq.

42. Le Clerc translated the *Abstract of the Essay* which he published in the *Bibliothèque Universelle Historique* of 1688 (Vol. III, pp. 49-142), under the title *Extrait d'un Livre Anglois qui n'est pas encore publié, intitulé Essai Philosophique concernant l'Entendement Humain,* under the wakeful guidance of Locke himself who had a sound knowledge of French.

For the rest COSTE is a good witness of the care with which Locke followed the translation of his works: see *Avertissement* to the French translation of the *Essai Philosophique concernant l'Entendement Humain,* cit. p. X et seq.; cf. my ed. *Introd.* p. XLII n. 2; p. XLIII n.1.

43. Locke regretted this to Limborch in a *Post-scriptum* to the letter quoted and dated 29 Oct. 1697: "linguae latinae dissuetudine, quae expedite scribere prohibet," in *Familiar Letters* in *Locke's Works*[1], III, p. 625.

44. As had happened with his translation of the *Abstract* and as Coste testifies: "[...] je seroi souvent demeuré court sans l'assistance de M. Locke qui a eu la bonté de revoir ma Traduction [...] et si j'ai pris quelque liberté (car on ne peut pas s'en passer) c'a toujours été sous le bon plaisir de M. Locke qui entend assez bien le Francois." *Avertissement,* cit. p. X and XIV.

intimate terms so that when Locke founded the Dry Club in London, one of his usual "clubs"[45] and a meeting place for discussion among philosopher friends, Popple was named as Secretary of the club which statute, for us a very important detail, laid upon its members an absolute respect for the widest freedom of faith and thought.[46] We also know that in 1692, when the *Third Letter concerning Toleration* came out, Locke sent a few copies to his dearest and most trusted friends among these, along with Ashley, Firmin, Newton and Le Clerc, was also Popple;[47] this is clear proof that Locke not only recognised that Popple had a serious interest in the question of toleration that was being debated at that time, but also that Locke's relationship with him had long been firmly based on mutual respect and friendship.

Perhaps it would not be far from the truth if one said that the friendship must have begun in the years about 1670, that is to say when Locke was introduced by Ashley to the group round Firmin; Firmin's London house in Lombard Street had become a place of meeting and refuge for the English Unitarians.[48] That Locke should have got to know the Socinian merchant Popple at that time, perhaps through business contact with Firmin and Ashley, is anything but improbable; what in any case is certain is that when he returned to England after the exile in Holland, Locke renewed his contacts with Firmin and the Unitarians around him, and if he did not renew a long-standing friendship with Popple, certain it is that he associated with the Unitarian, who had become known in those years for a little work called *A Rational Catechism* of rigorous anti-trinitarian inspiration.

Now, in the Spring of 1689 English Unitarian circles were in turmoil

45. For the Clubs set up by Locke and for the effect they had on his character and intellectual life cf. CRANSTON op. cit. p. 117, 282 seq., 361 seq.; BAYLE (*Oeuvres Diverses*, IV, p. 643) wrote that he had found "du plaisir et du profit" in the meetings of the Lanthern Club set up by Locke in Rotterdam.

46. The statute of the Dry Club: "*Rules of the Dry Club: For the Amicable Improvement of Mixed Conversation*" can be found in the Lovelace Collection of the Bodleian Library (MSS Locke, c 25, f 56-57) and is in Popple's handwriting. The first condition of admission for members asks "Whether he has an Universal Charity and Good will to all men, as Men, of what Church or Profession of Religion soever they are?"

For the photocopy of the Statute of the Dry Club I am indebted to the kindness of Mr. K.E. Butler, Deputy to Mr. Vivian Ridler, Printer to the University at the University Press, Oxford, whom I here thank publicly.

47. Cf. CRANSTON, cit. p. 368.

48. Cf. FOX BOURNE, op. cit. I, p. 310 seq.; CRANSTON, op. cit. p. 127.

caused by the injustice of the Act of Toleration which alongside the Catholics excluded the Unitarians themselves as absolute heretics. In Firmin's circle the question of religious liberty must therefore have been more than ever alive, and Locke, whose hidden Sociniansim inclined him, as we shall see, to share the delusion of the Unitarians, can certainly have been no stranger to the discussions and recriminations of the anti-trinitarians at whose head was Firmin.

A proof of Locke's contacts with Firmin's circle when he returned to England and the feelings of the broad-minded philosopher towards the cause of the Unitarians is the fact that, on the eve of the passing of the Act of Toleration and when the Unitarians were already afraid of their future, Locke sent Le Clerc in Holland *A Brief History of the Unitarians Called also Socinians* so that he might spread a knowledge of it through the *Bibliothèque Universelle;* the expenses of publishing this work were paid by the philanthropist Firmin himself.[49] That in exchange Locke should have arranged to circulate that anonymous *Epistola de Tolerantia* among the English Unitarians of Firmin's circle as soon as he had received it from Holland seems to us anything but a risky supposition; that work made explicit the reasons for universal religious toleration among the various Christian churches and so coincided perfectly with the protest made by the Unitarians against any limitation or discrimination. Certain it is that hardly had Locke received a few copies of the *Epistola* from Limborch, when, as we have seen, Popple began the translation of it[50] with Locke's knowledge, so that Le Clerc

49. In his letter of 12th Feb. 1689 (see BONNO, op. cit. pp. 35-36) LE CLERC had asked Locke to send him any books his friends wanted to make known through the *Bibliothèque* "deça la mer," and Locke replied promising to send him *A Brief History of the Unitarians called also Socinians. In four Letters written to a Friend*, London, 1687 (cf. BONNO, op. cit. p. 37) published at Firmin's expense (ibid. p. 25). At the beginning of July the book had not yet reached LE CLERC (BONNO, op. cit. pp. 38-39) whose "compte-rendu" did not appear till the 1689 December number of the *Bibliothèque* (vol. V, pp. 364-366). In January 1692 Firmin was to send Le Clerc "avec quelques civilites" some works on Toleration (BONNO, op. cit. pp. 49-50) which could include Locke's first two letters but certainly not the third as BONNO thinks (op. cit. p. 49, n. 74) because it is dated 20th June.

50. It is worth remembering that even in the letter of 10th September, when, that is, Locke informed Limborch that the English translation had been finished, Locke himself complained that, in spite of the entreaties made to Limborch and the assurances received from him, the *Epistola* could not yet be obtained on the London book-market: "Miror Bibliopolam vestrorum vel nostrorum negligentiam " Locke wrote, "*Epistola de Tolerantia* [...] apud nos nullibi reperire

was able to write with knowledge of the matter that the *Epistola* "n'eut pas plutôt vu le jour qu'un de ses amis la traduisit en Anglois."

5. That Locke then had frequent contact with Popple while the translation was being done and that he followed that translation very closely is also documented by the correspondence between Locke and Limborch.[51] We know in fact that when the Arminian theologian was told by his philosopher friend that someone was translating the *Epistola* into English, he from his side told Locke that a Dutch and a French translation were in hand and that therefore the *Epistola* could soon be read in four languages.[52] On 10th September Locke told Limborch that the English translation was finished asking at the same time for a copy of the translations that had appeared in Holland: "Traductionem et belgicam et gallicam quaeso mittas."[53] However, the French translation,

possum venalem" (cf. my ed. *Introd.* p. XXXIII). Popple could not therefore have got the *Epistola* in a bookshop. It is true that some friend might have sent him a copy from Holland. But who? Perhaps that Daranda who revealed to his Arminian friends, kept in the dark by Limborch, that the author of the *Epistola* was reported in London to be Locke (cf. CRANSTON, op. cit. pp. 332-333) and who later suggested that Locke, Popple and Sir Francis Masham should help Le Clerc out of the extreme poverty into which he had fallen? (cf. CRANSTON, op. cit. p. 416 n. 2). But I do not see why one should have recourse to the hypothesis that a not very well identified friend of Popple's should have sent him a copy of the *Epistola* from Holland, when Locke had already received some copies from Limborch and was himself in contact with Popple. And why, then, if Locke was sending English books to Holland so that they might be better known "deça la mer," could he not in turn have arranged for English books published in Holland to be circulated among his English friends? Such a hypothesis would fall in the matter being examined only if it were shown that Locke's contacts with Popple began as FOX BOURNE supposes (op. cit. II, p. 154) after the translation of the *Epistola*, but we have seen that this was not the case.

If this were not the case, one could not explain how Locke new that "aliquem anglum" had begun and brought to completion the job of translation. I believe I can maintain against EBBINGHAUS (II, ed. cit. p. 136-137) the conclusion which I had already reached (cf. my ed. *Introd.*, p. XXXIII) namely that Locke provided Popple with the Latin copy from which the English translation was made, I believe I can maintain that naturally until the contrary is proved or at least until new facts are brought to light for a different conjecture.

51. Cf. my ed. *Introd.* p. XXXV et seq. and especially p. XL.

52. Limborch to Locke (BL MSS Locke 18 July 1689 c. 14 f. 26[2]) quoted by KLIBANSKY, French ed. *Préface*, p. XXXII seq.

53. Locke to Limborch 10 Sept. 1689 MSS R.L. B.a. 256°; my ed. *Introd.* p. XL.

entrusted to Le Cène, who, as we know from Le Clerc, could not have been the man best suited to such a job,[54] although finished would never be printed,[55] while no trace of the Dutch translation has been found in the libraries of Holland,[56] in spite of what Limborch said about it.[57] All the same the fact is worth noting that even if Le Clerc hints at a Dutch translation in Volume XV of the *Bibliothèque*[58] he makes no further mention of it in the *Avertissement* to the *Oeuvres Diverses* in which the French translation of the letter was published in 1710. Nor is there any mention of it under the entry *Locke* in the big dictionary of Moreri.

However that may be, Locke knew from Limborch that a French and a Dutch translation had already come out or were on the point of coming out in Holland and asked for a copy of each. This was on the 10th September. On the 30th September Limborch replied that it was unlikely that the French translation would be published: "Gallica versio non est impressa: an imprimenda incertus sum."[59] On the 3rd October

54. Le Clerc, in writing to Locke, gave his opinion of Le Cène (cf. BONNO, op. cit. p. 38 n. 2) in the following words: "M. Le Cène qui a fait le volume XIII [of the *Bibliothèque*] l'a fait si misérablement, que malgré les corrections infinies que j'y ai fait, j'en ai honte moi-même."
55. Limborch to Locke 18th July 1689 quoted by Klibansky; see note 52 above.
56. For the Dutch translations I found in the Libraries of Leyden and The Hague and how these were made from the English text and not the Latin one see my ed. *Introd.* pp. XXXVI-XL. After the evidence adduced by KLIBANSKY (French ed. *Préface*, p. XXI) it seems all the same that one must accept that a Dutch translation was made before the English one. It is, however, strange that no record of this translation should have been preserved and that the existing Dutch translations, though referring to an earlier translation should all turn out to be from Popple's text.
57. On 16th Sept. of the new calendar Limborch wrote to Locke (BL. MSS Locke c. 14 f. 30²) ap. KLIBANSKY, French ed. *Préface*, p. XXI: "verum Belgice in officinis nostris prostat, et a pluribus maximo cum applauso legitur." On the 30th Sept. he apparently sent to Locke a copy of the Dutch translation: "Versionis Belgicae vides hic exemplar" (Limborch to Locke, 30 Sept. new calend. 1689, BL MSS Locke c. 14 f. 32ᵛ ap. KLIBANSKY cit. ib.).
58. In a summary of the *Epistola* which appeared in vol. XV of the *Bibliothèque* art. XIV pp. 402-412 only in the winter of 1690 (cf. my ed. *Introd.* p. XXX n. 3) Le Clerc wrote (p. 412): "Ce livre [the *Epistola*] a si fort plû en Angleterre, et ici, qu'on l'a traduit d'abord en Anglois, et en Flamand. Il est déja imprimé en ces deux langues, et peut être qu'on la verra encore en François."
59. Quoted by KLIBANSKY, French ed. *Préf.* p. XXXIII n. 3.

meanwhile the English translation was licensed by the censor and appeared shortly afterwards set in type by Churchill with the following notice given by Popple in the translation: "The ensuing *Letter concerning Toleration* first printed in Latin this very year in Holland, has already been translated both into Dutch and French."[60] Who told Popple first that the manuscript had been submitted to the censor and then that a French and a Dutch translation had already appeared in Holland? In my view I do not see who else could have done it but Locke.[61]

Given that Locke was a friend of Popple's and that he knew perfectly well that the latter had started and completed the English translation of the *Epistola* between June and September 1689, nothing prevents one from believing that it was Locke himself who told Popple of the news received from Limborch about the Dutch and French translations which, according to Limborch, had already appeared in Holland.

6. If, then, Locke knew about the work of Popple, to whom he had given the copy of the *Epistola* from which the English translation was made, as all the foregoing allows us to believe, and certainly passed on the news received from Limborch about the Dutch and French translations, then when he wrote in the codicil to his will that the *Epistola* had been translated "without my privity" he could certainly not have meant "without my knowledge;" but rather that the translation had been done without his "consent".[62] Having kept quiet about,

60. My ed. *Introd.* p. 3.
61. According to KLIBANSKY (French ed. *Préf.* XXIII) on the other hand, Popple learned of the French translation from Dutch friends, wrongly concluding that the translation itself had already been published.

But in reality Klibansky, who has also produced conclusive proofs about the translations that had been made, or planned and not completed, in Holland, proofs drawn from the Limborch-Locke correspondence, has not on the other hand taken into account that part of the Locke-Limborch correspondence which shows that Locke was aware of the fact that Popple was translating the *Epistola* into English, nor has he given enough attention to Locke's relations with the Socinian merchant. Because, if he had done so, he would not then have concluded that "Popple, qui avait des amis aux Pays Bas, avait donc [?] appris qu'une traduction française était en cours et avait conclus à tort que la publication était acquise," from the moment that he, Klibansky, realised that Popple had a friend closer at hand who was perfectly informed about the circumstances of that translation and hence very well able to pass on news that he in his turn had received from Limborch. In any case Klibansky's assertion remains, at least for the present, unsupported by any proof whatsoever.

62. For the interpretation of "privity" in the meaning of "consent" see my ed. *Introd.* p. XXXIV n. 2.

138

or having denied to Popple the fact that he was the author of the *Epistola*, he was not called upon to make such an endorsement as there had been no prior agreement between him and Popple[63] just as on his part there had been no request for the *Epistola* to be translated. This was quite certainly an act of honesty and modesty but misinterpreted it has led to Popple being severely judged and to Locke being accused of mendacity.[64]

In support of the accuracy of the interpretation, which we have already given elsewhere[65] and confirmed above, we recall that a similar "endorsement" on the part of the author to the translation of his work into another language was given by Locke himself with regard to Coste's French translation of the *Essay concerning Human Understanding* where it stood as a guarantee of the reliability and faithfulness of that same translation.[66]

63. Let the reader recall that the entry "privity" in the Oxford English Dictionary, 1961, Vol. III, note 6 is given as "any relation between two parties recognised by law." Cf. my ed. *Introd.* p. XXXIV n. 2.

64. CRANSTON, op. cit., p. 320, in fact accused Locke of mendacity, claiming that though Locke knew Popple was translating the *Epistola*, he still said that the translation had been done without his knowledge; this of course is to interpret Locke's phrase in the sense given it by Coste.

65. Cf. my ed. *Introd.* p. XXXIV and n. 2.

66. In the hope of rendering a valuable service to the students of Locke I record here in full the following example of "privity" in the sense of "consent" left us by Locke with regard to Coste's French translation of the *Essay* and published in 1700. This is from the third edition of the *Essai Philosophique concernant l'Entendement Humain* [...] *par* M. LOCKE, *traduit de l'Anglois par* M. COSTE [...], Amsterdam, MDCCXXV, p. XL: "Monsieur Locke au Libraire. La netteté d'Esprit et la connoissance de la Langue Francoise, dont M. Coste a deja donné au Public des preuves si visibles, pouvoient vous être un assez bon garant de l'excellence de son travail sur mon *Essay*, sans qu'il fût necessaire que vous m'en demandassiez mon sentiment. Si j'étois capable de juger de ce qui est écrit proprement et élegamment en Francois, je me croirois obligé de vous envoyer un grand éloge de cette Traduction dont j'ai ouï dire que quelques personnes, plus habiles que moi dans la Langue Francoise, ont assuré qu'elle pouvoit passer pour un original. Mais ce que je puis dire à l'égard du point sur lequel vous souhaitez de savoir mon sentiment, c'est que M. Coste m'a lû cette Version d'un bout à l'autre avant que de vous l'envoyer, et que tous les endroits que j'ai remarqué s'éloigner de mes pensées, ont été ramenez au sens de l'Original, ce qui n'étoit pas facile dans des Notions aussi abstraites que le sont quelques-unes de mon *Essay*, les deux Langues n'ayant pas toujours des mots et des expressions qui se répondent si juste l'une à l'autre qu'elles remplissent toute l'exactitude philosophique; mais la justesse d'esprit de M. Coste et la souplesse de sa Plume lui ont fait trouver les moyens

A guarantee of the legitimacy and reliability of Popple's translation was equally given by Locke through the mere fact of having left the Bodleian Library a copy of the *Letter* along with one of the *Epistola* and of other works "dont M. Locke se reconnoit l'auteur," with the clear intention of fully acknowledging the authorship of, and the responsibility for the English edition of the *Epistola*.[67] And if Locke acknowledged the authorship of, and responsibility for that *Letter concerning Toleration* the reason is to be sought not only in the fact that that *First Letter* was continued in a *Second* and a *Third Letter concerning Toleration* but also in the fact that Popple's translation and Preface had turned the *Epistola* into a new and different work to which the *Second* and the *Third Letter concerning Toleration* were linked and formed sequels, even in their titles; this was not the case with regard to the *Epistola*.[68] That is to say that when Popple bent Locke's tract to suit a different historical situation and also conferred on it a completely different meaning, Locke did not for that reason feel himself betrayed in thought and feeling.

On the contrary, Locke fully shared the feelings expressed by Popple in the introduction to the *Letter* and he himself has left an open testimony to the fact. Already on the eve of his return to England, when he told Limborch[69] of Parliament's moves with regard to religious liberty, Locke dropped his usual caution and openly expressed his mistrust of the attitude of the Anglican Episcopate,[70] and asked himself whether this body was acting in its own interests or in the common interests: "In parlamento de tolerantia jam agi coeptum est sub duplice titulo, *Comprehensio* scil [icet] et *Indulgentia.* Prima ecclesiae pomoeria extenda significat, ut ablata caerimoniarum parte plures comprehendat. Altera tolerantiam significat eorum qui, oblatis conditionibus ecclesiae

de corriger toutes ces fautes que j'ai découvertes à mesure qu'il me lisoit ce qu'il avoit traduit. De sorte que je puis dire au Lecteur que je présume qu'il trouvera dans cet Ouvrage toutes les qualités qu'on peut désirer dans une bonne Traduction."

67. Cf. my ed. *Introd.* pp. XLV-XLVI. It has already been said that KLI-BANSKY (French ed. *Préf.* p. VIII) has now ended up by admitting that Locke by the act of donating the Bodleian Library a copy of the *Letter* reinforced Popple's translation with his own authority. So Klibansky too has taken up a position against the views of Ebbinghaus and Waismann.

68. Ref. in my ed. *Introd.* pp. XLIV-XLV.

69. Locke to Limborch, 12 March 1689 in *Familiar Letters* in *The Works of J. Locke*, ed. 1714, cit. III, p. 603.

70. On the question see TREVELYAN, *The English Revolution*, cit. p. 159.

Anglicanae, se unire vel nolunt vel non possunt. Quam laxa vel sctricta haec futura sint, vix dum scio, hoc saltem sentio, clerum episcopalem his aliisque rebus quae hic aguntur non multum favere, an cum suo vel reɪp[sa] commodo ipsi videant." These same words are found again almost literally in Popple's *Introduction* and it cannot be mere chance: "It is neither *Declarations of Indulgence* nor *Acts of Comprehension*, such as have yet been practised or projected amongst us, that can do the work. The first will palliate, the second increase our evil [...] I cannot, therefore, but hope that this *Discourse* [...] will be esteemed highly reasonable by all men that have souls large enough to prefer the true interest of the public before that of a party."[71]

So, when the *Act of Indulgence*, commonly but improperly called the *Act of Toleration,* was passed in May 1689 Locke wrote again to Limborch: "Tolerantiam apud nos jam tandum lege stabilita [...] Non ea forsan latitudine qua tu et tui similes veri et sine ambitione vel invidia Christiani optarent;"[72] in this way he interpreted not only the disappointment of his Remonstrant friend[73] but also his own disappointment at seeing vanish the hope for a universal liberty covering all churches. Consequently Popple's words "Absolute liberty, just and true liberty, equal and impartial liberty is the thing that we stand in need of," if they really are Popple's, are not for that reason not shared, or subscribed to, by Locke. As the liberty claimed in these words is the liberty of conscience and worship of which the Unitarians had need above all, "the thing that we stand in need of" and not an absolute civil liberty, unfettered that is to say from the ties of law and of the civil justice;[74] a religious liberty, in other words, which as such is removed from the competence of the civil justice and, if necessary, enjoyed even if he opposes it: "a perfect uncontrollable [religious] liberty which he may freely use without or contrary to the magistrate's command,"[75] since everyone has "an absolute and universal right to toleration"[76] as Locke had expressed himself since 1667 in the *Essay concerning Toleration.*

71. My ed. of Locke's *A Letter concerning Toleration, To the Reader*, p. 3.
72. Locke to Limborch 6 June 1689 in *Familiar Letters*, cit. III, p. 604.
73. The view of the Remonstrants is given by Le Clerc who defines the *Act of Toleration* merely as "une démarche vers la paix," in BONNO, op. cit., p. 38.
74. That it is a matter here of religious liberty and not of civil liberty is not clear to Klibansky: see note 25 above.
75. J. LOCKE, *An Essay concerning Toleration*, in J. LOCKE, *Scritti editi ed inediti sulla Tolleranza*, ed. by C.A. VIANO, Turin, 1961, p. 85.
76. *An Essay*, cit. p. 83.

141

So the motives for which Locke immediately took a position alongside the Unitarians in the politico-religious controversy raised by the Act of Toleration became clear; at first he took his position covertly and indirectly, offering them the defence of the arguments of the *Epistola* in favour of an indiscriminate religious liberty; and then directly and openly with the *Second* and the *Third Letter on Toleration* which were to form the episodes of a struggle in favour of the Unitarians and from which Locke could not escape. Popple's *Preface* therefore perfectly interpreted Locke's thought and feeling, which were to reveal only some years later and much more explicitly than in the *Reasonableness* how close his sympathy was with the Socinians in their struggle against the exclusion of the Unitarians from religious toleration.

It ought to be clear from what has been said so far how a discussion on the fidelity of the English text to the Latin original becomes quite irrelevant, if it is true that the *Epistola* and the *Letter* ought to be considered completely original and independent works rather than the latter being a translation of the former. They underline two different historical situations to which Locke's feelings were perfectly atuned and which the two works in their diversity of tone and style perfectly reflect. The very fact that Locke should have wanted the *Epistola* and the *Letter,* in contrast to his other works that were translated while he was still alive, to be kept for posterity one beside the other can in my view mean nothing else. If, then, the *Letter* has outlived the *Epistola,* that confirms the fact that the former has had more influence on history than the latter, and more than the latter has aroused and assisted a ferment of ideas still alive today. That ought to be borne in mind by anyone who disputes the good fortune that Popple's work has enjoyed and demands its removal from the list of Locke's works.

7. Besides, there are elements by which to evaluate the English text of the *Epistola*, elements which though still conjectural are no less significant.

The *Letter* was put into circulation in the autumn of 1689 and, as had already happened in Holland with the *Epistola*,[77] its appearance immediately raised the question of the Author's identity; a question, it is easy to suppose, that was all the more urgent, the deeper was the effect of the *Letter* on the politico-religious controversy of the moment. And

77. Cf. my ed. *Introd.* p. XXVII seq.

if Limborch had initially been able to elude the curiosity of the Arminian friends in Holland, in England by contrast Locke's name was quickly
mentioned and widely circulated and soon crossed the Channel so that
Limborch, pressed by the most insistent of Locke's Dutch friends, could
no longer keep the secret.[78] Someone therefore told Locke that as the
name of the author of the *Epistola* was known in England, so he would
have made it just as well known in Holland. Locke was frightened by the
news and had hard words with his theologian friend who had betrayed a
secret he had sworn to keep. And although Limborch might reassure
Locke on the descretion of his Dutch friends, the silence had now been
broken and, if respect for the man dissuaded Bayle from making the
fact public,[79] the fact remains that the *Epistola* was no longer anonymous either in England or in Holland.

For the rest, if Locke himself had kept quiet about or denied being
the author of the *Epistola* before April 1690, he would have had difficulty in keeping the secret from his Unitarian friends after Proast's attack on the *Letter concerning Toleration.*[80]

The fact that Proast, rejecting Locke's clear distinction between civil
society and religious society and hence the aims and the limitations of
each one, should have defended the magistracy's right to intervene in
religious matters inevitably required a rectification from the Unitarians
who saw their cause being compromised. But a reply to Proast could
not, and in fact did not, come from anyone but the author of the
Letter. It is extremely important for our purposes to note the circumstances that, while the anonymous pamphlet of Proast had the *imprimatur* of 9th April, Locke had already finished his *Second Letter* on the
27th May.

It is frankly inconceivable that a man like Locke, who agonized for
years over his writings, leaving them unedited for years on end, should
have decided to write, and in a very few days did write, the 32 pages of
folio which make up the reply to Proast unless, with the need to defend
his ideas, he had not been urgently entreated to forestall and annul the

78. The incident has been reconstructed by CRANSTON, op. cit., p. 332-
333.

79. Cf. my ed. *Introd.* p. XXVIII seq.

80. Proast's anonymous pamphlet *The Argument of the Letter concerning
Toleration, Briefly consider'd and answer'd*, Oxford, 1690, had the imprimatur
of 9th April 1690 and was put into circulation in late April or early May of that
year.

dangerous effects which Proast's subtle arguments might have had on a practical level in the dispute opened by the Act of Toleration.

It is clear, in fact, that in replying to Proast with a *Second Letter on Toleration* Locke put himself in the centre of that dispute and provided the Unitarians with another valid argument for their defence. It is very probable, though not demonstrable, that Locke was pressed to do that by the Unitarians themselves; in any case it is certain that when he decided to answer Proast, Locke did not overlook the fact that in so doing he revealed himself by implication as the author of the *First Letter.* Besides the secret of who wrote the *Letter* had now been broken and Locke knew it;[81] nor, even if he had wanted to, could he have kept the secret any longer from Churchill and Popple, from the moment he handed the publisher the manuscript of a *Second Letter,* which formed a sequel to the *First Letter*, which had been translated by Popple and to which the very title referred. With what right otherwise would he have appropriated the title of a work by giving another as a sequel to it if he had not confessed to Churchill and his Unitarian friends, who had made that first letter into a weapon of their fight, that he himself was the author of them both?

Now, one should note that the *Second Letter*, which was finished on the 27th of May and licensed on the 27th June came from Churchill's press not before the end of July 1690. Meanwhile, towards the end of June, whilst the manuscript of the *Second Letter* was still in the hands of the censor, there appeared a *Second Edition corrected* of the *Letter concerning Toleration.* Who had supervised this second edition of the *Letter*? But if it was no longer a secret for anyone that Locke was its author, and least of all could it have been a secret for Popple and Churchill, could Popple have taken care of the second edition? And can one still maintain that the second edition was produced "à l'insû de M. Locke"?

The preface *To the Reader* of the first edition of Locke's complete works[82] indirectly but inequivocally denies that by noting that the *"Two Treatises of Government* were never till now published from a copy corrected by Locke himself,"[83] but it makes no reference to the

81. See CRANSTON, op. cit., p. 360 and p. 366 which will tell us and document how, three years after the publication of the *Letter* it had become recognized that Locke was the author of the first two *Letters concerning Toleration* and how Locke himself no longer denied this.

82. *The Works of J. Locke*, cit. I ed. 1714.

83. And Locke himself complained of this in the codicil to his will which has

144

First Letter concerning Toleration, which is therefore by implication included among those works "printed from copies corrected and enlarged under Locke's own hand." Now the editor of *Locke's Works* of 1714 was, along with Sam Manship, that John Churchill, heir and successor to Awnsham Churchill whose name starts to appear in the frontispiece of Locke's works beginning precisely with the *Second Letter concerning Toleration*.[84] John Churchill must therefore have known very well whether the *First Letter* had been "corrected and enlarged" by Locke personally and, in other words, what had really happened in 1690, when, that is to say, the second edition of the *Letter* appeared, a short while after Locke himself had, as has been said above, handed over the manuscript of the *Second Letter* so that it might be submitted to the censor. So much so that in the same *Preface* of the 1714 edition the codicil to Locke's will, which mentions those of Locke's works that had appeared anonymously or under a pseudonym, is reproduced but with a radical change in the sense that no mention is made of the "privity" lacking from the English translation,[85] which therefore allows one to believe that the text of the first *Letter* was in reality "corrected and enlarged under Locke's own hand."

As for me, I shall continue to believe for the foregoing reasons, so long as proof to the contrary is not produced, that Locke personally supervised the second edition of the *Letter* to which the open dispute with Proast promised a wider circulation. Besides, the few formal retouches, the suppression of some arbitrary insertions and the abundant use of cursive, so typical of Locke's writing, clearly reveal the hand of Locke.[86]

In conclusion the fact remains firmly established that the *Epistola* was not published without Locke's knowledge, as has been, and still is, believed; but rather that Locke followed Popple's work very closely, clearly acknowledging the authorship of that *Letter concerning Tolera-*

already been quoted. In that codicil speaking of the *Two Treatises of Government* he wrote: "where of Mr. Churchill has publish'd several Editions, but all very incorrect." For the story of the Text see *Locke's Two Treatises of Government. A critical edition with Introd. and notes by* P. LASLETT, Cambridge, 1960, *Introduction*, p. 3 seq. and p. 164 seq.

84. Cf. my ed. *Introd.* p. XLIV.

85. It is found reproduced in my ed. of the version of the 1714 Ed. of *Locke's Works, Introd.*, p. XLIII seq.

86. The variants of the first two editions of the *Letter* have been studied by me in my edition.

tion translated by his Socinian friend to which he gave sequels with a *Second* and a *Third Letter concerning Toleration* and in so doing entered directly into the dispute against the limitations of the Act of Toleration, to which Popple's Preface had destined the *First Letter.* Furthermore, since there is reason to believe that the second corrected edition of the *Letter* was personally supervised by Locke, the *Letter concerning Toleration* has the right to be regarded not as a translation of the *Epistola*, whether faithful or unfaithful does not matter, but rather as an original and independent work of Locke's, to which the great influence it exercised in history assures an indisputable place of privilege in comparison with the *Epistola*.

Athens, Spring 1967

LOCKE'S EPISTOLA ON TOLERATION FROM THE
TRANSLATION OF POPPLE TO THAT OF GOUGH

1. In 1689 there appeared two editions of the celebrated *Epistola* of Locke on toleration, both anonymously: a Latin one in Gouda and an English one in London. The first was brought out by the Arminian Limborch, Locke being absent; the second by the Unitarian Popple who translated the Latin of Gouda into English with Locke's knowledge.

However, the Latin edition was soon forgotten and was never reprinted, except for the two editions by Hollis of 1765 and 1785; the English edition in contrast was quickly accepted into the corpus of Locke's works and was published by itself over and over again.

In 1957 Ebbinghaus reprinted Popple's English edition yet again with a German version facing it and so started the recent editions of this work of Locke's in the series "La Philosophie et la Communauté Mondiale" supervised by Klibansky.[1] But once Ebbinghaus had made a close comparison of the original Latin version of Gouda with the English translation of London and found a whole series of "alterations and errors" (*Abänderungen und Fehlern*),[2] Klibansky decided to exclude Popple's translation from the subsequent editions of that series, because that translation seemed to be corrupt and unreliable, and to use the Latin text of Gouda with a modern version opposite.[3]

1. JOHN LOCKE, *Ein Brief über Toleranz. Englisch-Deutsch übersetzt, eingeleitet und in Anmerkungen erlautert* von JULIUS EBBINGHAUS, Hamburg, Meiner, 1957; second edition with a *Nachwort zum Englischen Text*, as 1st ed., 1966.
2. V. EBBINGHAUS, ed.cit., p. VII and p. 127 et seq.; II ed., *Nachwort*, p. 136 seq. and the *Anmerkungen*, p. 130 seq.
3. In fact Klibansky, who had stated in a preface to Ebbinghaus's English/German version that the purpose of the series "La Philosophie et la Communauté Mondiale" was to produce reliable editions of the original texts *(die Ausgaben der Originaltext)*, in the following Latin/Italian version (*Lettera sulla Tolleranza, Testo latino e versione italiana. Premessa di* R. KLIBANSKY. *Introduzione di* E. DE MARCHI. *Trad. di* L. FORMIGARI, Firenze, La Nuova Italia, 1961) he wrote that "Popple, while trying to remain faithful to Locke's text, inserted modifica-

147

Even when Klibansky realized that Popple's translation had not been made, as he himself had believed, without Locke's knowledge[4] and that Locke himself had guaranteed its authenticity and faithfulness,[5] the ban set on the English text was not raised and, even if more embarrassing, Klibansky managed to find reasons for not doing so.

In the meantime, in 1963, I published my own edition of the Latin text and Popple's translation,[6] with an introductory study in which, among other things, I maintained that even if Popple's work was not always faithful to what Locke had written in Latin, nevertheless it was not unfaithful to Locke's thinking.[7]

Furthermore, as I wrote earlier, a better knowledge of the circumstances in which the original Latin and English translations were each

tions here and there which in certain cases ended up by distorting the original meaning. We have therefore preferred," Klibansky continued, "to place the Latin text before the reader, a text which has not been reprinted for some two centuries" (p. VIII).

From then on the English text has not been reprinted in that series, except in the second edition of Ebbinghaus.

A Latin/Spanish edition, Montreal, 1962, with translation, introduction and notes by A. WAISMANN and the same preface by KLIBANSKY): then a Latin/Polish edition (Warsaw, 1963) with the usual preface by KLIBANSKY, the same introduction by E. DE MARCHI and the translation by Z. OGONOWSKY.

In 1964 there appeared the Latin/French edition with translation, introduction and notes by R. POLIN and with a fuller and more careful *Préface* by KLIBANSKY who softened his assessment of Popple's translation whose modifications now were seen as altering only "un peu" the original meaning. This same Latin/French edition was reprinted in 1965 and 1967 (PVF).

On these editions of the series supervised by Klibansky see *supra, The Socinianism of Locke and the English edition of the Letter concerning Toleration*.

4. Compare the 1964 Latin/French edition pp. VII-VIII with the 1961 Latin/ Italian edition p. VII and the Latin/Spanish edition p. VII.

5. Compare the Latin/Italian edition p. VII and the Latin/Spanish edition p. VII with the 1964 Latin/French edition p. VII where Klibansky writes: "Locke recconnu être l'auteur de l'*Epistola* et avalisa en même temps de son autorité la traduction de Popple." Hence also his revised assessment of Popple's translation. See n. 3 above.

6. JOHN LOCKE, *A Letter Concerning Toleration. Latin and English texts revised and edited with variants and an Introduction by* MARIO MONTUORI, Martinus Nijhoff, The Hague, 1963, repr. here, v. *supra*. For further details and clarifications of the points raised in my *Introduction* see also the paper *Locke's Socinianism and the English edition of the Letter concerning Toleration*, cit.

7. See my edition, *Introduction*, p. XXXI, and note 2; pp. XLII-XLIII and note 1; p. L.

written, circumstances reconstructed by me for the first time, led me to believe that Popple's translation is as reliable as, if not actually more reliable than, the Latin original[8] and that in any case the second English edition of 1690 ought to be regarded as a new version of the *Epistola de Tolerantia* in English rather than a translation of the Latin original, whether faithful or not is beside the point.[9]

My arguments failed to convince Ebbinghaus who, clearing himself with a few words of rejection, held fast to the literal comparison of the two versions and asserted that to the errors and deviations of Popple's text there was added a tendency of form which being absent from the personality and style of Locke made it impossible to accept that the English text carried any authenticity (*Authentizität*) in regard to the original Latin one.[10]

These arguments of mine, to which Ebbinghaus had paid little attention, were taken more seriously by Klibansky and Gough in their most recent edition of the *Epistola*, which appeared in the same series supervised by Klibansky: John Locke, *Epistola de Tolerantia, A Letter on Toleration. Latin Text edited with a Preface* by Raymond Klibansky. *English Translation with Introduction and Notes* by J.W. Gough, Oxford, At the Clarendon Press, 1968.

In the introduction to the texts that these scholars each revised both Klibansky and Gough accept my historical and textual researches[11] and

---

8. cf. my edition, *Introduction,* p. XLI.

9. cf. my edition, *Introduction,* p. XLVI; *The Socinianism of Locke*, cit. p. 145 et seq.

10. cf. EBBINGHAUS, 1966[2], *Nachwort,* p. 136 et seq.

11. I feel obliged to draw the readers attention to the fact that both Klibansky and Gough, if they have drawn some of their own conclusions from my researches, have carefully avoided giving credit to the precedence of my work. Since it is a matter of conclusions of considerable importance, I believe it is right and proper that this fact should be known. Mine in fact are the observations that the *Postscriptum* would have been added to the *Epistola* in due course (cf. my ed. *Introd.* p. XXIV-XXV with KLIBANSKY's Preface, pp. IX–X); that the *Epistola* is not a "personal letter" (cf. my ed., *Introd.* p. XXV) from Locke "addressed to his Remonstrant theologian friend, Philip Limborch," as GOUGH and KLIBANSKY believed in accordance with the *comunis opinio* (J.W. GOUGH, *John Locke's Political Philosophy,* Oxford 1950, p. 195; *The Second Treatise of Government and A Letter Concerning Toleration,* by J. LOCKE, *ed. with an Intr. by* J.W. GOUGH, Oxford 1956, p. X, ed. 1966 p. XI; and KLIBANSKY, ed. Latin/French 1964, *Préface* p. XVIII; ed. 1967, s.l.) but a "libellus" or "Tractatus de Tolerantia per modum Epistolae scriptus" (cf. my ed. *Introd.* p. XXVI)

draw a number of conclusions from them. Yet as regards the reliability I claimed for the English text, while the former confirms his disagreement,[12] the latter unexpectedly joins him.[13]

However, in repudiating my arguments neither Klibansky nor Gough appear to have opposed them with other more valid ones in support of their reasons for rejecting the English text. On the contrary I would say that their objections are often based on misunderstandings or on failure to examine the problems themselves closely enough, as I hope will become clear in the discussion that follows.

2. It is even embarassing to point out how the suspicion which modern editors have of the English edition of the *Epistola* clearly has its origin

dedicated to Limborch (my ed. *Introd.* pp. XXV and XXVII compared with KLIBANSKY, *Preface* p. IX; Gough, *Introd.* p. I) that the respondent of the *Epistola* is not Limborch as he would have been given a polemical position very far from the one he held (my ed. *Introd.*, pp. XXVI-XXVII, compared with GOUGH, *Introd.*, p. I). Mine also is the observation that the Revocation of the Edict of Nantes and the emotions aroused by the brutal "dragonnades" may have given rise to the *Epistola* (my ed. pp. XV-XVII; and *The Socinianism of Locke*, p. 132 compared with KLIBANSKY, *Preface* p. XVII). Also mine is the remark that where Locke writes "suae [...] cohortes" Popple translates "his dragoons" so making the memory of the *dragonnades* more explicit and immediate (my ed. *Introd.*, p. XVII n. 1), an observation taken up word for word by GOUGH, p. 65 and n.6, p. 156. Mine, too, is the remark of Popple's disappointment about the exclusion of the Unitarians from the benefits of Toleration in so far as he himself was a Unitarian or Socinian (cf. my ed. *Introd.* p. XXXV and n.1 with GOUGH, *Introd.*, p. 167); as also the allusion, taken up by GOUGH in exactly the same context, to the covert way in which LE CLERC refers to the writings received by Locke on the Toleration (cf. my ed. *Introd.* p. XXIII with GOUGH, *Introd.* p. 45. where Gough repeats the mistake I myself had made: cf. *The Socinianism of Locke*, p. 141 n. 49) without mentioning other texts and documents examined for the first time by me.

12. It has already been stated above that from the 1962 Latin/Italian edition on, Klibansky found that Popple had in some cases distorted the original meaning of the Latin text, hence his decision to substitute Gough's English version for that of Popple.

13. Unexpected certainly Gough' lightning conversion; after having published four editions of the *Epistola* in Popple's translation in the twenty years from 1946 to 1966, the first three of which followed the 1698 text while the fourth followed that of 1690 (*The Second Treatise of Government* [...] and *A Letter Concerning Toleration* by J. LOCKE, *edited by* J.W. GOUGH, Oxford 1946,1948, 1956, 1966) he suddenly realises the unreliability of the published texts and hence the convenience of substituting a "version in modern English" for the traditional one by Popple.

in a false interpretation of a phrase of Locke's. When Locke gave to the famous Oxford library those of his works that had been published anonymously or under a pseudonym, he wrote a codicil to his will in which he stated, it is true, that the *Epistola*, which had appeared in Latin in Gouda, had been translated immediately afterwards into English "without my privity."[14] This phrase, interpreted by Coste as meaning "à l'insû de Mr. Locke"[15] has given rise to the mistaken belief that the translation of the *Epistola* was made and published without Locke's knowledge.

Against this belief, of which Klibansky was both heir and victim,[16] I pointed out that not only was Locke fully aware of the fact that Popple had begun and completed the translation,[17] but also that he had followed the translation very closely[18] and lastly that it was Locke himself who must have provided Popple with the copy of the Latin text used for the translation.[19]

In reply to my not entirely unfounded theory Klibansky, though by now persuaded that the English translation had not been made without Locke's knowledge, nevertheless puts forward the view that Popple might have received a copy of the *Epistola* from Holland before Locke received those sent by Limborch, and hence that the work of translation "had begun before Locke himself received a copy of his book."[20] As new evidence Klibansky records what Locke himself wrote to Limborch in his letter of 6 June 1689: "I understand that some Englishman is already engaged in translating the little book on

14. See my ed. *Introd.* p. XXXII, n.2.

15. No one had demonstrated Coste's responsibility for the mistaken belief before I did so (see my ed. *Introd.* p. XXXII n.2); now GOUGH appropriates this observation (GOUGH, *Introd.* p. 44 n. 2).

16. In the Latin/Italian edition KLIBANSKY (*Premessa*, p. VII) in fact translated the passage in the codicil to Locke's will referring to the *Epistola de Tolerantia* as if it meant that it had been "translated into English without his, Locke's, knowledge;" see also the Latin/Spanish version, p. VII. In the Latin/French edition of 1964 on the other hand KLIBANSKY wrote with reference to the same passage "et traduite ensuite en anglais *without my privity*. Cette expression un peu ambigue – Klibansky went on – ne signifie pas nécessairement, comme les biographes récents de Locke l'ont voulu (!), que Locke prétend avoir ignoré que l'on préparait une traduction, mais – en ce conteste – qu'elle se faisait sans la partecipation active du philosophe."

17. Cf. my ed. *Introd.* p. XXXII et seq.

18. Cf. my ed. *Introd.* p. XXXIII et seq. and p. XL et seq.

19. Cf. my ed. *Introd.* p. XXXIII et seq.

20. Cf. KLIBANSKY, *Preface*, p. XLI and p. XXI.

toleration," and ends by deducing from that 'already': "obviously, the translator undertook his task independently of the author."[21]

But it should be noted that Klibansky's deduction rests on an erroneous translation of Locke's Latin. Locke, in point of fact, expressed himself in the letter quoted by Klibansky as follows: "In vertendo de tolerantia libellum aliquem anglum iam iam occupatum intelligo."[22]

Now the duplication of the temporal adverb *iam* "indique l'instantanéité de l'action," as one can read in Ernout-Meillet s.v. Hence, in the passage quoted the two actions "intelligo" and "occupatum" are to be considered as taking place at the same time; this means literally that the translation was begun at the very moment in which Locke came to know of it and informed Limborch about it. For this reason I would not translate the Latin with the phrase "is already engaged," because *already* gives a false precedence to the "occupatum" as compared with the "intelligo," but more exactly with: "is just (just now) engaged" that is "il vient de s'engager" or "vi ha appena (or ora) messo mano."

Once Locke's Latin has been correctly rendered, Klibansky's objection fails, since it maintains that the English translation was begun before Locke himself had received a copy of his book. It fails because, with the iteration of the adverb *iam*, Locke clearly states that the work of translation actually began as he was writing to Limborch and therefore this took place a few days after, not before, he had received the copies of the *Epistola* sent him by Limborch from Holland.[23]

In any case, how could Popple have received a copy of the *Epistola* before Locke, when it had just appeared in Gouda and at a time when the London booksellers were able to obtain it only in early October, when, that is to say, the translation was already finished?[24]

In this connection Klibansky supposes that Furly[25] might have got hold of a copy of the *Epistola* as soon as it had been published in neighbouring Gouda and, knowing his friend Popple's interest in

21. Cf. KLIBANSKY, *Ibid.*
22. Cf. my ed. *Introd.* p. XXXIII.
23. Cf. my ed. *Introd.* p. XXXII; KLIBANSKY, *Preface*, p. XIX.
24. Cf. my ed. *Introd.* p. XXXIII; KLIBANSKY, *Preface*, p. XXXVII & n. 4.
25. On Benjamin Furly, English merchant, polyglot and bibliophile, who sheltered Locke during the last two years of his exile in Holland in his house in Rotterdam, cf. M. CRANSTON, *John Locke, A Biography*, London, 1957, p. 280 et seq.

the problem of toleration, might have taken him a copy when he visited England[26] in early May.

Although subject to a double condition, this hypothesis is in itself not entirely impossible but what makes it historically unacceptable is the fact that it is not supported by any evidence whatsoever. Now, in historical research a hypothesis is all the more valid the closer it adheres to the documents that sustain the topic, in the context of which the hypothesis is made.

Therefore, if we know from uncontrovertible evidence:

— that Locke was a friend of Popple's;[27]

— that Locke, on returning to England, immediately got in touch with the Unitarians of Firmin's Group to which Popple himself belonged;[28]

— that Locke received the three copies of the *Epistola* sent to him by Limborch not later than 20-22nd May;[29]

— that Locke was perfectly aware of the fact that Popple had just begun to translate the *Epistola;*[30]

26. Cf. KLIBANSKY, *Preface,* p. XXXI, p. XLI; GOUGH, *Introd.* p. 49.

27. Cf. my ed. *Introd.* p. XXX n. 4; *The Socinianism of Locke,* v. *supra* p. 130 n. 28, and the corroboration of KLIBANSKY, *Preface*, p. XXII, n.1.

28. *The Socinianism of Locke,* v. *supra* p. 134.

29. Cf. my ed. *Introd.* p. XXXII; KLIBANSKY, *Préface,* p. XIX. Limborch had sent Locke 3 copies of the *Epistola,* each one bound *(compacta)* with the *De Pace Ecclesiastica* of Strimesio, with the letter dated 16th May 1689. Cf. CRANSTON, *John Locke,* op. cit. p. 320, n.7.

In the same letter Limborch informed Locke that 6 other copies of the *Epistola* alone *(incompacta)* had been sent to Furly in Rotterdam for forwarding to London (cf. KLIBANSKY, *ibid.*). However on the 6th June Locke (MSS RL.B. a 256 1), while telling Limborch that he had received the 3 copies directed to him (compacta recte accepi), complained that he had not yet received the copies sent him by hand of Furly (incompacta nondum ad manus meas pervenerunt). From this one can deduce, either that Furly had left for England before the 16th May and hence that the copies of the *Epistola* intended for Locke remained a long while at Furly's address, or that Furly left for England a considerable time after the 16th May since by the 6th June Locke had not received the 6 copies intended for him. In the first case Furly could not have had a copy of the *Epistola* to hand at a time when Limborch himself did not have one; in the second case Furly would have arrived in England some time after 20th to 22nd May when Locke received the copies sent him by Limborch; in either case it seems that one should rule out Klibansky's hypothesis that Popple might have received a copy of the *Epistola* before Locke himself received his.

30. Cf. my ed. *Introd.* p. XXXIII; KLIBANSKY, *Preface,* p. XXII n. 3; p. XLI where Klibansky wrongly translates Locke's Latin (see above).

153

– that Locke also knew on the 10th September that Popple had by then finished the work of translation (*Epistola de Tolerantia* iam in anglicanum sermonem versa est);[31]

– that, while Popple was translating the *Epistola*, Locke kept in touch with his Unitarian friend to whom he gave the information about the French and Dutch translations which must have already appeared in Holland, information which can be found in Popple's own introduction to his translation;[32]

– that when the translation was finished the *Epistola* was still not to be found on the London book market.[33]

then my conjecture, that it was Locke himself who provided Popple with the copy of the *Epistola* from which the English translation was made, is endorsed by the evidence of a whole series of facts with which the conjecture is entirely compatible.

The same cannot be said of Klibansky's hypothesis,[34] which intervenes like a *deus ex machina* and relies on two conditions which are difficult to accept in a serious study: the first, that Furly *might have* obtained a copy of the *Epistola* when it had hardly come out in neighbouring Gouda; the second, that Furly, knowing of Popple's interest in the problem of toleration, *might have* handed it personally to his Unitarian friend when he returned to England in early May.

The only thing certain about this hypothesis is Furly's friendship with Popple.[35] But Locke was also a friend of Popple's,[36] and if Furly "may well have acquired the book then recently published in neighbouring Gouda" by the 20-22 May, Locke had certainly received the three copies sent him by Limborch; if, finally, Furly – always by way of hypothesis – "(may well) have taken the *Epistola* with him when he went to England early in May 1689" Locke certainly had a copy of the *Epistola* to hand and knew not only of Popple's interest in the problem of toleration, but he himself, as I have demonstrated elsewhere, being of the Unitarian faith, had lived, and lived intensely, through the drama

---

31. Cf. my ed. *Introd.* p. XXXIII; KLIBANSKY, *Preface*, p. XXII n. 3.

32. Cf. my ed. *Introd.* p. XXXIV et seq.; *The Socinianism of Locke*, v. *supra* p. 136.

33. Cf. my ed. *Introd.* p. XXXIII; KLIBANSKY, *Preface*, p. XXXVII and n.4.

34. KLIBANSKY, *Preface*, p. XLI n.2 which is echoed by GOUGH, *Introd.* p. 49 op.cit.

35. cf. KLIBANSKY, *Preface*, p. XXII n.l.; GOUGH, *Introd.* p. 49.

36. See above n. 27 at p. 159.

of Popple and all the Unitarians excluded by the Act of Toleration.[37] If, for this reason, and in order to support the cause of the Unitarians, Locke himself sent Le Clerc in Holland a copy of the *Brief History of the Unitarians called also Socinians*[38] so that it might be made known in Europe, it is perfectly legitimate to believe that Locke might have arranged to circulate that anonymous *Epistola,* as soon as it had been received from Holland, among his Unitarian friends grouped round Firmin; that *Epistola,* which denied to the civil authorities the right of legislating on religious matters: "cura salutis animarum nullo modo pertinere potest ad magistratum civilem,"[39] fell in perfectly with the motives of the Unitarians, who protested against an Act of Parliament that had declared them absolute heretics and so excluded them from the benefits of toleration.[40]

Of the two objections advanced by Klibansky and discussed above, one has been shown to be an erroneous translation of Locke's Latin and the other quite unjustified and remote from such textual evidence as is available to us for a supposition on the matter.

For this reason I believe I can reasonably and legitimately maintain my supposition against Klibansky that it was Locke himself who provided Popple with the copy he used for the translation and, until there is proof to the contrary, no one but Locke.

3. But the matter on which Klibansky most sharply disagrees is that which concerns the fidelity of Popple's translation to the Latin original.[41]

There is no doubt that Popple's translation is not exactly a model of fidelity. But, in order to assess its reliability, what is to be understood as fidelity in Popple's translation? Fidelity to Locke's thought or fidelity to the letter of the Latin text? In other words, if Popple is not always a faithful translator, does his infedelity distort the contents or alter the form, tone and style of Locke's writing?

For my part I maintained that Popple's translation "renders very faithfully the sense of the original and in no case, or so it seems to me,

37. On this matter see my study, already quoted several times: *The Socinianism of Locke and the Eng. ed. of the Letter on Toleration*, op. cit. esp. p. 124 et seq. and p. 134 et seq.
38. Cf. *The Socinianism of Locke,* p 135.
39. Cf. my ed. p. 20.
40. Cf. *The Socinianism of Locke,* p. 140 s.
41. See KLIBANSKY, *Preface*, p. XLI.

does Popple distort Locke's thoughts."[42] I noted, with regards to the variants and errors pointed out by Ebbinghaus[43] "certainly, if we make a word by word comparison of the English and Latin texts, it is not difficult to discover some inaccuracies and a few liberties, but it does not appear that Popple's translation "in some cases" distorts the "original meaning" as is claimed by Klibansky.[44] I therefore denied that Popple had misrepresented Locke's thinking even if his translation does not lack discrepancies and liberties.

Klibansky, instead, objects to my comments that the passages in which Popple departs from Locke's text are "too numerous and too significant to be ignored."[45] In support of these "so numerous and important" passages in which Popple is believed to have misrepresented Locke's thinking, Klibansky refers the reader to those pointed out in the note to Gough's translation. Gough himself, while stressing a number of differences between his translation (a version in modern [English]) and that of Popple ([a version] in seventeenth century English),[46] looses a whole tirade against me, who had asserted, against Klibansky, that "Popple [...] renders very faithfully the sense of the original and nowhere distorts Locke's thoughts,"[47] and, surprisingly, he ends by concluding in the following terms that "on the whole it [Popple's

42. cf. my ed. *Introd.* p. XXXI.
43. EBBINGHAUS, ed. English/German, 1957, *Vorwort*, p. VII.
44. cf. my ed. *Introd.* p. XXXI n.2.
45. KLIBANSKY, *Preface*, p. XLI. Let us remember that Klibansky, as on other occasions, even with regard to Popple's fidelity, changed his opinion several times; for the Ebbinghaus edition that reproduced it, Popple's translation was in fact the "Original text" of Locke's writing. cf. *ibid: Zur Schriftenreihe "La Philosophie et la Communauté Mondiale."* In the Latin/Italian (1961), Latin/Spanish (1962) and Latin/Polish (1963) editions the Latin text was preferred to the English one because, as Klibansky noted, "Popple, though trying to remain faithful to Locke's text, introduced modifications here and there, which in some cases end by altering the original meaning." (p. VIII). In the Latin/French edition of 1964 and in the following ones of 1965 and 1967 he modifies the fore-going judgement by finding that those same modifications introduced by Popple "finissent pour altérer un peu le sens originale," (p. XIX); finally in the 1968 Latin/ English edition Klibansky holds the passages in which Popple departs from Locke's text as being "too numerous and too significant." In this way, with a new and different set of reasons he rejects my assertion that Popple nowhere distorted Locke's thinking. cf. my ed. *Introd.* p. XXXI.
46. Differences that are listed in the notes to Gough's translation (see p. 156 et seq.).
47. GOUGH, *Introduction*, p. 43.

work] succeeded in reproducing Locke's meaning," even if it was not a "literal translation" and even if there are many places where "it departs in some degree from the actual wording of the Latin."[48]

Which is exactly what I myself had said. What else did I say?

Besides, before me Fox Bourne[49] and Viano[50] and after me also Polin[51] were of my opinion. In the Latin/French, which appeared in the same series supervised by Klibansky, Polin wrote as follows: "si William Popple a été fidèle au sens générale de l'oeuvre [...], il a suivi de façon peu stricte le détail du texte."

And so? Well, there is the proof that Klibansky and Gough have proved nothing, but what I myself had proved and that is that notwithstanding "some inaccuracies and a few liberties" Popple's translation "renders very faithfully the sense of the original." If then Klibansky and Gough prefer to believe that they have demonstrated the contrary, readers will have difficulty believing it.

4. The third argument that Klibansky opposes to my thesis is this: that given the "discrepancies" revealed by Gough "it is improbable that Locke should have supervised and checked the [Popple's] translation."[52]

Ebbinghaus had already made the same objection to my view. For him the deviations (*Abweichungen*) he revealed in the English text stand to show that Locke did not revise Popple's translation.[53]

I had maintained, in fact, that the considerations set out above[54] allowed one the reasonable belief that Locke did follow and revise the translation that his friend Popple was making of his work.[55] I felt able to confirm my conjecture observing that if the *Epistola* had been published by Limborch in Locke's absence,[56] Popple's translation was, on the contrary, made with Locke's knowledge and in his presence. If,

48. GOUGH, *Introduction*, p. 50.

49. H.R. FOX BOURNE, *The Life of John Locke,* London 1876, II, p. 54.

50. Cf. JOHN LOCKE, *Scritti editi ed inediti sulla tolleranza,* edited by C.A. VIANO, Turin 1961, *Introduction,* p.12.

51. Cf. the Latin/French edition of 1964, 1965 & 1967, POLIN, *Introduction,* p. XXXVIII.

52. KLIBANSKY, *Preface,* p. XLI; see also GOUGH, *Introduction,* pp. 43 and 46; and compare my ed. *Introd.* pp. XL and XLV.

53. Cf. EBBINGHAUS, *Nachwort,* II ed. p. 138.

54. see above p. 159 et seq.

55. Cf. my ed. *Introd.* p. XL.

56. Cf. my ed. *Introd.* p. XLI.

therefore, it is probable, but not demonstrable, that Limborch edited Locke's manuscript accurately[57] it is quite certain that Locke had frequent contact with Popple while the translation was in progress.[58]

Now, to suppose that Locke, having kept silent about, or having denied to Popple, his authorship of the *Epistola,* took no interest whatsoever in the translation of his work that his Unitarian friend had begun, seems to me to contradict above all what Le Clerc and Coste testify to the thoroughness with which Locke followed the translation of his work into other languages.

One could, it is true, object that it is precisely this thoroughness on Locke's part that prevents one from thinking that he himself could have followed and revised Popple's translation from the moment that it contained, as I myself have noted, "some inaccuracies and a few liberties" and, in fact, all those *discrepancies* pointed out by Gough and before him by Ebbinghaus. But an objection in this sense could only be valid if the translations made under Locke's supervision were free of those *Abweichungen* and *discrepancies,* which in the view of Ebbinghaus, of Klibansky and of Gough prevent one from thinking that Locke "supervised and checked" Popple's translation.

But we have irrefutable proofs to the contrary; proofs clearly overlooked by Ebbinghaus, Klibansky and Gough, and overlooked even after I had made explicit reference to them.[59]

Let us, therefore, once again take Book I of the *Abstract* of the *Essay*, published by Lord King from Locke's manuscript[60] and subject it to a "word-by-word" comparison with Le Clerc's French translation.[61]

Locke wrote: "In the thoughts I have had concerning the Understanding, I have endeavoured to prove that the mind is at first *rasa tabula.* But that being only to remove the prejudice that lies in some men's mind, I think it best, in this short view I design here of my principles, to pass by all that preliminary debate which makes the first book, since I pretend to show in what follows the original from whence,

57. Cf. my ed. *Introd.* p. XXXII et seq.
58. Cf. my ed. *Introd.* p. XL; *The Socinianism, supra* p. 136 et seq.
59. Cf. my ed. *Introd.* p. XLII and n.1.
60. *Abstract of the Essay*, from LORD KING, *The Life of J. Locke,* 2 vols. London 1830, II, pp. 231-293.
61. *Extrait d'un livre anglois qui n'est pas encore publié, intitulé Essay Philosophique concernant l'Entendement (...) Communiqué par* MONSIEUR LOCKE, in *Bibliothèque Universelle et Historique,* Tome VIII, 1688, pp. 49-293.

and the ways whereby, we receive all the ideas our understandings are employed about in thinking."

Here, then, is Le Clerc's translation with the variations in italics: "Dans les pensées que j'ai eues, concernant *nôtre* Entendement, j'ai tâché *d'abord* de prouver que *nôtre* Esprit est au commencement *ce qu'on appelle tabula rasa; c'est à dire, sans idées & sans connoissance.* Mais comme ce n'a été que pour *détruire* les préjugez de quelques *Philosophes, j'ai cru* que dans ce petit *Abrégé* de mes principes, *je devois* passer toutes les disputes préliminaires, qui composent le premier Livre. Je prétends de montrer, dans les suivans, *la source de laquelle nous tirons toutes les idées, qui entrent dans nos raisonnemens, & la maniere dont elles nous viennent."*

Well, there is not a single page of Popple's translation in which it is possible to collect such great *Abweichungen* and *discrepancies* nor, for good measure, so "numerous and [...] significant," as those noted in these few lines of Le Clerc's translation which are here reproduced. Yet Locke, though he knew French well, does not seem to have been outraged by Le Clerc's translation,[62] since he immediately assumed responsibility for it and authorised its publication under his own name.

That is valid also and with even greater force for Coste's translation into French of the *Essay concerning Human Understanding.* Right at the beginning of the book, in the *Epistle to the Reader* Locke writes:[63] "Reader, I here put into thy hands, what has been the Diversion of some of my idle and heavy Hours: If it has the good luck to prove so of any of thine, and thou hast but half so much Pleasure in reading, as I had in writing it, thou wilt as little think thy Money, as I do my Pains, ill bestow'd. Mistake not this, for a Commendation of my Work; nor conclude, because I was pleas'd with the doing of it, that therefore I am

62. As WAISMANN shows himself to be, more than the other editors of the series directed by Klibansky. In the *Notes* of the Latin/Spanish edition, 1962, p. 107, he deplores the "considerables faltas" found in the English translation and writes: "We firmly believe that Popple's well-known English translation, whether from a philological or philosophical point of view, which concerns the very contents of Locke's thought, is unworthy of the reputation it has enjoyed and still enjoys. It is very far from being a faithful translation, it is full of arbitrary interpretations and is exaggeratedly periphrastic and ornate where Locke's style is simple and plain." For this reason Waismann uses his "honrado esfuerzo" to present a version as close as possible to the Latin text. So faithful and modern is this text, as Waismann wants it to be (ib. p. 107) that in place of the "dragoons" evocatively used by Popple, Waismann more modernly uses "los esbirros," p. 9.

63. I quote from the I ed. of *Locke's Works,* 1714, vol. I, p. VI.

fondly taken with it now it is done. He that "hawks at Larks and Sparrows, has no less Sport, though a much less considerable Quarry, than he that flies at nobler Game: And he is little acquainted with the Subject of his Treatise, the UNDERSTANDING, who does not know, that as it is the most elevated Faculty of the Soul, so it is employ'd with a greater and more constant Delight, than any of the other. Its Searches after Truth, are a sort of Hawking and Hunting, wherein the very Pursuit makes a great part of the Pleasure."

And here is how Coste[64] translated this passage: "Voici, *cher Lecteur, ce qui a fait le divertissement de quelques heures de loisir que je n'étois pas d'humeur d'employer à autre chose. Si cet Ouvrage* a le bonheur d'occuper *de la même manière quelque petite partie d'un temps où vous serez bien aise de vous relâcher de vos affaires plus importantes,* et que vous preniez seulement la moitié tant de plaisir à le lire que j'en ai eu à le composer, vous n'aurez pas, je croi, plus de regret à votre argent que j'en ai eu à ma peine. N'allez pas prendre ceci pour un Eloge de mon Livre, ni *vous figurer que*, puisque j'ai pris du plaisir à le faire, je l'admire à présent qu'il est fait. *Vous auriez tort de m'attribuer une telle pensée.* Quoi que celui qui chasse aux Alouettes ou aux Moineaux, n'en puisse pas retirer un grand profit, il ne se divertit pas moins que ̃celui qui court *un Cerf ou un Sanglier. D'ailleurs, il faut avoir fort peu de connoissance du sujet de ce Livre, je veux dire* l'ENTENDEMENT, *pour ne pas savoir*, que, comme c'est la plus sublime Faculté de l'Ame, il n'y en a point aussi dont l'exercise soit accompagné d'une plus grande & d'une plus constante *satisfaction.* Les recherches *où l'Entendement s'engage* pour trouver la Vérité, sont une espèce de chasse, où la poursuite même fait une grande partie du plaisir."

No more is needed, I think, to underline the opinion of a meticulous translator of the *Essay* who, quite rightly, writes[65] that: "as Locke is plain, direct and rough, a friend of things and shy (where possible) of generality and any sort of ritual, so Coste is pompous and diffuse, rich in ornaments and verbal rotundities." Yet for his part Coste wrote: "Je me suis [...] fait une affaire de suivre scrupuleusement mon Auteur sans m'en écarter le moins du monde et si j'ai pris quelque liberté (car on ne

---

64. I quote from the third edition (Amsterdam, 1735) of the *Essai Philosophique concernant l'Entendement Humain par* M. LOCKE, *trad. de l'Anglois par* M. COSTE, *Préface de l'Auteur*, p. XXX. Italics are mine.

65. V.C. PELLIZZI, *Avvertenza del Traduttore*, from J. Locke, *Saggio sulla Intelligenza Umana*, Bari, 1951, Vol. I, p. XXIII.

peut pas s'en passer) ç'a toujours été sous le bon plaisir de M. Locke qui entend assez bien le François"[66] and "qui a eu la bonté de revoir ma traduction."[67]

It is worth to add here the invaluable evidence on this point given by Le Clerc, *Eloge historique de feu Mr. Locke*, in *Oeuvres Diverses de Monsieur J. Locke*, Rotterdam, 1710, p. LV, who goes so far as to prefer the French translation of the *Human Understanding* to Locke's original in English, pointing out that the French translation was made by Coste in Locke's house and under the supervision of Locke himself. "Ce fut aussi la même année, que son Ouvrage de l'*Entendement* parut en folio, pour la première fois, en Anglois. Il a été publié en cette même Langue trois fois depuis, en 1694, en 1697 et en 1700. Cette dernière année, on le publia en François à Amsterdam, chez H. Scheltre. Mr. Coste, qui demeroit alors dans la même maison que l'Auteur, le traduisit avec beaucoup de soin, de fidelité et de netteté, sous ses yeux, et cette version est très estimée. Elle a fait connoitre ses sentiments de çà la mer, avec plus d'étendue que l'Abregé, qui avoit paru en 1688, ne pouvoit le faire. Comme l'Auteur étoit present, il corrigea divers endroits de l'Original, pour les rendre plus clairs et plus faciles à traduire et revit la Version avec soin; ce qui fait qu'elle n'est guère inférieure à l'Anglois et qu'elle est souvent plus claire." In fact Locke himself declares: "M. Coste m'a lu cette version d'un bout à l'autre," and he goes on to assure the reader "qu'il trouvera dans cet Ouvrage toutes les qualités qu'on peut désirer dans une bonne Traduction."[68]

Well then, after this judgment of Locke's on Coste's translation, a translation moreover that was done in his own house and under his own eyes, the appeal to the *Abweichungen* or *discrepancies* does not seem to be enough to reject my supposition that Locke himself followed and

66. See *Avertissement du Traducteur,* foreword to *Essai Philosophique,* op. cit. p. XIV. On the difficulties Coste found in translating Locke's English into French, see what somewhat surprisingly Coste himself writes in the *Préface du Traducteur* to the translation of the *Thoughts concerning Education,* (Amsterdam 1708,[3] pp. XXVII-XXVIII) as well as that in the *Avertissement* to the *Essay Philosophique,* op. cir. esp. p. XV et seq.

67. See *Essay Philosophique,* op. cit. *Avertissement,* p. X.

68. *Essay Philosophique,* op.cit. *Monsieur Locke au Libraire,* p. XL. In my paper *The Socinianism of Locke and the English Edition of the Letter on Toleration* already quoted, this notice of *Mr Locke au Libraire* is given in full as an example of "privity" in the meaning of "consent" or agreement of the author to the translation of his work.

revised Popple's translation. It does not seem so because the objection of Ebbinghaus and Klibansky could be valid if, and only if, it were shown that there, where *Abweichungen* and *discrepancies* are found in the translations of Locke's works, it is certain that Locke himself did not follow and revise those translations; but, as we have seen, this is not the case. On the contrary, just as Locke assumed responsibility for Le Clerc's translation and guaranteed the faithfulness of Coste's translation, so Locke "avalisa [...] de son autorité la traduction de Popple," as even Klibansky himself has let slip.[69] This is so, because clearly Locke for his part "so long as the original sense of his writing was respected, did not deny his translators certain independence of interpretation and style"[70] for the simple reason that, as Coste wrote "on ne peut pas s'en passer."

5. That Locke did not follow and revise the translation of the *Epistola* that Popple was making or had made seems to Klibansky[71] to be confirmed by Locke himself when he wanted to clarify in the codicil to his will that the English translation of the *Epistola* had been made "without my privity."

According to Klibansky, who had already stumbled over this expression earlier,[72] Locke wanted to say that the *Epistola* had been translated into English "without his having an active share in it."[73] If one could

---

69. KLIBANSKY, *Préface,* to the Latin/French edition (op.cit. p. VII). In the earlier Latin/Italian (p. VII) and Latin/Spanish (p. VII) Klibansky had said the opposite. In the Latin/English edition KLIBANSKY, *Preface*, attenuates Locke's recognition of the English translation while GOUGH simply denies it (*Introd.* p. 46). For the contrary see my ed. *Introd.* p. XLV et seq., *The Socinianism of Locke*, p. 145.

70. My ed. *Introd.* p. XLIII; see also p. L. One should also recall what Coste wrote on this subject, COSTE, *Avertissement* to Locke's *Essay Philosophique*, op. cit. p. XIX): "Quoique [...] Mr. Locke m'eut laissé une entière liberté d'employer les tours que je jugerois les plus propres à esprimer ses pensées."

71. KLIBANSKY, *Preface*, p. XLI.

72. In the editions before the Latin/French one and until 1963 Klibansky had in fact translated Locke's phrase as "without my having knowledge of it," as it had always been translated from Coste on.

73. KLIBANSKY, *Preface*, p. XLII. It was in the Latin/French edition of 1964 that Klibansky gave an interpretation of Locke's phrase "without my privity" as meaning "qu'elle se faisait sans la partecipation active du philosophe," p. VII seq; this interpretation was maintained in the Latin/English edition and adopted by Gough (*Introd.*, p.45) who takes it to mean exactly "without my

really interpret Locke's phrase "without my privity" in the sense proposed by Klibansky and followed by Gough, my proposition, that Locke had closely followed Popple's work and that he had personally supervised the "Second Edition corrected" of the *Epistola,* which appeared in 1690, would certainly fail. But the fact remains that Klibansky's interpretation can be maintained only by misreading Locke.

It is, in fact, worth remembering that the clause quoted, namely "without my privity," is found, as has been said, in a codicil to the will by which Locke left the Oxford library those of his works that had appeared anonymously or under a pseudonym and of which he admitted being the author. Among the works mentioned by Locke there was the *Epistola* itself, and Locke stated explicitly that it had been written in Latin and published at Gouda in 1689 "and afterwards translated into English without my privity." That one can, in this context, take "without my privity," to mean, as Klibansky has done, "without my having taken an active part in the translation" seems to me quite unjustified.

It seems unjustified because if Locke was certainly old and dying when he dictated the codicil, he was not for this reason insensible to the point of lacking mental equilibrium. Because if indeed, in mentioning those works of his that had appeared anonymously or under a pseudonym, Locke alludes with the *Epistola* to the English translation, it cannot in my view have meant anything but that that translation had also appeared anonymously in 1689 and not that it had been made without his active participation. And the anonymity of the English translation is confirmed by the clause "without my privity," which is to be understood, as I have already shown,[74] in the legal sense of "consent," that is to say, without the consent or assent of a party with a functional interest, so, in the case under examination, the endorsement of the author to the translator of his work. Locke never gave this endorsement, which he was not called upon to make either to the translator or to the editor in 1689, since he had kept quiet about or even denied to Popple that he had written the *Epistola,* and hence the anonymity of the English translation.

An example of "privity" as "consent" is, furthermore, given by

---

active participation." The example which Gough provides in this sense (*ibid.* n.6) if it can be considered valid in the context in which Klibansky's interpretaion might be acceptable, cannot be so considered in our case for reasons I set out in the text.

74. cf. my ed. *Introd.* p. XXXIV and n.2.

Locke himself when he addressed the "libraire" to guarantee the excellence of the French translation of the *Essay* made by Coste;[75] there the statement that "M. Coste has read me the version from beginning to end before sending it to you" presupposes a previous agreement between the two parties, that is to say between the author and the translator concerning the work, which the one is to do on the text of the other and the respective rights deriving from that work; hence my interpretation of "privity" as "consent" applied, as in our case, to every "relation between two parties recognised by law."[76]

Perhaps it is not even necessary at this point to add that my interpretation of "privity" as "consent" does not contradict what I have written in the *Introduction* to my edition of the *Epistola,* namely that after Proast's attack Locke himself may have personally supervised the second edition of the *Letter,* for the obvious reason that Locke, as one can see from the phrase "without my privity," wanted to make clear that the English translation had appeared, like the *Epistola,* anonymously, and not that he had or did not have a hand in the translation into English of the *Epistola.* If Locke had intended to state this, as Klibansky and Gough believe, that clarification would have been quite out of place in the context where it is found.

6. It is precisely with regard to the "Second edition corrected" of the *Letter*, that Gough[77] rejects my hypothesis,[78] which proposed that, after the penetrating criticism to which Proast had subjected the *Letter,* Locke himself supervised this edition, intended as it was for a wider circulation.

In Gough's view, instead, the second edition came out in March 1690 and therefore "before Proast's pamphlet was published."[79] If this had been the case, there certainly would have been no reason for Locke to prepare a second edition of the *Letter.* In fact Proast's attack, by obliging Locke to an immediate reply,[80] revealed him as the author

---

75. The letter *Mr. Locke au Libraire* is in the French translation of the *Essay* already quoted, p. XL. It is reproduced in full in the *Socinianism of Locke,* p. 145 n. 66.
76. cf. my ed. *Introd.* p. XXXIV and n.2.
77. GOUGH, *Introd.* p. 46.
78. My ed. *Introd.* p. XLV.
79. GOUGH, *Introd.* p. 46; KLIBANSKY, *Preface,* p. XXII.
80. My ed. *Introd.* p. XLIV et seq; *The Socinianism of Locke,* p. 149.

of the *Letter*, both to Popple and to the editor Churchill,[81] assuming that neither of them had known who had really written the *Letter*.[82] Now if the second edition of the *Letter* had appeared after Proast's pamphlet, it would have been difficult for Popple to have supervised the second edition of the *Letter*, from the moment that Locke had already handed the editor a *Second Letter concerning Toleration*, which was a sequel to the first even in its title;[83] if, on the other hand, it precedes Proast's attack, it is likely that the second edition would have been published with few modifications by Popple.

But Klibansky decides that the second edition of the *Letter* preceded Proast's reply because the latter says in his *Introduction* that "he knows of the existence of two editions of the treatise he is attacking."[84] And, in fact, in March 1690, when he was writing the *Preface* to his anonymous pamphlet, Proast could have known of only two editions of the work he was preparing to criticize: the Latin one, which had arrived on the London book market in October 1689[85] and the first English edition that came out in November 1689. If the "Second edition corrected" had appeared in March 1690 Proast would have known of three editions not two.

If, then, this and not something else is the argument Gough relies on to reject my hypothesis, I do not think he has succeeded. Also that hypothesis is supported by first-hand evidence it is difficult to refute and to which Gough himself cannot have been entirely indifferent seeing that they confirm the reliability of Popple's translation, which he, Gough, published, re-published and kept alive for a good twenty years,[86] before disavowing himself and Popple. Instead, in answer to the evidence I gave of the fact that both the French translation and the Dutch translation of this tract of Locke's were made from the English

---

81. My ed. *Introd.* ibid.; *The Socinianism of Locke*, op. cit. ibid.

82. My ed. *Introd.* p. XXIX; *The Socinianism of Locke*, p. 148.

83. PROAST's Anonymous pamphlet. *The Argument of the Letter concerning Toleration, briefly consider'd and answer'd*, Oxford, 1690, bears the *imprimatur* of 9th April 1690 and was put into circulation some time towards the end of April, or at the beginning of May.

The *Second Letter* was ended and dated the 27th May, after being handed over to the editor.

84. KLIBANSKY, *Preface*, p. XXII and n.4.

85. KLIBANSKY, *Preface*, p. XXVII and n.2.

86. See above n.3 p. 208.

text and not from the Latin original,[87] Gough limits himself to objecting that I find it "significant"[88] but does not say why I should not. He does not say why I should not find "significant" the fact that in the Arminian circle itself, with Limborch, the theologian and the spiritual head of the Remonstrants, still alive, a man who liked to call himself – wrongly – the addressee of the *Epistola*,[89] Popple's translation should have been preferred to the Latin original to the extent that the translation rather than the original should have been the base for the subsequent French and Dutch translations.

For his part Klibansky admits that the Dutch translation that has come down to us follows Popple's version,[90] but as for the French translation he maintains that "the translator makes occasional use of Popple's English version, but on the whole, the French is based on the Latin text."[91] To give an example of this Klibansky can find nothing better than to quote these four words of the Latin text: "alios ad hilaritatem otium (*scil.:* in societatem redigit)." Popple translates this into English: "other, for want of Business, have their Clubs for Claret," while the French version, which, according to Klibansky, follows the Latin text, has: "l'envie de se divertir fait que les autres ont leur rendez-vous."[92]

Frankly, the example chosen by Klibansky could hardly have been less happy; because the phrase "leur rendez-vous" is a very good translation of "their Clubs for Claret" agreeably summoned up by Popple,

87. My ed. *Introd.* pp. XXVI-XLIII.
88. GOUGH, *Introd.* p. 46. Thus GOUGH (*Introd.* p. 47) considers it to be of slight importance that the editor Churchill, in transcribing the above-quoted codicil to Locke's will, should have omitted the clause "without my privity" in relation to the English translation of the *Epistola*. I am and remain persuaded of the contrary. cf. my ed. *Introd.* XLIV: *The Socinianism of Locke*, p. 156.
89. My ed. *Introd.* p. XXII seq.
90. KLIBANSKY, *Preface*, p. XXVII: see my ed. *Introd.* p.XXXVIII seq. Klibansky points out (*ibid.*n 2) the error I made (my ed. *Introd.* p. XXXVII) in dating the copy of the *Verzameling* to 1724 instead of 1734. The mistake was confirmed by Mr. Verwer of the Library of the Rijksuniversiteit of Leyden who kindly sent me photocopies of the frontispiece and whom I take the opportunity to thank publicly.
91. KLIBANSKY, *Preface*, p. XXIX. Klibansky himself (*ibid.* n.1) puts into doubt the fact that it was Le Clerc who translated the *Letter* into French. See my ed. *Introd.* p. XLI.
92. KLIBANSKY, *Preface,* p. XXIX n.3.

formerly a winemerchant at Bordeaux who must have remembered those "Clubs for Claret" as pleasant places for the meetings or gatherings ("ont ieur rendez-vous") of all those who were idle "for want of Business" and met to sing the praises of the good Bordeaux claret: "Benedetto quel claretto che si spilla in Avignone" as people used to sing even in Italy at that time!

But, leaving aside the 4 words chosen as an example by Klibansky, in any case too few to decide one way or the other, Polin himself, who translated the *Epistola* in the series "Philosophy and the World Community," once again contradicting Klibansky, declares[93] that the French translation which appeared in Rotterdam in 1710 is "manifestement traduite en français à partir de l'anglais et non à partir du Latin." Which is exactly what I myself said.[94] And, I repeat, it seems to me "significant" for the reliability of the English text, repudiated by the editors of "Philosophy and the World Community" series, that the first translations of Locke's script on toleration should have been made, not on the Latin text which was published when Locke was abroad, but rather on the English version published instead with Locke's knowledge and presence, and perhaps in the second edition by Locke himself. If then one takes into account that the French translation issued from the circle of the Remonstrants while Limborch was still alive, this circumstance seems to me to be all the more decisive for the purpose of rehabilitating the English text preferred, and not without a certain justification, to the Latin one by the contemporaries themselves.

7. All the foregoing has of course no weight for the modern editors of Locke's *Letter;* Gough, rather, is even surprised that I should find it "significant." For that reason they devote themselves to substituting Popple's translation with one of their modern versions which may free the original Latin one from the heavy mantle of neglect Popple put upon it. There is of course nothing to be said against substituting modern versions for Popple's one if by so doing one aims at a wider dissemination of the *Epistola* because to do this is certainly useful and worthwhile. The case is very different if the reason for the rejection is the unreliability of Popple's English, which is precisely what Klibansky and Waismann claim. Even worse if, independently of the literary value of

93. POLIN, *Introduction,* to the Latin/French ed., 1964, p. XXVIII.
94. My ed. *Introd.* p. XLI where the Latin text, the French text and the English text are compared.

the text, one overlooks or ignores the value of that same text as an historical document, which is precisely what Ebbinghaus and Gough have done.

What, according to Ebbinghaus, makes Popple's translation inacceptable, while on the whole he does not find it bad (*schlecht*)[95] is not so much the variants and errors found in it as the demagogic (*Demogogen*) and tribunitial (*Volksredners*)[96] tone which resounding in Popple's English belies the sobriety and realism (*Nüchternheit und Sachlichkeit*)[97] of Locke's Latin. For that reason Gough, who takes over Ebbinghaus's argument, writes that what justifies "a new translation" of Locke's *Epistola* "is not so much Popple's occasional inaccuracy" as the tendency "to inflate and exaggerate" already deplored in Popple's language.[98]

It is undeniable that Popple has this tendency, but I do not think that this can justify a "version in modern" for that of Popple.

I do not think so because independently of the quite justified conjectures that can be made to confirm its reliability, Popple's English must be judged in relation to the particular historic and spiritual situation in which it took life and form,[99] such as the exclusion of the English Unitarians from the benefits of the Act of Toleration and must not be compared to the Latin text written in another historical climate and in another spiritual environment and intended furthermore to be kept hidden and inactive among Locke's secret papers.

Only a person who has forgotten the circumstance that Popple put the sober Latin of Locke into the middle of a politico-religious controversy, for which it was at first not intended, and made it into the cry of protest of the Unitarians, disappointed and offended by an act of Parliament that judged them to be absolute heretics, can mistake the tone which Popple gave to Locke's *Epistola* for that of a tribune. The truth is that Popple translated the Latin text "ab irato," but that text in its sobriety of tone and style admirably fitted the reasons the English Unitarians had for their protest; against the discriminations imposed by the political power in religious matters they demanded "absolute

95. EBBINGHAUS, English/German edition, 1966[2], *Nachwort*, p. 138.
96. EBBINGHAUS, op.cit. p.137.
97. EBBINGHAUS, *ibid.*
98. GOUGH, *Introduction*, p. 51.
99. For all that follows I refer the reader to my paper, *The Socinianism of Locke* (cit.). where the argument is amply considered and scrupulously documented.

168

liberty, just and true liberty, equal and impartial liberty." Liberty, that is to say, not to be judged by Parliament in matters of faith, and therefore an absolute religious liberty, not absolute civil liberty as Klibansky[100] and Gough[101] believe; this is not what Popple asks, but only that one liberty, which even for Locke could and should have been removed from the competence of the civil magistracy, and hence absolute in its enjoyment.[102]

Now, it is precisely the *animus* that pervades the English text and which is expressed in its excited tone that makes the *Letter,* in reality, quite different from the *Epistola;* they are two different texts that reflect two different historical situations, namely the Revocation of the Edict of Nantes which was the origin of the *Epistola,* and the exclusion of the Unitarians from the religious toleration that was the cause of the translation into English;[103] the *Letter* destined to become the heart and voice of the protest of the Unitarians; the *Epistola,* instead, to remain secret among Locke's papers.

While, for that reason the English text has become an unsuppressible document of politico-religious controversy, which stands at the surface of modern liberal conscience, hence its universal diffusion; the Latin text, in contrast, had no history or fortune, not even among the very Arminians of Holland who knew Locke's *Epistola* in Popple's English translation rather than in the Latin of Locke. And since Locke himself was not a stranger to the Unitarians' protest,[104] so the *Letter Concerning Toleration* ought to be considered not so much a translation of the Latin text, but rather as an independent and original work to which its great effectiveness in history assures a place of indisputable privilege in relation to the *Epistola.*

---

100. KLIBANSKY, Latin/Italian ed. p. IX, and the subsequent editions; see in this connection *The Socinianism of Locke,* p. 128 n. 25.

101. J.W. GOUGH, *John Locke's Political Philosophy,* Oxford 1950, p. 191; *Introd.* p. 47 where, among other things in n.2 Gough says he is not convinced as regards this matter by what I said in my edition (*Introd.* p. XXXIV, n.3). I must point out that Gough says I talk of "absolute liberty" without specifying that I mean religious liberty.

102. LOCKE, *Epistola,* my ed. p.20. "Cura salutis animarum nullo mdo pertinere potest ad magistratum civilem." Cf. *The Socinianism of Locke,* p. 128 s.

103. My ed. *Introd.* p. XV et seq.; *The Socinianism of Locke,* op.cit. p. 10 et seq.

104. See what I have said on this subject in my paper, *The Socinianism of Locke,* p. 124 seq.

Let modern versions be made and welcome also to Gough's one with all the "discrepancies" between Popple's English and the original Latin text carefully set out in a row to demonstrate the translator's infidelity to Locke's script and above all that regrettable tendency "to inflate and exaggerate"; but to try to replace Popple's English version with that of Gough means in reality to try to replace a text which has worked in history precisely because of the controversial character of Popple's tone and style, with a cold and modern cast of a Latin text that has practically had no history.

Athens, Winter 1969

ON KLIBANSKY AND LOCKE'S
"EPISTOLA DE TOLERANTIA"

Raymond Klibansky persists with his praiseworthy efforts to make Locke's celebrated *Epistola on Toleration* available, and known, to an ever wider circle of readers in every language and in every country. He has done this in the series "Philosophie et Communauté Mondiale" where he has supervised modern versions set side by side with the Latin text of Gouda suitably emended. After the editions in German, Italian, Spanish, French and English, Klibansky has in fact supervised the Latin/Hungarian version[1] which appeared a few years ago in Budapest and which may perhaps be followed by others still.

Like the preceding editions, the present one with the Latin text supervised by Klibansky and the translation of Màtrai Làszlò has a lengthy Preface by Klibansky himself which does not depart far, as regards contents, from the Prefaces to the preceding editions of the *Epistola*. That is to say that Klibansky repeats, amongst other things already known, that although the second English edition, which appeared a year after the first one, is to be preferred to it, Popple's english is nevertheless often unreliable. It is desirable, therefore, to publish, as he has done, modern versions to replace that of Popple, and that the much discussed phrase "without my privity" does not mean, as Locke's modern editory have always believed – so Klibansky declares – that Locke was unaware of the translation of his work that his Unitarian friend had been making, but rather that the translation had been made without any direct participation by Locke himself. In spite of a clear indication in Popple's *Preface* to the English edition that an earlier Dutch edition had been made, Klibansky claims all the same that he found a late Dutch edition of 1732. Klibansky also says that the

---

1. JOHN LOCKE, *Levél a Vallási Türelemrol*, [*Epistola de Tolerantia*], *Latin Szöveg és Magyar Fordítás - Szovegkritika és Elóyzó: Raymond Klibanski - Bevezetés*: Mátrai László - Akadémiai Kiadó, Budapest, 1973.

two different interpretations of the enigmatic initials that hide the names of the author and recipient of the *Epistola* in the frontispiece of the Gouda edition provided by Le Clerc and Lady Masham respectively could only have been suggested by Limborch who whould have liked to be the recipient of the *Epistola* and to whom both Le Clerc and Lady Masham turned for an explanation, and so on.

I have already dealt at some length with Klibansky and his editions of the *Epistola* in some of my writings on the subject (see above my ed. of *A Letter concerning Toleration*; *The Socinianism of Locke*; *Locke's Epistola on Toleration*) where I also reveal the carefree way in which he or one of his collaborators appropriate certain of the results of my historical and textual research and frankly I believed that Klibansky would have taken the next opportunity to set matters right. Alas! I was mistaken.

In point of fact, not only has Klibansky not made amends, but, rather he has studiously avoided mentioning my name for good or ill and has continued to present as his own, things that I have said and repeated several times. Only when Klibansky believed or wanted to believe that he had caught me making a mistake, did he allude to my edition of the·*Epistola*. "A contemporary critic" Klibansky wrote on p. 24, "declares that the author of the *Epistola* borrowed an example of the *Commentaire Philosophique*. In this context it should be observed that the *Commentaire* was not published until October 1686, that is to say 8 or 9 months after the *Epistola* was published. It is therefore inadmissible that Bayle's work could have had any influence at all on Locke's tract."

Since I have reason to believe that "the contemporary critic" to whom Klibansky alludes could only have been me, I find myself obliged to point out that all I said was that "in the September/November (1689) issue of the Histoire [which nevertheless appeared many months later|, De Beauval, himself the author of a *Tolérance des Réligions* (Rotterdam 1684) [...] gave a graceful summary of the *Epistola* (p. 20-26) noting a point of contact with Bayle's *Commentaire* (pp. 23-24) and attributing the *Epistola* to Jacques Bernard." (See above, my ed. of *A Letter Concerning Toleration*, cit. Introd. p. XXVIII, n. 5). It is clear that I did not speak of Bayle's influence on Locke but simply referred to the fact that the summariser of the *Epistola*, who already knew the *Commentaire*, had noted 'a point of contact' between the two works. That was all! But it makes no odds − Klibansky's nature is such that he does not like to pay his debts. Of course, this does not diminish his merits as a scholar and a tireless editor; it only shows an unconquerable weakness

that the kind reader, no less than the writer of this note, will have no difficulty in forgiving.

London, summer 1976

THREE LETTERS FROM LOCKE TO LIMBORCH
ON THE UNITY OF GOD

1. Only a few months after the publication in London of the *Reasonableness of Christianity*[1] Locke was accused by his critics of being a Socinian and an atheist[2] and this in spite of the fact that the work was anonymous.[3]

1. *The Reasonableness of Christianity as delivered in the Scriptures*, London, printed for Awnsham and John Churchill at the Black Swan in Pater-Noster-Row, London 1695.

Awnsham Churchill was the first English editor of Locke, whose *A Letter concerning Toleration* he published in 1689. After 1690, when the *Second Letter concerning Toleration* appeared, the name of Awnsham's heir and successor John Churchill is always added. It is to John Churchill in collaboration with Sam. Manship that we owe the first edition in folio of *Locke's Works in Three Volumes* published in London in 1714. Before the appearance of the *Reasonableness of Christianity* Locke had published a number of works at the house Awnsham and then, as mentioned above, Awnsham and John Churchill, namely: *A Letter concerning Toleration*, 1689; the *Second Edition* of the same *Letter concerning Toleration*, 1690; *A Second Letter concerning Toleration*, 1690; *Two Treatises of Government*, 1690; *Some Considerations of the Consequences of the Lowering of Interest and the Raising of the Value of Money*, 1692; *Some Thoughts concerning Education*, 1693; the re-printing, with large additions, of the second edition of the *Essay concerning Human Understanding, In four Books*, 1694; and then, in 1695, the *Reasonableness*.

2. The fact that the work was published by Locke's usual publisher did not help to preserve its anonymity and Locke's name began to be at the centre of religious controversy from the time the *Letter concerning Toleration* was published. V. *supra*, *A Letter concerning Toleration, Introd.* p. XXVII et seq. XLIII et seq.; and also *The Socinianism of Locke and the English Edition of the Letter concerning Toleration*, p. 145.

Locke admitted to being the author of the *Reasonableness* in a codicil of 15th Sept. 1704 to his will; see Lovelace Collection in the Bodleian Library, Oxford (BL. MSS. LOCKE, b. c-14) published by LORD KING, *The Life of J. Locke with extracts from his Correspondence, journals and common-place books. New ed. with considerable additions*, 2 vols., London, 1830, II pp. 51-53. In this he at last admitted writing the works that had appeared either anonymously or under a pseudonym.

3. JOHN EDWARDS, when he opened the hostile discussion on Locke's work

John Edwards,[4] openly referring to Locke as "the gentleman who wrote the *Human Understanding* and *Education*"[5] drew attention to the fact that whoever asserted that every Christian should limit his belief to this, "that Jesus is the Messiah"[6] thereby denied "the Holy Trinity:

with *Some Thoughts concerning the several causes and Occasions of Atheism, especially in the present Age. With some Brief Reflections on Socinianism, And on a late Book entitled the Reasonableness of Christianity as delivered in the Scriptures*, London 1695 (p. 113), was the first to assert that the author of the *Reasonableness* was "all over Socinianized" and that "a Socinian is an Atheist, or [...] one that favours the cause of Atheism" (p. 75).

Locke immediately, before the end of 1695, replied to Edwards' accusation with an anonymous *Vindication of the Reasonableness of Christianity as delivered in the Scriptures from Mr. Edwards' Reflections*.

Edwards made a sharp reply a year later in a pamphlet with the title *Socinianism Unmasked* in which he accused the anonymous author of the *Reasonableness* of "irreligion and Atheism" and asked him to reveal his identity: "Appear no more in masquerade; away with this mummery and show yourself what you are [...] Throw off your visor then, and speak out like a man" p. 69. Locke replied again in 1697 with a *Second Vindication of the Reasonableness of Christianity*; and again Edwards replied in the same year with the *Socinian Creed; or a brief account of the professed tract and doctrines of the foreign and English Socinians: wherein is showed the tendency of them to irreligion and atheism* [...], London, 1697.

For the history of the controversy and in general for the critics of the *Reasonableness* see FOX BOURNE, *The Life of J. Locke*, 2 vols., London, 1876 II, pp. 282-292 & pp. 408-415.

The literature arising out of the controversy is covered by H.O. CHRISTOPHERSEN, *A Bibliographical Introduction to the Study of John Locke*, Oslo, 1930, espec. p. 58 et seq. For the argument between Edwards and Locke and in particular on the essence of Locke's Christian belief see also M. CRANSTON, *J. Locke. A Biography*, London, p. 390 et seq., p. 409 et seq.; C.A. VIANO, *John Locke, Dal Razionalismo all'Illuminismo*, Turin, 1960, p. 374 et seq.; and R. CRIPPA, *Studi sulla coscienza etica e religiosa del Seicento. Esperienza e libertà in G. Locke*, Milan, 1960, p. 135 et seq.

4. On John Edwards, 1637-1716, uncompromising calvinist and unwavering polemicist, and on the writings he dedicated to criticising the *Reasonableness* v. n. 3 above.

5. J. EDWARDS, *Some Thoughts concerning the several Causes and Occasions of Atheism* [...], *op. cit. 113.*

6. J. LOCKE, *The Reasonableness of Christianity*, which is quoted here is from *J. Locke's Works in Three Volumes*, Printed for John Churchill and Sam. Manship, London, 1714, vol. II, pp. 471-553 esp. 479 et seq. & 520 et seq. But the whole of Locke's work aims at showing, on the basis of passages from the Scriptures, that Christ is the Messiah and that the belief in Jesus the Messiah is the condition of salvation: "it is plain that the Gospel was written to induce them

176

Father, Son and Holy Ghost" and revealed himself as "all over Socinianized".[7]

Edward Stillingfleet,[8] Bishop of Worcester made the same accusation against Locke, both from the pulpit[9] and in a closely argued dis-

into a belief of this Proposition; That Jesus of Nazareth was the Messiah, which if they believed, they should have life," p. 480.

7. J. EDWARDS, *Some Thoughts concerning the several causes and Occasions of Atheism* [...], op. cit., p. 113. Locke comes back to this accusation time and again in *A Vindication of the Reasonableness of Christianity* [...], which I have quoted from *Locke's Works*, Vol. II, pp. 543-553 et passim; where he opposes with the view that "Socinianism is not the fault of the Book [...] there is not one word of Socinianism in it," p. 547. Locke's defence against the accusation of Socinianism is the more serious, the more Edwards insisted on identifying socinianism with atheism: "a Socinian is an Atheist" Edwards had written, op. cit. p. 75, or at least: "one that favours the Cause of Atheism."

8. On Stillingfleet see J. TULLOCK, *Rational Theology and Christian philosophy in England in the XVII century*, London, 1874[2], vol. I, chap. VII; FOX BOURNE, *The Life of John Locke*, op. cit. II, pp. 420-438.

For the circumstances that gave rise to Stillingfleet's attack concerning "some Unitarian Treatises, published nearly at the same time" it is useful to see the account which LORD KING gives in *The Life of John Locke*, Vol. I, pp. 359 sqq. and before him J. LE CLERC, *Eloge historique de feu M. Locke*, in *Oeuvres Diverses de M.J. Locke*, Rotterdam, 1710, pp. LXVIII sqq.

9. See Locke to Molineux dated 22 February 1697 in *Some Familiar Letters. Locke's Works*, cit. Vol. III[1], p. 555. A. CARLINI, *La filosofia di Locke*, 2 vols., Florence, 1929, Vol. II, p. 274 sqq. and R. ASHCRAFT, *Faith and Knowledge in Locke's philosophy*, in *John Locke: Problems and Perspectives. A collection of new essays* ed. by J.W. YOLTON, Cambridge, 1969, p. 201, and lately E.S. de Beer, *The Correspondence of John Locke*, Vol. VI, Oxford, 1981, p. 5, following an outdated view, as inexplicable now as it was formerly, identify William Sherlock rather than Edward Stillingfleet as the person referred to by Locke in the words "For a Man of no small Name, as you know Dr. S.–– is, has been pleased to declare against my Doctrine of no innate Ideas, from the Pulpit in the Temple, and as I told, charged it with little less than Atheism." In Molineux's letter to Locke of 3 Feb. 1697 quoted in *Some Familiar Letters* in *Locke's Works*[1], cit. III p. 554, to which Locke replied with the extract quoted above, Molineux was referring explicitly to the Bishop of Worcester that is to say to Stillingfleet, whom he called "A Man of great Name." So it is clear that Locke was alluding to Stillingfleet when he mentions what the latter had been pleased to say from the pulpit "in an Harangue to a *Sunday's Auditory*" concerning "An Essay on Human Understanding" and that Stillingfleet was the "Man of no small Name" and the "Great Man". Again, addressing Stillingfleet in the *Letter to the Right Reverend Edward Lord Bishop of Worcester* in *Locke's Works*[1], Vol. I, p. 344, Locke repeats, with clear mental reference to what both he and Molineux had said about Stillingfleet, "Your Lordship's Name is of so great Authority in

177

course in the *Vindication of the Trinity*[10] basing it not so much on the arguments of the *Reasonableness* as on the *Essay concerning Human Understanding*[11] and especially on the criticism of Descartes' innate

the Learned World". In my view therefore there is nothing that leads one to suppose that the person referred to is Sherlock, "a powerful non-juror who changed his mind in 1690", (CRANSTON, *J. Locke. A Biography*, p. 471, No. 4) and who dedicated himself stubbornly to combatting socinianism and who ended by being nothing less than the Bishop of London. Furthermore Sherlock entered the field against Locke only in 1704 with *A Discourse concerning the Happiness of Good Men and punishment of the Wicked in the next World*, a work which Locke did not take very seriously, finding it "too subtle" for him and declaring himself content with his own "mediocrity" when confronted by so "extraordinary and sublime a way of reasoning". (CRANSTON, op. cit. p. 471)

10. E. STILLINGFLEET, *Learned Discourse in Vindication of the Doctrine of the Trinity*, London, 1696.

To the Bishop of Worcester's *Discourse* Locke replied with *A Letter to the Right Rev. Edward Ld Bishop of Worcester, concerning some Passages relating to Mr. Locke's Essay on Human Understanding in a late Discourse of his Lordship's in Vindication of the Trinity*, by J. LOCKE, Gent. London, 1697, in *Locke's Works*[1], ed. cit. I, pp. 343-387. The same year Stillingfleet replied in his turn to Locke's letter with *The Bishop of Worcester's Answer to Mr. Locke's Letter concerning some passages relating to his Essay* [...], to which Locke replied, still in the same year, 1697, with *Mr. Locke's Reply to the Right Rev. The Lord Bishop of Worcester's Answer to his Letter concerning etc.*, op. cit. pp. 388-499. Stillingfleet returned to the fray in the following year with *The Bishop of Worcester's Answer to Mr. Locke's Second Letter: wherein his Notion of Ideas is proved to be inconsistent with itself, and with the Articles of the Christian Faith*. Locke had the last word with the longest of his replies to Stillingfleet which was published in 1699 but in fact finished by, and dated, 4 May 1698 (op. cit. 432-575): *Mr. Locke's Reply to the Right Rev, the Lord Bishop of Worcester's answer to his Second Letter* [...]. In spite of Le Clerc's disapproval of the polemic started by Stillingfleet and of his style and language (cf. LORD KING, *Life of John Locke*, op. cit. p. 362) the resulting battle of words is of considerable interest as it helps us to a better understanding of Locke's thinking, since it was Stillingfleet who first obliged Locke to reveal it, in spite of the latter's reticence.

For the polemic between Locke and Stillingfleet, besides the longer treatment by FOX-BOURNE (op. cit.), see also the shorter but essential summary by CRANSTON, *J. Locke*, op. cit., pp. 410 sqq.

11. In the *Discourse in Vindication of the Doctrine of the Trinity*, the chapter headed *Objections against the Trinity in Point of Reason, answered*, pp. 233 et seq., is devoted entirely to Locke's *Essay on Human Intelligence*. In that Essay the denial of innate ideas and his criticism of the conception of substance were held by Stillingfleet to lead to a denial of the Trinity. In the *Letter to the Rev. Edward Lord Bishop of Worcester* Locke replied (op. cit. p. 343): "in my whole

ideas. He shows how Locke's criticism of the idea of substance[12] denies the basis of the doctrine of the Trinity[13] and so associates Locke with the "gentlemen of this new way of Reasoning," namely with the Unitarians and the Socinians.[14]

The more openly his name was mentioned, the more seriously did Locke take the accusation and he reacted immediately against both men by firmly refusing to confess himself a Unitarian let alone a Socinian. In fact it is surprising that a man as prudent — one might even say as timorous — as Locke[15] should have decided to make an immediate reply to his accusers, and this in spite of Molineux' advice to avoid getting into an argument with Stillingfleet, "a man of great name," over a matter which seemed to him "not of that moment."[16] So, if in spite of that advice he decided to reply, the explanation is that Locke sincerely loathed the accusation of Socinianism.

But the fact that Locke may not have liked to see himself confused with the Socinians and for that reason firmly rejected the charge declaring himself to be what he had always been, within the serious schism of the Christian church, "Evangelicus, ego Christianus sum, non pap-

Essay, I think there is not to be found any thing like an objection against the Trinity" and he goes on to examine Stillingfleet's arguments one by one; first of all those concerning the criticism of the conception of substance (*Discourse in Vindication*, pp. 233-252 & *A Letter*, pp. 344-373) and then those that refer directly to the Trinity (*Discourse in Vindication*, pp. 252-259 & *A Letter*, pp. 373-386).

For the polemics that resulted from the *Essay* and the literature born of these polemics after Stillingfleet's attack and in connection with the *Reasonableness* see CHRISTOPHERSEN, *A Bibliographical Introduction to the Study of John Locke*, op. cit. pp. 29-57.

12. Stillingfleet quite simply accused Locke of having "discarded Substance out of the reasonable part of the World." *Vindication of the Trinity*, p. 234.

13. STILLINGFLEET, *Vindication of the Trinity*, p. 252.

14. See especially Locke's *Reply* to the answer to his *Letter* (op. cit. p. 388 et seq.) in which Locke insists on dissociating himself from the Unitarians and the Socinians.

15. J. LE CLERC in his *Eloge Historique de feu Mr. Locke*, which first appeared in the *Bibliothèque Choisie*, Vol. VI, 1705, p. 342 et seq. and reprinted in *Oeuvres Diverses de Mr Locke*, Rotterdam, 1710, from which we quote, on p. XLVI, described Locke as "plutot timide, que courageux." In my view also, other well known episodes in Locke's life, allow one to speak unhesitatingly of his "timorousness."

16. See the letter from Molineux to Locke dated 3 Feb. 1697 in *Some Familiar Letters* in *Locke's Works*, Vol. III, p. 554.

ista,"[17] is not enough to allow us to decide whether he was really Socinian or whether the theoretical bases of his philosophical thinking had carried him to theological conclusions which, although they might be close to, and confused with, Unitarian and Socinian principles, were in fact of quite a different origin.

More recent and more measured[18] judgment of Locke's thinking, although accepting the reasoning of Edwards and Stillingfleet, tends nevertheless to the view that the *Reasonableness of Christianity* bears witness only to a coincidence of conclusions or to a convergence of the theological meditations towards Unitarian and Socinian principles and that he did not adhere fundamentally to the essentially Unitarian and Socinian principles of the rational theology of the Arminians. The view is that at the bottom Locke remained closer to the latitudinarian wing of the Anglican church than to the Unitarian beliefs of the Dutch Remonstrants.

In contrast, however, three of the letters Locke wrote to Limborch[19] provide the Dutch theologian with a rational proof of the unity

17. See Locke's letters to Limborch dated 4th Oct. 1698 in *Some Familiar Letters, Locke's Works*[1] Vol. III, p. 634. Locke explains a little further on what he means by evangelical and papist: "Inter christiani nominis professores duas ego tantum agnosco classes, evangelicos et papistas. Hos qui tanquam infallibile dominium sibi arrogant in aliorum conscientias. Illos qui quaerentes unice veritatem, illam et sibi et aliis, argumentis solum rationibusque persuasam volunt; aliorum erroribus faciles, suae imbecilitatis haud immemores; veniam fragilitati et ignorantiae humanae dantes patentesque vicissim."

18. We refer particularly to the works already quoted above, namely M. CRANSTON, *J. Locke*, op. cit., especially p. 390; R. AARON, *J. Locke*, 1937, London, 1955[2], p. 38, p. 292 et seq. especially p. 298; R. CRIPPA, *Studi sulla coscienza etica e religiosa del Seicento. Esperienza e liberta in J. Locke*, cit. p. 158; and C.A. VIANO, *J. Locke. Dal razionalismo all'Illuminismo*, cit. p. 376; to these one might add, at least as far as they agree on the grounds of Edwards' and Stillingfleet's conclusions: R. ASHCRAFT, *Faith and knowledge in Locke's philosophy*, in *J. Locke. Problems and Perspectives*, ed. by YOLTON op. cit. especially p. 200 et seq. and lastly J.D. MABBOLT, *John Locke*, London, 1973, especially p. 136.

19. On Limborch see my note No. 2 on p. XVIII of the *Introduction* to my edition of the *Letter concerning Toleration*. Latin and English texts (in this volume), and the exhaustive monograph by A.P. BARNOUW, *Philippus van Limborch*, Den Haag, 1963.

The three letters from Locke to Limborch to which we refer, are published at the end of this introductory study in tl.ir original and inedited form. We shall speak about these in the *Bibliographical Note*.

of God and show Locke to be avowedly unitarian and socinian. "Ego sane nunquam dubitavi [...] numen illud [Deum] esse unicum."[20]

I have already referred to these three letters from Locke to Limborch on the unity of God and partly quoted from them in an earlier study[21] aimed at demonstrating, alongside Locke's basic Socinianism, his participation in the English edition of the *Epistola de Tolerantia* produced for anti-Trinitarian circles by the Socinian, Popple. I believe it is opportune to publish these three letters in their entirety, taking them from the fuller manuscript versions[22] rather than from the shorter and reticent printed ones. Until now these letters have had scant consideration or they have more often been totally overlooked, yet a careful study of them could help to define Locke's position more accurately in the great religious controversies of his time and also to determine the significance of the man and his work.

2. In the spring of 1695 Locke confided to Limborch that during the winter he had written a book ("cogitata mea in chartam conjeci") which aimed at demonstrating "ex intenta et accurata *N. Testamenti* lectione [...] in quo consisteret fides Christiana."[23]

The book about which Locke informed Limborch in this roundabout way was *The Reasonableness of Christianity as delivered in the Scriptures*,[24] which had been published anonymously in London in the April of that year. The very fact that it had been published anonymously was the reason why Locke recommended Limborch to be careful not to reveal the identity of the writer; Limborch had already disappointed Locke[25] in this respect several times. "Haec tibi in aurem dicta sunto; nam me hoc tractasse argumentum tibi solo communicatum volo."[26]

20. Locke to Limborch dated 29 Oct., 1697 – the latin postscript to the first letter published here.

21. V. *supra*, The Socinianism of Locke and the English edition of the Letter concerning Toleration, p. 124 and notes 16 and 17.

22. On the editions of these letters see *Bibliographical Note* below.

23. Locke to Limborch, 10-5-1695 in *Some Familiar Letters* from *Locke's Works*, Vol. III, p. 616.

24. See above note 1.

25. With reference to Limborch's disclosure of the authorship of the anonymous *Epistola de Tolerantia*, much to Locke's dismay and resentment, see my introduction to J. LOCKE, *A Letter concerning Toleration*, op. cit., p. XXIII, note 1 and p. XXIX et seq.

26. Locke to Limborch, 10th May 1695, cit.

Locke's recommendation was all the more urgent as he was open and generous in the recognition of the work's indebtedness to the *Theologia Christiana* of his Arminian friend. "Pro *Theologia* tua *Christiana* iam denuo a me reddendae sunt gratiae, non quod Bibliothecam volumine, sed me scientia auxerit."[27]

Limborch, who did not know English,[28] could not take cognizance of the work Locke announced to him until the Summer of 1696[29] when the French translation of the *Reasonableness* appeared. "Prodiit nuper apud nos," he wrote to Locke, "tractatus Anglici quod *Religio Christiana*, qualis nobis est representata in Scriptura Sacra, sit summe rationalis, versio Gallica."[30]

27. Locke to Limborch, 10th May 1695, cit. The *Theologia Christiana ad praxin pietatis ac promotionem pacis Christianae unice directa*, appeared in Amsterdam in 1686, that is to say three years after Locke had sought refuge in Holland and had met the Arminians there, in particular Limborch, who more than anyone else had given Locke the comfort of his own friendship. At that time Locke was working on the *Essay concerning Human Understanding* and on the *Two Treatises of Government*. The long conversations with the Arminian theologian, about which we have firm evidence, had a deep influence on Locke's thinking, and Locke himself bears witness to this once again in the letter to which we refer.

28. Limborch did not know English; Locke did not speak French fluently, a language they both could read. For that reason not only their correspondence but also their conversation was in Latin, a language in which Limborch had the advantage of greater knowledge and more practice in speaking.

Not all correspondence between Locke and Limborch has been published, although it has been thoroughly investigated and for the most part known. |The huge exchange of letters between Locke and his correspondents is in the course of being published by Esmond de Beer who has so far published the first five of eight volumes: E.S. DE BEER, *The Correspondence of John Locke in eight Volumes*, Oxford Clarendon Press, Vol. I, 1976 et seq. It is easy to foresee that once this precious, and for the most part hitherto unedited, material has been published, students of Locke will be urged to reconsider several aspects of Locke's spiritual biography that are now unquestioned.|

29. Translated by Coste, the *Reasonableness* appeared under the title *Le Christianisme raisonnable tel qu'il est represente par l'Ecriture Sainte* in Amsterdam in 1696. Coste was later taken on by Locke as secretary and translator of his works.

But even before the *Reasonableness* had appeared in French, J. Le Clerc had already spoken accurately about it in Holland in *La Bibliothèque Choisie*, Vol. II, article 8 (cf. *Eloge Historique de feu Mr. Locke* in *Oeuvres Diverses*, op. cit. p. LXVII).

30. Limborch to Locke [14/24 July] 1696, in *Some Fam. Let.* = *Locke's W.*[1], III, pp. 617-618.

Limborch read *Le Christianisme Raisonnable* with eagerness and pleasure because he saw his own thoughts reflected there. "Ego summa cum voluptate lectioni illius incumbo, et in precipuo (quot toto libro de fidei Christianae objecto tractat) argumento illi prorsus assentior."[31]

But, as has happened with the *Epistola de Tolerantia*, which had been attributed to Limborch himself, because it was seen to be "selon ses principes,"[32] so, when the *Christianisme Raisonnable* appeared, the author was sought — and not wrongly — in the circle of the Remonstrants and among Limborch's friends. "Illius [tractatus] autorem volunt multi esse amicum meum."[33] However, Limborch kept the secret, though it was not destined to last long as both in England and in Holland itself it was open to everyone.[34]

In the same letter Limborch, as if to show the care with which he had read the work, drew Locke's attention to the fact that the French translation of verse 7 of the second *Epistola* of John — "qua ratione eum Anglice expresserit autor, ignoro" — "[...] lequels ne confessent point, que Jesus, le Messie, soit venu en chair" is a poor interpretation of the original text which would be better rendered by "qui non confitentur Jesum Messiam qui in carne venit."[35]

The point for a unitarian theologian like Limborch was of considerable importance and the subtle discussion he added demonstrates this. In fact Locke admitted the exactness of the point: "quod monuisti de loco Johannis tecum sentio: idem est in versione nostra, quem in Gallica observasti error"[36] and he then asked Limborch to re-read the whole tract and to make known his and other people's opinions. "Cum vero totum perlegeris, et tuam et aliorum de tractatu illo sententiam scire vellem."[37]

31. Limborch to Locke, cit.
32. For the various attributions of the *Epistola* see my *Introduction* pp. XXVIII, XXIX.
33. Limborch to Locke [14/24 July] 1696, cit.
34. It should be remembered that J. Edwards had identified Locke as the author of the *Reasonableness* (see above p. 176) without any shadow of doubt in spite of the anonymity of the work.
35. Limborch to Locke [14/24 July] 1696, cit.
36. Locke to Limborch, 3rd September 1696 in *Some Fam. Let.* = *Locke's Works*, III, pp. 618-619.
37. Locke to Limborch, cit. id.

But it was only several months later that Limborch was able to respond to Locke's request "Legi totum tractatum a capite ad calcem: nec unica lectione contentus, eum relegi,"[38] and to give the opinion for which he had been asked. This opinion was one of complete agreement, especially as regards the central question in the work. "Imprimis placent mihi duo: methodus accurata historiae evangelicae, quam cap. IX tradit, et per quam varia loca in evangeliis, in speciem obscura, feliciter admodum interpretatur; et perspicua illa deductio argumentorum, quibus ostendit cur D. Jesus Christus in terris degens, non expressis verbis docuerit, se esse Messiam."[39]

Limborch found this last "deductio argumentorum" especially important for the unitarian thesis and the satisfaction of the Arminian theologian bears witness to the worth of Locke's contribution to that thesis.

As for the comments, these referred to Adam's fall and to the doctrine of the redemption, to the immortal nature of Adam and how this is to be understood and finally to the significance of "eternal life" in some passages of the Scriptures;[40] but in reality it was only a matter of a few marginal comments as Limborch himself admitted. "Verum exigua haec sunt, et extra principalem autoris scopum"[41]: that is to say they do not touch on the substance of Locke's arguments to which Limborch adhered without reservation.

In the meantime the *Reasonableness*[42] was ever more the subject of discussions and polemics, both in England, where acceptance of the dogma of the Trinity was still required by law and Unitarians were excluded from religious toleration,[43] and abroad particularly in Holland, where the general dislike of Socinianism[44] was given an extra reason in the arguments of the anti-unitarian theologians by the Cartesian doctrine of substance. The Remonstrants on the other hand found a new and valid support to the Unitarian faith in the *Reasonableness*, just as

38. Limborch to Locke, 26th March 1697 in *Some Fam. Let.* = *Locke's Works*, III, pp. 619-622, cit. at p. 619.
39. Limborch to Locke, cit. *Locke's Works*, III, pp. 619-620.
40. Limborch to Locke, cit. *Locke's Works*, III, p. 620.
41. Limborch to Locke, cit.
42. See preceding note no. 3.
43. See my study *The Socinianism of Locke*, cit. p. 136 and the notes there.
44. I would refer to my earlier studies, *Introd.* to the *Letter concerning Toleration* (cit.), *The Socinianism of Locke* (cit.) and *Locke's Epistola on Toleration from the Translation of Popple to that of Gough.*

they had found arguments in the *Letter Concerning Toleration* to support the religious toleration they demanded against the persecutions and menaces to which they were continuously subjected.[45]

It is therefore very understandable that the Arminians should discuss these matter among themselves and with Limborch too, especially as Limborch himself was tempted to stimulate the discussion in order to refer to Locke the opinions of the others on these points.

In fact Limborch wrote to Locke on the 8th of October, 1697: "Hac aestate, cum viris aliquot primariis, sermonem de variis habui: inter alia incidit sermo de tractatu de quo in superioribus meis judicium meum scripsi."[46] Everybody, Limborch added, had praised the book highly: "omnes eum summopere laudabant" and that one person had even complained, "non satis placere affirmabat" that the brevity of the title did not correspond to the dignity of the work: "libro magnifico exilem praefixisse titulum."[47] Another, though highly appreciative of the author and his work, put a precise question, which, by insisting on an equally precise reply, asked Locke in practice to take an unequivocal position on the question of the Unity of God. "Idem ille vir primarius affirmabat," Limborch wrote,[48] "se argumenta quaedam irrefragabilia requirere, quibus probetur Ens aeternum, seu per se existens, seu undique perfectum, esse tantum unicum."

Whoever put this question – and it is not easy to identify him[49] – certainly went deeper than Limborch who had contented himself with

---

45. Idem.
46. Limborch to Locke, 8 Oct. 1697 in *Some Fam. Let. = Locke's Works*[1], III, pp. 623-624, cit. p. 623.
47. Do p. 623.
48. Do. pp. 623-624.
49. In the letter of 8 Oct. 1697 quoted above Limborch alludes to the unnamed person in this way: "idem qui tibi ante hac Sladum nostrum commendatum esse voluit." Of Slade or Sladus, a Dutch doctor who went to seek his fortune in England and died there from an apoplectic stroke, four letters to Locke have been preserved in the Lovelace Collection (B.L. Mss. LOCKE c. 18 ff. 112-117). Compare CRANSTON, *J. Locke*, cit. p. 328 n. 3. The letters may perhaps give the name of the person who recommended Sladus to the philosopher and who is here concealed by Limborch, who refers to him as "vir magnificus." But whoever he is we shall certainly know from the imminent publication of Locke's *Epistolario* which E. de Beer has in hand, p. IX note 49.

[According to E. De Beer, *The Correspondence of John Locke*, vol. VI, Oxford, 1981, Letter 2318, p. 206, Letter 2352, p. 1697, the "vir *magnificens*" seems to be Mr. Johannes Hudde, the burgomaster of the City of Amsterdam.]

conceiving the Unity to consist in the reduction of Jesus to the Messiah that lies at the centre of *The Reasonableness of Christianity*.

The unnamed person put one other question to Limborch, less wily but no less pertinent: "Quaesivit ex me," Limborch wrote, "num illo tractatu [*de Intellecto Umano*] etiam unitatem entis a se existentis adstruxisset?"[50]

Limborch, himself, did not know what to reply, "utpote lingua mihi ignota conscriptum [*tractatum illum*] numquam legerim."[51] However Limborch begged Locke on behalf of the anonymous questioner, "ut si in tractatu tuo *de Intellecto Humano* quaestionem hanc [de unitate entis] intactam reliqueris, illius adstructione tractatum augere velis, unitatemque entis independentis solide adstruere."[52]

Locke answered Limborch on the 29th of the same month with the first of the three letters in French which are here published. This letter was originally conceived and written down in a far fuller and more circumstantial form than that sent to Limborch and it appeared later in *Some Familiar Letters between Mr. Locke and several of his Friends* (*Locke's Works*,[1] III, pp. 624-25). In publishing here the first of the Three Letters from Locke to Limborch on the Unity of God we have preferred to follow the unedited version which seems to us to be more spontaneous and therefore more intimately revealing of Locke's thinking.

It may surprise the reader that these three letters from Locke to Limborch, and only these three letters, which discuss the unity of God should be written in French rather than in Latin, which was more familiar to both of them than French. As neither knew the native language of the other Latin was constantly used in the copious correspondence that ran without a break from 1689 to 1704 between the English philosopher and the Dutch theologian.[53]

In a Latin *post-script* to the first of the three letters[54] Locke excused himself regretting that his lack of practice in Latin prevented him

50. Limborch to Locke, cit. *Locke's Works*[1], III, p. 624.
51. Limborch to Locke, cit. ib.
52. Limborch to Locke, cit. ib.
53. The last letter from Locke to Limborch (published in *Some Fam. Let.* = *Locke's Works*[1], III, p. 688) is dated 4th August 1704. Locke died on the 28th Oct. of that same year. This is a most dignified letter, written when Locke was ill and almost at the point of death. In it he tells of his pain at being separated from a dear friend.
54. It is reprinted here in full with the first letter in French.

from writing fluently "lingua Latinae dissuetudine, quae expedite scribere prohibet" and even that, as his letter had to pass the scrutiny of such learned minds, he had preferred to write it in a "lingua vernacula" and so had entrusted the translation to a Frenchman "Galloque in suam linguam vertendam tradidi."

It is doubtful whether Limborch, who knew the timid nature of the philosopher, believed in the excuse, and the exaggerated praise that he gave to Locke's Latin[55] when he replied, he who was the better Latin scholar, leads one to suppose that he did not believe it at all; nor can we, who have better facts to judge by, believe it either.

The fact remains that when Limborch, in the name of the anonymous "vir magnificus" requested an argument that would be an irrefutable proof of the Unity of God: "Ens aeternum seu per se existens, seu undique perfectum, esse tantum unicum" (cit.) and, regretting the lack of such a proof in Grotius,[56] asked whether one had already been given in the *Essay on Human Understanding* and, if it had not, whether one would be included in the next edition. Locke untertook an extensive reply that was by and large fairly relevant to the questions Limborch had put to him in the name of someone else.

But these were questions the answers to which Locke had always preferred to keep to himself, keeping quiet with everyone about his belief in the unity of God and about the proofs on which it was based,

55. Limborch to Locke, the 11th October 1698 in *Some Fam. Let.* = *Locke's Works*[1], III, p. 626, wrote about Locke's Latin as follows: "Quod vero linguae latinae dissuetudine praetexis quae expedite scribere prohibet, plane me in ruborem dedit [...] Epistolae tuae omnes, etiam veloci calamo scriptae, sunt non tantum purae et tersae, sed et vividae ac elegantes; quae si tibi displiceant, quid de me judices non difficile mihi est colligere." Is this generous praise only? or is there a touch of kindly irony in it as well?

56. Limborch to Locke, 8th Oct. 1698 in *Some Fam. Let.* from *Locke's Works*[1], III, p. 624. "Desiderabat quaedam in argumentis Hugonis Grotii, libro primo *De Veritate Religionis Christianae*." Locke replied *en passant* in the Latin *post-script* to the first letter in French: "Ad unitatem Dei quod attinet, Grotii, fateor, in loco a te citato, argumenta non abunde satisfaciut." The reader can refer to H. GROTIUS, *De Veritate Religioni Christiane*, Leiden, 1627, I, III, where Unity is given as the first of God's attributes. "Once the existence of a divinity is demonstrated, we then go on to his attributes: of these the first to be met is the following: that there are no gods but one God." For Locke, however, who found Grotius' argument not entirely satisfactory, unity is implicit and understood in the other attributes of God, since it is their very basis. So the proposition God is itself an affirmation of unity.

proofs that he was careful not to provide, not only in the *Essay Concerning Human Understanding* but also in the anonymous *Reasonableness of Christianity*. After Stillingfleet and Edwards had uncovered the unitarianism implicit in these works he was even less disposed to provide them.

However, when asked for these proofs by Limborch who assured him of the greatest possible discretion about any reply that Locke might give, Locke could not refuse and prepared a long and, though verbose, fairly exhaustive reply. He preferred this time to write his reply in his own language rather than in the colloquial Latin he normally used in this correspondence. The reason was not his disuse of Latin, which was taken up again in the subsequent correspondence, but rather to be able to work out his thoughts well and to be better able to weigh the words he used to express them. This can be seen from the much corrected manuscripts which were handed for translation to Coste,[57] who was accustomed to translate Locke's writings under the author's close surveillance.[58]

But the reply turned out to be too long or at least it seemed so to Locke and above all too binding, and as such, if it had become known outside the narrow circle of friends for whom it was intended, it could once again have stirred the arguments round his name and above all have justified all those, who not entirely wrongly accused him of Socinianism.

57. On Pierre Coste, recommended to Locke by Le Clerc see the letter from Le Clerc to Locke dated 8th July, 1695 in BONNO, *Lettres Inédites de Le Clerc à Locke*, Berkeley and Los Angeles, 1959, p. 86. As the philosopher's secretary and the established translator of his works see BONNO, op. cit., *Introduction*, p. 22.

58. For the French translation of Locke's works done by Coste see what Coste himself writes in *Avertissement du Traducteur* to the *Essai Philosophique concernant l'Entendement Humain par M. LOCKE trad. de l'Anglois par M. COSTE*, Troisième ed., Amsterdam, MDCCXXXV, pp. IX and XVIII and especially what Locke himself writes in the open letter *Monsieur Locke au Libraire* in *Essai Philosophique*, op. cit., p. XV.

With regard to the faithfulness of the translation of Locke's works and in particular of the *Epistola de Tolerantia*, which was disputed and rejected by modern editors, I take the liberty of referring to the introduction to my edition of the *Letter concerning Toleration* (cit. especially p. XXI et seq.), to my study *The Socinianism of Locke*, (cit. passim) and once again to the article *Locke's Epistola on Toleration from the Translation of Popple to that of Gough*, cit. In this last reference the matter is examined once again on the basis of documents that the scholars in question have not so far refuted.

Among the manuscripts of Locke preserved by the Bodleian Library in Oxford there is in fact a first version of the letter in French dated 29th Oct. 1697 (Mss Locke c. 24. fs 156-^{r}-7^v), much more extensive, as is indicated above, than the one subsequently sent to Limborch and published in *Familiar Letters* in *Locke's Works*,[1] III, p. 624-5. The earlier version is translated and copied out in Coste's elegant calligraphy and Locke has added at the front in his own writing "Je suis, Monsieur, Votre très humble et très obéissant serviteur," but he has not signed it.

In the first version of his letter Locke reveals for the first time and, what really counts, with unexpected openness, the unitarian premise of the demonstration of the existence of God that was put forward in the *Essay Concerning Human Understanding* Part IV Chapter X, adding that the Unity of God is implicit in the very proposition of his existence: "L'idée de Dieu sur laquelle j'ai raisonné [*Essay Concerning Human Understanding* IV, X, espec. 1-12] c'est celle d'un Etre Eternel, tout Puissant et *Omniscient.* Des attributs, etant une fois reconnus en Dieu, nous conduisent aisement, si je ne me trompe, à l'unité de Dieu. Car si Dieu est tout puissant et *Omniscient,* je ne croy pas qu'il puisse avoir deux Etres de cette nature " (fs 156^r-156^v).

But such an assertion unequivocally exposed the unitarian and Socinian framework of his theologico-philosophical thinking of which he had been accused by Stillingfleet and Edwards, an accusation that he had firmly denied. This must have frightened Locke, "plutot timide que courageux"[59] as he was, so instead of signing and sending the letter, which was already complete, he preferred instead to cross out with a thick stroke of the pen more than three of the four pages that made up his reply including the demonstration of the unity of God deduced from his divine attributes, and he noted in the margin that these pages had been eliminated: "omitted in the letter I sent."

However, once the three central pages had been eliminated, the reply to Limborch became vague and elusive and Locke himself must have realized this for, in the margin of the first page (f.156^r) he inserted three lines in his own hand which, although they made the reply sent to Limborch more pertinent in spite of their succinctness, still contained two admissions no less important and revealing:

I, that he would willingly have inserted the demonstration of the

---

59. It is so defined by J. LE CLERC, *Eloge historique ae feu Mr. Locke*, in the *Bibliothèque Choisie*, VI, 1705, p. 342 et seq., reprinted in *Oeuvres Diverses de Mr. Locke*, Rotterdam, 1710, p. 46.

unity of God in the fourth edition of the *Essay Concerning Human Understanding* which was in preparation: "J'aurois volontiers satisfait à votre désir, ou au désir d'aucun de vos amis en y insérant dans la IVe edition [de l'Essay concernant l'Entendement que le libraire se dispose a faire⁶⁰] les preuves de l'unité de Dieu qui se presentent a mon esprit";

II, that he was inclined to believe that the Unity of God could be demonstrated as clearly as his existence: "Je suis enclin à croire que l'unité de Dieu peut être établie sur des preuves qui ne laisseront aucun sujet d'en douter" (ib.).

Then why did he not either give in the letter or insert in the *Essay* the demonstration of the Unity of God of which he is so sure of being able to give an irrefutable proof? Because "J'aime la paix," Locke excuses himself, "et il y a des gens dans le monde qui aiment si fort les criailleries et les vaines contestations, que je doute si je dois fournir de nouveaux sujets de dispute" (ib.).

However, in the Latin post-script⁶¹ to the same letter in French and marked as personal to Limborch only, Locke allowed himself to go as far as this explicit declaration: "Putasne tamen quespiam, qui Deum agnoscit, posse dubitare Numen illud esse unicum? Ego sane nunquam dubitavi." Clearly Locke. if he had wished to be cautious or even reticent in the letter that Limborch would show to, and discuss with, his friends, felt unable to withhold this frank declaration of faith to the Arminian pastor and theologian, who on his side must have been well aware of Locke's true sentiments. But it is typical of Locke that he immediately added: "Sed hoc tibi soli dictum sit." Locke never felt that he could be too prudent.

3. In the meantime let us note that Locke has explicitly admitted that he has always been a unitarian or believed in the unity of God; that for Locke the unity of God can be rationally and irrefutably demonstrated; that the rational proof of the unity of God could have found a place in

---

60. The IVth ed. of the *Essay concerning Human Understanding* "with large additions," was printed by A. & J. Churchill and S. Manship in London towards the end of 1699 but dated 1700. For the "additions" inserted in this edition see A. CAMPBELL-FRASER, *An Essay conc. Hum. Underst. by J. Locke, collated and annot.* [...], Oxford, 1894, esp. Vol. I, p. 380; Vol. II, p. 129 n. 2; p. 131 n. 2.

61. Locke to Limborch, 29th October 1797 in *Some Fam. Let. = Locke's Works*, III, p. 625. It is reprinted below.

the *Essay Concerning Human Understanding;* and finally that the only reason why he did not insert this proof in the fourth edition of the *Essay* was for love of peace.

That Locke was timorous is well known; that he knew, as even Kant was to know and say later on, that if it is always necessary to say the truth it is not always necessary to speak,[62] is clearly the case here; but that from his point of view he was not entirely wrong, no one would wish to deny. It has already been stated above that in England acceptance of the dogma of the Trinity was required by law and Locke, after returning from Holland to England in the following of William and Mary, would not have put himself outside the law — *a partibus infidelium* — for anything in the world. It has also been stated that Stillingfleet had already uncovered, if not the Socinian roots of the *Essay Concerning Human Understanding* at least its convergence with socianism in its criticism of the Cartesian idea of substance.

Two years earlier Locke had complained to Molineux about the attack made on him by the Bishop of Worcester, who had accused Locke of atheism and Socinianism because of his criticism of innate ideas in the *Essay Concerning Human Understanding.* On that occasion he had been violently censured from the pulpit by the Bishop and did not even have the protection of anonymity that he had had when Edwards had attacked the *Reasonableness of Christianity.* "For a man of no small name," wrote Locke, "as you know Dr. S[tillingfleet][63] is, has been pleased to declare against my Doctrine of no innate Ideas, from the Pulpit in the Temple, and, as I have been told, charged it with little less than atheism [...] "My book," Locke went on, "crept into the world about six or seven years ago, without any opposition, and has since passed among some for useful, and, the least favorable, for innocent. But, as it seems to me, it is agreed by some men that it should no longer do so."[64] With Limborch and his friends Locke was more ex-

62. This expedient maxim, that sounds improbable coming from Kant, was found written in pencil on the margin of one of the philosopher's manuscripts of the categorical imperative, when this was censured during a disputation in the university faculty. It is referred to in the posthumous *Kant* by P. MARTINETTI which was edited by M. DAL PRA and published by Bocca of Turin more than 25 years ago, when I read the book. Now, at the time of writing, I no longer have the book available and ask the reader to excuse me for this summary reference.

63. Locke to Molineux, 22 Feb. 1697 in *Some Fam. Let.* = *Locke's Works,* III, p. 555. I have shown above (note 9) that the person referred to here is Stillingfleet and not Sherlock.

64. Locke to Molineux, cit. ib.

plicit: "Il y a sept ans que ce livre [*l'Essai conc. l'Entendement*] a été publié. La premiere, et la seconde édition ont eû le bonheur d'être generalement bien reçuës: mais la dernière n'a pas eû le même avantage. Après un silence de cinq ou six années on commence d'y découvrir je ne sais quelles fautes dont on ne s'étoit point aperçu auparavant; et ce qu'il y a de singulier, on prétend trouver matiere a des controverses de religion dans cet ouvrage, ou je n'ai eû dessin de traiter que de question de pure speculation philosophique."[65] But even if he is more explicit, he is no more truthful; in fact, knowing that the letter would be read by Limborch's friends, Locke says something that is definitely not true.

The fact is that Locke knew very well, even before the *Essay* was published in London, what sort of "controverses de religion" his book of so-called "pure speculation philosophique"[66] was going to encounter. So much so that when the *Abregé* in French of the *Essay* was published in the *Bibliotheque Universelle* of Le Clerc[67] in Holland in 1688 Locke left out the whole of the first book which dealt with the criticism of Descartes' innate ideas.

Locke justified this omission with a few words, but they were very revealing, especially as they appeared in the French translation of Le

65. Locke to Limborch, 29th Oct. 1697, in *Some Fam. Let. = Locke's Works*, III, p. 624.

66. All the same Locke could not escape from the fact that his radical denial of innate ideas and especially of the innate idea of God (*Essay concerning Human Understanding*, I, III, 8) and of substance (I, III, 19) could, as he himself said, appear to some people to overturn the "long-established foundations of knowledge and certainty" (ib. trans. Pellizzi). But he was honest in declaring that the aim of his investigation had only been the truth (ib.) without concerning himself in any way to leave or to follow any authority whatever (ib.) convinced as he was that if "we (human beings) proposed seeking the truth by following our own thoughts rather than those of others greater progress would be made in the knowledge of things" (ib.). The attack on the followers of Descartes was only too obvious even if it was extended to all those who in his day marched under the banner of Descartes or Aristotle. Still, Locke knew very well that he would be censured for over-turning the "long-established foundations of knowledge and certainty" by the Cartesians, whose leaders he accused of being authoritarian and whose disciples of being mentally lazy. So it was that he took good care, for the reasons we have already seen, not to publish in the *Abregé* of the *Essay* the book containing the criticism of innate ideas.

67. *Extrait d'un livre anglois qui n'est pas encore publié, intitulé Essai Philosophique concernant l'Entendement* [...] *comuniqué par Monsieur Locke* in *Bibliothèque Universelle et Historique*, Vol. VIII, Amsterdam, (Jan.) 1688), pp. 49-142. The original English text was published by LORD KING with the title *Abstract of the Essay* in *The Life of J. Locke* (cit. II, pp. 231-293).

Clerc,[68] which immediately calls to mind the words quoted above: "Mais j'aime la paix, et [...] je doute si je dois [...] fournir de nouveaux sujets de dispute."

"Dans les pensées que j'ai eues, concernant notre Entendement,"[69] the *Abrégé* began, "j'ai tâché d'abord de prouver que nôtre Esprit est au commencement ce qu'on appelle *tabula rasa;* c'est à dire, sans idées et sans connoissance. Mais comme ça n'a été que pour detruire les préjugez de quelques Philosophes, j'ai cru que dans ce petit *Abregé* de mes principes, je devois passer toutes les Disputes préliminaires, qui composent le premier Livre. Je prétends de montrer, dans le suivans, la source de laquelle nous tirons toutes les idées, qui entrent dans nos raisonnemens, et la manière dont elles nous viennent."

That the "source de laquelle nous tirons toutes les idées" is very different from the one postulated by Descartes and that "les quelques philosophes" whose prejudices he wanted to destroy are the Cartesians with their doctrine of innate ideas is only too obvious in spite of the covert way it is put forward. But the name of Descartes or Cartesianism or any other one that might have given rise to polemics is avoided not only here in the introduction but also in the body of the *Abregé* that has been cut hard.[70] The reason is that in Holland, as Moreri[71] had already shown and modern research has clearly brought to light,[72] the

68. For the linguistic variations between Locke's original manuscript and Le Clerc's translation into French see my article quoted above: *Locke's Epistola on Toleration from the Translation of Popple to that of Gough.*

69. *Extrait d'un livre* [...] *intitulé Essai Philosophique concernant l'Entendement* [...], cit. p. 49.

70. The reference is to the numerous omissions especially in Book II of the *Extract* which makes clear Locke's intention to avoid every possible cause for a dispute with the Cartesians of Holland.

71. *Le Grand Dictionnaire Historique ou le Mélange Curieux de l'Histoire Sacrée et Profane* [...] *par* LOUIS MORERI, XVIII ed., Amsterdam, MDCCXL, 8 Tomm. Sub. v. *Cartesius.* With the years the edition referred to has been enriched with numerous additions by many hands including that of Le Clerc. If, on the one hand, this has expanded Moreri's time scale, on the other it has made a considerable change in the spirit of the work, which started life as Catholic and was brought up to date by Protestants, Calvinists and Remonstrants. Nevertheless the *Grand Dictionnaire Historique* of Moreri is precious evidence of European culture at the end of the 17th century and the beginning of the 18th, especially of the religious disputes of the time.

72. See especially the valuable miscellany *Descartes et le cartesianisme hollandais. Etudes et Documents*, Paris-Amsterdam 1950, and the bibliographies quoted in each of the papers collected there. The study by J. YOLTON, *John*

philosophy of Descartes in general and the theory of inborn ideas in particular had become a matter of theological dispute, even during the life-time of Descartes. The dispute took place in the renowned schools and universities of Holland between Cartesians and anti-Cartesians, between reformers and traditionalists, and between theologians like Heidamus, Cocceius, and Vittich on one side and Voetius on the other.[73] This was so much the case that it has been rightly noted that the spread of Cartesian ideas in the United Provinces is due in the final analysis to the propaganda of the Cartesian theologians themselves.[74]

However, already with Heidamus, that is to say the first Cartesian theologian of Leyden, the Socinians are called to account and with them the Arminians from the time of the Synod of Dordrecht are accused of having favoured with their schism the entry into Holland of the Socinians.[75] Nobody but Bayle, making his own the accusation of the Gomarists, wrote these words: "Tous les Arminiens savans sont sociniens pour le moins [...] nos calvinistes se font un honneur et un merite de s'eloigner d'une secte qui est l'egout de tous les Athées, Deistes et Sociniens de l'Europe."[76] If these were the feelings that so strenuous a defender of religious liberty as Bayle[77] harboured towards the Arminians, how much less tender must have been the feelings of the Gomarists, implacable enemies as they were of the followers of Arminius.[78]

Locke and the Way of Ideas, Oxford 1956, pp. 1-71, is excellent for the story of the spread in Europe of the doctrine of Descartes and innate ideas.

73. Compare especially C.L THIJSSEN-SCHOUTE, *Le Cartesianisme aux Pays Bas*, in AA. VV., *Descartes et le cartésianisme hollandais*, op. cit. p. 183 et seq. and P. DIBON, *Note Bibliographique sur les Cartésiens hollandais*, in op. cit. p. 261 et seq.

74. P. DIBON, *Note Bibliographique sur les Cartésiens hollandais*, in *Descartes et le cartésianisme hollandais*, op. cit. p. 263 and p. 278.

75. Compare my *Introduction* to the *Letter concerning Toleration*, cit. p. XXIV-XXV and the accompanying notes where I put forward a conjecture which was then surreptitiously appropriated by other people. See also *Locke's Epistola on Toleration from the Translation of Popple to that of Gough*, note 1, about the Latin post-script to the *Epistola* on schism and heresy which seems to me to have been put in later at Limborch's request in defence of the Arminians who were being persecuted by the Gomarists or Counter-remonstrants because the latter held them to be schismatics and heretics.

76. P. BAYLE, *Oeuvres Diverses*, The Hague 1737, IV, p. 623.

77. On Bayle's intolerant attitude to the Arminians of Holland compare E. LABROUSSE, *P. Bayle*, I, The Hague, 1963, pp. 262-3.

78. See note 75 above.

Locke's criticsm of Cartesianism, especially if it started from an Arminian background such as the *Bilbiothèque Universelle* of Le Clerc, could therefore have provoked those who supported the theory of inborn ideas to a dangerous philosophic and theological argument which might even have put the continued existence of the Arminians in danger, and even have led to the risk of Locke being extradited, for the Arminians had welcomed him and hidden him in their homes.[79] Neither Le Clerc nor Limborch, who was the recognized spiritual head of the Arminians, and far less Locke himself, would have wanted to expose themselves to such a risk.[80] A summary of Book I of the *Essay on Human Understanding,* precisely because it would have caused these "controverses de religion" which it aroused when the complete edition of the work appeared with its criticism of Descartes theory of innate ideas, was therefore totally suppressed in the *Abregé* of the *Bibliothèque Universelle*; the text we read does not reflect what Locke would have liked to say freely but only what Locke limited himself to saying[81] out of a love of peace.

79. The fact that LIMBORCH'S *Theologia Christiana ad praxin pietatis ac promotionem pacis unice directa,* Amsterdam, 1686, had come out two years earlier without provoking too much uproar did not mean that, if the acceptance by the spiritual head of the Arminians of the "anti-innate" thesis was tolerated (*Theol. Christ.*, 1, 2, 5, and also note 81 below), the same toleration could be extended to the criticism of Descartes' innate ideas by the English philosopher who had taken refuge in Holland; the very profession of faith by the Arminians was the object of continuous censorship and condemnation, so acceptance of Locke's position with its theological implications would have brought support to the detested Arminian minority.

80. The hypothesis that Book I of the *Essay* was omitted from the *Abregé* of the *Bibliothèque Universelle* because the criticism of Descartes' innate ideas was directed to the Cambridge neo-platonists and therefore quite superfluous in an extract that appeared in Holland, as Carlini holds (CARLINI, *La Filosofia di Locke*, cit., II, pp. 25-26, and *Locke* — with an extensive selected anthology, Milan, 1969, p. 157 note 1) is totally unfounded and overlooks the real cultural and historic situation in Holland at the end of the 17th century especially the position of the Arminians in the philosophic and religious disputes raised by the penetration of Cartesian ideas into Holland.

81. Further to this point we can add that Cartesian theologians, especially those of Holland, no less than the neo-platonists of Cambridge and the Cartesians of Europe, were the target of Locke's polemic against innate ideas.

The very fact that Locke had thought it inopportune to include Book I of the *Essay* in the *Abregé* published in Holland shows in my view that Locke expected to be accused of having over-turned "the ancient foundations of knowledge and wisdom" (*Essay conc. Hum. Und.*, I, III, 24 cit.) more by the Dutch

4. If the *Abregé* lacks the first book of the *Essay* for the reasons set out above, the *Essay* in its turn lacks the demonstration of the Unity of God, which, as we have seen, Locke himself thought to include there. In fact, once denied the *a priori* nature of the ideas of infinity and substance and the idea of God itself, the very basis of the Cartesian ontological argument, and the empirical nature of these ideas demonstrated, the negation of the dogma of Transubstantiation and hence of the Sacrament of the Eucharist was implicit in the empirical nature of these ideas.

Stillingfleet will not have taken long to understand it, or at least to suspect it, even if, before accusing the author of the *Essay Concerning Human Understanding* openly of atheism and socinianism he waited for the confirmation of it through Toland's *Christianity not Mysterious*;[82]

---

theologians than by the Cambridge neo-platonists, and this in spite of the fact that there was no reaction in Holland to the complete London edition of the *Essay*, at least so long as Toland (see note 82 below) did not draw the attention of theologians to Locke's criticism of the theory of innate ideas.

Furthermore, and this is the nub, Limborch had already taken up his position against the Cartesian theologians, by making Locke's theory of the "tabula rasa" itself the basis of his *Theologia Christiana*: "verisimilius tamen nobis est, nullam homini ideam esse innatam, sed intellectum ejus in nativitate tabulae esse instar rasae: nullamque nos rei notitiam aut perceptionem, nisi ministerio sensuum, ope institutionis, aut ratiocinationis acquirere." LIMBORCH, *Theol. Christ.*, cit. 1, 2, 5.

But if Limborch was openly Arminian and Unitarian and, by reason of his cloth as spiritual head of the Remonstrants, ready and willing to fight for his faith and if necessary to suffer for it as his predecessors had done, Locke on the contrary was not at all happy to be taken for an Arminian or Unitarian and had quite a different idea of the vocation of a martyr. In reply therefore to the question that AARON (*J. Locke*, cit. p. 88) asks repeatedly as to the target of Locke's criticism of the theory of innate ideas, "Against whom is the polemic directed?" we would agree with his answer that "Locke's polemic was meant for the Cartesians, for the schoolmen, for certain members of the Cambridge Platonist, and for those others, Herbert and the rest, who advocated the theory of innate ideas in any way" (p. 94). However we would add to the number of those "who advocated the theory of innate ideas in any way" the Cartesian theologians of Holland, precisely because by eliminating the first book of the *Essay* from the *Abregé* he showed that he wished to avoid getting directly into an argument with them while, as a refugee in Holland, he had been received by the Arminians and was hidden among them.

82. JOHN TOLAND, *Christianity not Mysterious*, London, 1696. On Toland and his relations with Locke: see FOX BOURNE, *The Life of John Locke*, cit. II, pp. 415-9. Toland's book is nothing more than a re-working of Locke's

this came from the *Reasonableness,* where the denial of the consubstantiation of the Son with the Father was made more explicit.

Both the *Reasonableness* and the *Essay* in fact implied, though they did not demonstrate, the Unity of God, in spite of the fact that a difference of substance between the Son and the Father necessarily leads to the predicate of the unitary nature of God. In reality Locke had begun to prepare for that demonstration with a series of notes which are none other than these "cogitata" or reflections which, as he had written to Limborch, he was at the time dedicating to the *Scriptures* during the winter of 1694 in order to understand the true essence of the Christian religion which was later to be the aim of the *Reasonableness.*[83]

Of these "notes," which were collected by Lord King and published in the *Life of John Locke* under the title given them by Locke himself, namely *Adversaria Theologica,*[84] two are especially interesting for our purposes: – the one on the Trinity[85] and the one on the divine nature of Christ,[86] which as Lord King points out "may be considered [...] as indications of his opinions."[87] The arguments are handled as a series of contradictions: *Trinitas – non-Trinitas*; *Christus Deus supremus – Christus non-Deus supremus* and the arguments for and against are collected under the thesis or the antithesis.

Now, if in the comparison *Trinitas – non Trinitas* Locke quotes only four passages from the *Old Testament* in favour of the thesis, namely *Gen.* I, 26; II, 22; IX, 6; *Isaiah* VI, he quotes a large number of passages from the *New Testament* in favour of the anti-thesis: "The Father alone is the most high God" (*Luke* I, 32, 35); "the Lord our Lord, the Lord is one" (*Mark* XII, 29)[88] and so on. So he sets against *Genesis* I, 26 the first of the sources quoted in favour of the Trinity: "it subverteth the

Reasonableness and inspired by the doctrines of the *Essay* carried to extreme Unitarian and Socianian conclusions. Hence Stillingfleet's polemic in which he associated Locke with Toland, "the gentlemen of this new way of Reasoning, that have almost discarded Substance out of the reasonable part of the World," (cit.) in the same accusation of socinianism.

83. See above p. 181 n. 22, and the letter of Locke to Limborch dated 10 May 1695 (cit. at note 22).

84. [JOHN LOCKE] *Adversaria Theologica,* from LORD KING, *The Life of John Locke* (cit. II, pp. 186-194).

85. *Adversaria Theologica, Trinitas-Non Trinitas* (from op. cit. pp. 187-9).

86. *Adversaria Theologica, Christus Deus Supremus-Christus non-Deus Supremus* (from op. cit. pp. 190-4).

87. LORD KING, *The Life of John Locke,* cit. II, p. 187.

88. *Adversaria Theologica,* cit. p. 187.

Unity of God, introducing three Gods."[89] In this way it becomes quite clear that what really interested Locke was not so much the research into the sources that were for or against the Trinity as the textual confirmation of the thesis of Unity at which he had already arrived and to which he already sincerely adhered. For the rest, had not Locke himself already confessed: "Ego sane numquam dubitavi [...] Numen illud [Deum] esse unicum?"[90] And it was precisely the unity of God that he was preparing to demonstrate when meditating on, and writing the *Reasonableness*. That is also shown by the contradiction: *Christus Deus Supremus – Christus non-Deus Supremus*, where the antithetical argument by distinguishing the Son from the Father, denies the Son consubstantiation with the Father: "He [Christus] is not equal to God"; "the Father is greater than he."[91] Christ, in fact, is only the Messiah and the Trinity a dogma against the evidence of the Scripture.[92]

However of these notes and of this careful biblical research which aimed at confirming the thesis of God's unity, and to which the discussion on the nature of Christ should logically have led, no trace remains in the *Reasonableness*. This book presupposes God's unity or takes it as understood and stops short of the point where Christ is reduced to the Messiah. Thus it avoids all discussion of the dogma of the Trinity, assent to which was required by law, as has been stated above. The reason for this was once again to avoid giving anyone who wanted it a pretext to drag Locke into other arguments and controversies. In short, it was the love of peace that brought the man to keep quiet about what the philosopher really thought.

Yet, even if Locke avoided setting out the textual proof of the unity of God in his books and kept quiet about, or even denied being a Unitarian, in his heart of hearts, as we have seen, he had not the slightest doubt that God was One; so much so that, when pressed by Limborch, he finally resolved to give, with his habitual secrecy, the demonstration of the unity of God that should have found a place in the *Essay on Human Understanding* and which he had prepared himself to give, but then did not give, in the *Reasonableness of Christianity*.

89. *Adversaria Theologica*, cit. ib.
90. See above page 190 and note 60.
91. *Adversaria Theologica*, cit. p. 190.
92. "Hc [Christus] is the Son of the most High, LUK. I, 32, and thereby distinguished from the most High [...] JOHN., XVI, 28." *Adversaria Theologica*, cit. p. 190.

5. Limborch delayed a long time in replying to Locke's letter of the 29th October, 1697, that is to say until the 11th March of the following year.[93] "Gratissimas tuas, 29 Octobris scriptas, recte accepi, viroque magnifico, ruius potissimum rogatu ad te scripsi, praelegi. Re ipsa de qua quaeritur a nemine sano in dubium vocari posse videtur: ipsa enim deitatis notio unitatem involvit, nec permittit, ut illa pluribus communis credi possit. Quare, me judice, nemo qui attente secum considerat quid voce Dei intelligamus, pluralitatem Deorum asserere potest".[94]

Limborch had no need to affirm his unitarian faith to Locke, to whom it was certainly already well known; but, in my view, if he does so here, it is only to overcome Locke's reluctance to give finally those proofs of the unity of God, which Locke had said he could give, by assuring him "sub promisso silentii," in order to make him better disposed, that whatever he said would not become either the material for argument or, much less, for dissemination.[95]

In renewing the prayer of the "vir magnificus" to Locke, Limborch formulates the question he puts as follows: "Requirit argumenta vir magnificus quibus solide demonstretur Ens independens et perfectum unicum tantum esse posse. Ex solide adstructa essentiae divinae unitate porro facili negotio omnia attributa divina, nostrumque tam erga Deum quam proximum officium deduci posse certissimus est."[96]

The "great person," Limborch adds, "Cartesium dicit unitatem illam non probasse, sed presupposuisse" and that he himself is searching for a demonstration of the unity of God "ipse sibi demonstrationem scripsit, sed eam aiebat subtiliorem esse" and that nevertheless "tua argumenta avidissime videre aiebat."[97]

In a later letter of 1st April[98] Limborch states the question of the "vir magnificus" rather differently: "Argumentum desiderat, quo probetur Ens, cuius existentia est necessaria, tantum posse esse unum; et quidem ut id argumentum a necessitate existentia desamatur, et a priori (ut in scholis leguntur) non a posteriori concludat, hoc est, ex

93. Limborch-Locke, 11 March 1698, in *Some Fam. Let.* = *Locke's Works*[1], III, pp. 625-26.
94. Limborch-Locke, cit. p. 625.
95. Limborch-Locke, cit. ib.
96. Limborch-Locke, cit. ib.
97. Limborch-Locke, cit. ib.
98. Limborch-Locke, 1st April 1698 in *Some Fam. Let.* = *Locke's Works*[1], III, pp. 627-628.

natura necessariae existentiae probetur eam pluribus non posse esse communem."[99]

Clearly the initial terms of the question are no longer the same. Locke was in fact being asked for "argumenta irrefragabilia" which would prove how the Eternal Being, existing in itself and perfect in every way, was of a necessity one, or in other words, that Locke should make explicit the unity of God which was presupposed in the attributes of the existence of God set out in the *Essay Concerning Human Understanding* and that, once deduced, the proof of the unity should be inserted in its place to complete and clarify the argument of the existence of God in the next edition of the *Essay*. Now, instead, he was being asked for a proof which was no longer the one presupposed, but not given, in the *Essay*, but rather another one, the one that is to say that the anonymous person wanted in conformity with his own different statement of the problem; this proof should proceed not from the divine attributes but rather "a necessitate existentiae desumatur": this was tantamount to wishing that Locke was a different philosopher from the one he had shown himself to be in the *Essay*. Locke's reply is dated the 2nd April[100] and so was unaware of this new formulation to which Limborch was to return in the next letter.

In publishing this second reply from Locke I have once again preferred to use the Bodleian manuscript (Mss. Locke c. 24 fs 158[r]-160[v]) including a passage erased from the letter which was sent to Limborch.

In replying to Limborch, Locke did not attempt a formulation of the proof of God's unity conforming to the expectation of the "great person", but rather made clear with his reply that he aimed at establishing for his enlightenment a useful comparison between the proof, which he believed he could arrive at in accord with the demonstration of the existence of God given in the *Essay*, and the other one reached, or thought to have been reached, by the "personne d'un genie si vaste." At the same time he insisted that Limborch should undertake to destroy his letter if he should ever ask him to do so. In fact Locke puts three precise conditions to Limborch for the demonstration of the unity of God which he was preparing to give: "La première, que

---

99. Limborch-Locke, cit. p. 628.
100. Locke-Limborch, 2 Apr. 1698 in *Some Fam. Let.* = *Locke's Works*[1], pp. 628-30.

200

que ces Messieurs me promettront de m'apprendre librement et sincerement leurs pensées sur ce que je dis: la seconde, que vous me promettez de jetter cette lettre au feu quand je vous prierai de le faire. A quoi je serois bien aisé que vous eussiez la bonté d'ajouter une troisième condition, c'est, que ces Messieurs me feront l'honneur de me communiquer les raisons sur lesquelles ils établissent eux mêmes l'Unité de Dieu."[101]

After that Locke re-states the question to be discussed in the following terms: "La question dont vous me parlez, se reduit a ceci, Comment l'Unité de Dieu peut être prouvée? ou en d'autres termes, Comment on peut prouver qu'il n'y a qu'un Dieu?"

Obviously, this was not what was wanted from Locke, who had been asked to make explicit the unity that Descartes had postulated but not demonstrated when he had put forward the idea of the Being existing in itself and necessarily. But Locke, who had briefly dealt with the argument in the passage of the letter that he later erased, had decided to do no more than set out his own proof of the Unity of God that was consistent with the premises formulated in the Essay and without entering the terrain to which the other man invited him. Above all he was not going to name Descartes or talk about him and the concept of substance.

"L'idée ordinaire, et à ce que je croi, la veritable idée qu'ont de Dieu ceux qui reconnoissent son existence," Locke wrote, "c'est qu'il est un Etre infini, eternel, incorporel et tout parfait. Or cette idée, une fois reconnue, il me semble fort aisé d'en deduire l'unité de Dieu. En effet un Etre qui est tout parfait, or pour ainsi dire, parfaitement parfait, ne peut être qu'unique; parce qu'un Etre tout parfait ne sauroit manquer d'aucun des attributs, perfections ou dégrez de perfections, qu'il luy importe plus de posseder, que d'en être privé. [...] Par la même idée de perfection nous venons à connoître, que Dieu est Omniscient. [...] On peut dire la même chose de la toute-presence de Dieu [...].[102]

In other words, Locke, re-tracing the arguments of the passage cut out of the first letter, answers the question which he himself had formulated, that is to say, that whoever admits the existence of God and admits at the same time that God is infinite, eternal, incorporeal, entirely perfect, omniscient, etc. admits thereby that God is one and

101. Locke-Limborch, cit. p. 628.
102. Locke-Limborch, cit. p. 629.

can only be one since the infinite, the incorporeal, the entirely perfect and the omniscient cannot be but one by virtue of each of these attributes. The Unity of God is therefore proved by Locke from God's own attributes. "Donc," Locke concludes, "il n'y a, ni ne saurait y avoir deux tout puissans, ni par conséquent deux Dieux. [...] Car de supposer deux êtres intelligens, qui connoissent, veulent et font incessamment la même chose, et qui n'ont pas une existence séparée, c'est supposer, en paroles, une pluralité, mais poser effectivement une simple unité."[103]

When Limborch had received Locke's reply, he discussed it with the person who had asked the question. It was only to be expected that the latter would not be satisfied: he wanted the unity of God to be deduced only after the necessity of God's existence had been proved. For Locke, instead, once the existence of God and his attributes had been admitted, the concept of his Unity followed self-evidently. The two positions turned out to be opposites from the beginning: for the "vir magnificus" the unity of God needed a prior rational demonstration of the existence of God; for Locke, on the other hand, the existence of God was taken as evident and his unity was subsequently deduced from his attributes.

"Verum ille querit argumentum non ex definitione Dei desumptum," Limborch insisted, "sed ex ipsa rationi naturali et per quod deducamur in definitionem Dei." Locke replied briefly on the 21st May, 1698 with the third letter which is printed below[105] (Mss. Locke c. 24 f 164^{IV}) and excuses himself for not having clearly understood, not the question but "le but de cet habil homme"; in his reply he did not in fact add anything new to what he had already written: on the contrary he repeats the argument he had previously given to prove the Unity of God: "Je croy que quiconque reflechira sur soy même, connoitra evidemment sans en pouvoir douter le moins du monde, qu'il y a eu de toute éternité un Etre intelligent. Je croy encore qu'il est evident à tout homme qui pense, qu'il y a aussi un Etre infini. Or je dis qu'il ne peut y avoir qu'un Etre infini, et que cet Etre infini doit être aussi l'Etre éternel; parce que, ce qui est infini doit avoir été infini de toute

103. Locke-Limborch, cit. ib.
104. Limborch-Locke, 16 May 1698 in *Some Fam. Let.* = *Locke's Works*[1], III, p. 630.
105. Locke-Limborch, 21 May 1698, in *Some Fam. Let.* = *Locke's Works*[1], III, p. 632.

éternité, car aucunes additions faites dans le temps, ne sauroient rendre une chose infinie, si elle ne l'est pas en elle même et pour elle même, de toute éternité. Telle étant la nature de l'infini qu'on n'en peut rien ôter, et qu'on n'y peut rien ajouter, d'où il suit que l'infini ne sauroit être separé en plus d'un, ni etre qu'un. C'est là, selon moi, une preuve *à priori* que l'Etre éternel independent n'est qu'un; et si nous y joignons l'idée de toutes les perfections possibles, nous avons l'idée d'un Dieu eternel, infini, omniscient et tout-puissant etc."[106]

To follow the discussion any further, now become a dialogue between deaf people, is of no interest to our purposes. For us it is enough to take account of the proof that Locke has given and clinched, careless of whether that proof was the one the others wanted him to give; that if he had done this, we could even have suspected that it was a matter of intellectual gymnastics that he did not take seriously; but this is not the case. Here we will add, in order to conclude, only that Locke became irritated by the persistence of the person in whose name Limborch questioned him without ever, on his side, deciding to give, as he had been asked to do, his proof of the Unity of God. Since he, Locke, had clearly given what he believed to be an *a priori* proof of the Unity of God; then let the bigwig give his, as had been agreed: "Rogo ut magnificum virum meo nomine adeas," wrote Locke to Limborch, "dicasque me magnopere rogare ut suam methodum, qua unitate entis per se existentis sibi que sufficientis adstruit, mihi indicare velit: quandoquidem mea ea de re argumentandi ratio ipsi non penitus satisfaciat."[107] But the "vir magnificus" in the end never gave his proof of the Unity of God for which Locke had asked him and we have perhaps lost nothing. At any rate we should be grateful to him for having induced Locke to give his own proof of the Unity of God and so for having led him to make a revelation of great interest for the understanding of his work.

6. If we now re-read Chapter X of Book IV of the *Essay Concerning Human Understanding*,[108] it will become clear to us that Locke has set out his own proof of the Unity of God and has done so with exact

---

106. Locke-Limborch, 21 May 1698, cit. p. 632 and below p. 218-219.
107. Locke-Limborch, 4-18 Oct. (1698) in *Some Fam. Let.* = *Locke's Works*[1], III, p. 634.
108. JOHN LOCKE, *An Essay concerning Human Understanding* = *Locke's Works*[1], I, pp. XXVIII-342.

conformity to the rational demonstration of the existence of God, which is the very subject of Chapter X of Book IV of the *Essay*.

Here Locke had assumed that God had not given us any innate idea of himself (*Essay* I, III, 8, 11 seq) but instead had provided us with sense, perception and reason, and hence the faculties needed to discover Him and to know Him, and so there was no need to go "farther than ourselves, and that undoubted knowledge we have of our own existence" (*Essay*, IV, X, 1). On the contrary, "from the consideration of ourselves, and what we infallibly find in our constitutions, our reason leads us to the knowledge of this certain and evident truth: that there is an Eternal, most powerful, and most knowing Being" (IV, X, 6), immaterial or thinking (IV, X, 11). "This discovery of the necessary existence of an eternal Mind," Locke concludes, "does sufficiently lead us into the knowledge of God" and of "all his attributes" (IV, X, 12).

Now, in giving Limborch the proof of the Unity of God, Locke comes once more to the following conclusion, which he had already reached in the *Essay* when starting from "the consideration of our selves", almost as if he was taking up a discourse briefly interrupted: "L'idée de Dieu sur laquelle j'ai raisonné" [in *Essay Concerning Human Understanding* IV, X, esp. 1-12], Locke in fact wrote in the deleted portion of the first letter, "c'est celle d'un Etre Eternel, tout-Puissant et Omniscient. Ces attributs, étant une fois reconnus en Dieu, nous conduisent aisement, si je ne me trompe, à l'Unité de Dieu. Car si Dieu est tout-puissant et Omniscient, je ne croy pas qu'il puisse entrer dans l'esprit d'une personne raisonnable qu'il puisse y avoir deux Etres de cette nature" (folios 156^r-156^v).

And in the second letter, picking up the same line of thought, he continued (folios 158^r-159^r): "En effet un être qui est tout parfait ou, pour ainsi dire, parfaitement parfait, ne peut être qu'unique, parce qu'un être tout parfait ne sauroit manquer d'aucun des attributs, perfections ou degréz de perfections." Of such, "l'être tout puissant" can be only one: "deux êtres tout puissans sont incompatibles; parce qu'on est obligé de supposer que l'un doit vouloir necessairement ce que l'autre veut; et en ce cas-là, l'un des deux, dont la volonté est nécessairement determinée par la volonté de l'autre, n'est pas libre [...] Donc, l'un des deux n'est pas tout-puissans. Donc il n'y a, ni ne sauroit y avoir deux tout-puissans, ni par conséquent, deux Dieux." Similarly omniscience can only be predicated from unity. "Par la même idée de perfection nous venons à connoitre que Dieu est omni-

scient. Or dans la supposition de deux êtres distincts qui ont un pouvoir et une volonté distincte, c'est une imperfection de ne pouvoir pas cacher ses pensées. Mais si l'un des deux cache ses pensées à l'autre, cet autre n'est pas omniscient, car non seulement il ne connoit pas tout ce qui peut être connu, mais il ne connoit pas même ce qu'un autre connoit. On peut dire la même chose de la toute-presence de Dieu [...] car de supposer deux êtres intelligens, qui connoissent, veulent et font incessamment la même chose, et qui n'ont pas une existence separée, c'est supposer, en paroles, une pluralité, mais poser effective- ment une simple unité."

This "preuve *a priori* que l'Etre éternel independent n'est qu'un," is hence deduced from the self-same nature of the attributes of God that were predicated in the *Essay*, attributes that by their very nature contradicted the idea of plurality, necessarily predicate the Unity of God. Hence the Unity, which is implied and understood in the *Essay*, is here made explicit and clear for the first time.

If this is so, we should have no difficulty in considering the three letters, which Locke wrote to Limborch and which we publish here, as being a coherent and integral conclusion to Chapter X of Book IV of the *Essay* and also the proof of the Unity of God as an inevitable inference from the knowledge of the existence of God which is its subject, and finally we should have no difficulty in considering the proof of the Unity of God as the one which could have been placed in this chapter of the *Essay* and which Locke left out for the sake of peace.

Can we then speak of Locke as being simply a Unitarian? I would say yes; simply a Unitarian and a Socinian as his contemporaries had supposed and suspected him of being; as modern scholars had correctly inferred not only from the *Reasonableness* but also from the "rational- ism" of Locke; and as these three letters, written by Locke to Limborch bear unequivocal witness for the first time.

With the proof of the Unity of God, deduced from the conclusion at which he had arrived in the *Essay* where he deals with the knowledge of God, Locke has given a different shape or rather has made the theological and religious mould of his thought more intelligible. He has also made much clearer the influence exercised on him by the continuous contact he had first with English unitarian and socinian circles and then with Dutch ones, and in particular with Arminian theology that he met for the first time in Grotius' *De Veritate Christianae Religionis*[109] and then in Limborch's *Theologia Christiana*

which he deeply imbibed and which Limborch had written under Locke's own eyes[110] and during long discussions with him.[111]

This is, at any rate, a proof that shows that even if Locke wanted to remain in his faith and, so to speak, faithful to his Church, Arminian influence had all the same carried him across the tenuous and movable boundaries that might still have existed between Latitudinarianism and Socinianism and beyond further into the Unitarian and Socinian field than he was prepared to admit.

But Locke has also given us a proof by his puzzling reticence which bears witness to the inner drama of Locke, the man who does not acknowledge what he really is, who denies in public what the philosopher thinks in secret, and who, in short refuses to recognize himself in his own thoughts.

But if, as we believe, by knowing the man better, we better understand the philosopher, then by knowing the weaknesses of Locke, the man we can better know the thinking of Locke, the philosopher.

109. Locke was familiar with Grotius' *De Veritate Christianae Religionis* (see W. Von Leyden app. JOHN LOCKE, *Essays on the Law of Nature* [...], ed. W. VON LEYDEN, Oxford, 1954. Intr. p. 20).

110. It has been stated earlier that Limborch's *Theologia Christiana* was published in Amsterdam in 1686, that is to say three years after Locke's arrival in Holland and the start of the association between the two men.

111. See Limborch's letter to Lady Masham dated 24th March 1705 (Mss. R.L. III D. 16-54): "[...] often visited him [Locke] in his solitude and conversed with him for many hours at a time," quoted by CRANSTON, *J. Locke* (cit. p. 253). On the reciprocal influence of these conversations comp. VIANO, *J. Locke* (cit. p. 378 et seq.); my *Introduction* to the *Letter concerning Toleration* (cit. p. XIX); BARNOUW, *Philip van Limborch* (cit. pp. 136-137), has pointed out Limborch's refusal of the theory of innate ideas of Descartes (*Theol. Christ.*, Books 1, 2, 5) as being clearly influenced "van zijn vriend Locke." But how much more Locke may have drawn on Arminian theological thought has been clearly shown by VIANO, *Locke* (cit., esp. p. 378 et seq.).

BIBLIOGRAPHICAL NOTE

The three letters written by Locke to Limborch published here bear the dates: London 29th Oct. 1697; Oates 2nd April 1698; and Oates 21st May 1698.

They were first published in *Some Familiar Letters between Mr. Locke and several of his friends,* (Print. for A. and J. Churchill, London, 1708), based on the originals in the possession of Limborch.

The *Familiar Letters* were then included in Vol. III of the first edition of the complete works of Locke: *The Works of John Locke Esqu.,* 3 Vols., London, Print for John Churchill at the Black Swan, in Pater-Noster-Row, MDCCXIV, respectively at pp. 624-625; pp. 628-630 and p. 632.

Le Clerc reprinted them and also translated into French the Latin letters to which Locke had replied: *Lettres diverses de Mr. Locke et de Mr. de Limborch, contenant quelques remarques sur deux Livres intitulez, le Christianisme Raisonnable et Essai concernant l'Entendement Humain,* added to the II ed. (I ed., Rotterdam, 1710) of the *Oeuvres Diverses de Monsieur Locke. Nouvelle Edition considérablement augmentée,* 2 Tomm., Amsterdam, chez Jean Frederic Bernard, MDCCXXXII, Vol. II respectively at pp. 263-268; pp. 277-285; pp. 293-296.

In the *Avertissement* to this second edition of Locke's *Oeuvres Diverses,* Le Clerc wrote as follows: "Les lettres, roulant sur deux sujets très importants, l'unité de Dieu et la liberté de l'homme, l'on peut considérer comme des eclaircissements utiles sur les matières les plus graves qui sont traitées dans l'*Essai concernant l'Entendement*" (*Avertissement,* cit. p. X).

The same three letters of Locke to Limborch are found in all the editions of *Locke's Works,* but, unless I am mistaken, they have never attracted the attention of scholars. Carlini, who looked at them, decided that they were quite without interest as their content was alien to Locke's thinking and the subject of a fortuitous and passing discussion. "The question was outside his system." A. CARLINI, *La Filosofia di J. Locke,* 2 Vols., Florence, 1928, I, p. LXII.

As far as I am aware, the first time these three letters were considered in a critical context that aimed at establishing Locke's religious thinking with lengthy passages of the first and second letter, was in my note: *Il socinianesimo di Locke e l'edizione inglese dell'Epistola sulla Tolleranza,* in the proceedings of the Accademia di Scienze Morali e Politiche of the Società Nazionale di Scienze, Lettere ed Arti, Naples, 1967; Vol. LXXVIII, pp. 30 of the extract, reprinted here as *The Socinianism of John Locke and the English edition of the Letter*

207

concerning Toleration, pp. 125-152.

Now in publishing the three letters of Locke to Limborch on the Unity of God in their entirety, instead of the printed editions based, as I have said above, on the letters owned by Limborch, I have used the drafts of each one written in French in Coste's own hand. These drafts, especially the first two, and in particular the first one, are fuller and more binding than the letters actually sent to Limborch. They are now in the Bodleian library of Oxford, where they are classified as follows:

I. Letter of Locke to Limborch, dated 29 October 1697. Mss. LOCKE c. 24 ff. 156^r-157^v; the draft in English is missing.

II. Letter of Locke to Limborch, dated 2 April 1698, Mss. LOCKE c. 24 ff. 158^r-166^v; draft in English in Locke's own hand, ib. 163^r.

III. Letter of Locke to Limborch, dated 21st May 1968, Mss. LOCKE c. 24 f. 164^{rv}, draft in English in Locke's own hand, ib. 163^r.

In the margin of page 157^v of the French draft of letter I there is this note in Locke's hand: "*Ib. All contained between the crochet p. 1 and this bar was omitted in letter I sent.*"

At the foot of the French draft of letter II, there is a note in Locke's hand which reads: "*J.L. to P. Limborch 21 feb. 1697-8,*" — this was later corrected in another hand: "*the date of present letter is April 2*" which is confirmed by the letter Limborch received. However, in the margin of page 158^r there is a note in Locke's hand which corrects the mistake made in the footnote: "*what is between this and the following bracket was omitted in my second letter of 2 April.*"

In this edition the passages between square brackets are those Locke struck out of the letters sent to Limborch. Square brackets to signify deletion were used by Locke himself.

As for the transcription of the manuscripts, I have limited myself to the smallest possible number of changes to the text except in a few points of little importance.

I am indebted to Mrs M. Clapinson, Assistant Keeper of Western Manuscripts at the Bodleian Library of Oxford for the photocopies of the three letters published here and take the opportunity to thank her publicly for her kindness.

London, Christmas 1973   M.M.

[The same three letters to Limborch by Locke on the Unity of God have recently been published by E. De Beer in his edition of the Locke's Letters, *The Correspondence of John Locke* in eight volumes, vol. VI, Oxford, 1981.

The first letter, dated 29th October 1697, on pp. 243-244 and in Appendix II, pp. 783-787; the second dated 28th April 1698, which De Beer dates 31st January 1698, on pp. 321-326, whilst the draft in English appears in Appendix II, pp. 788-791; the third letter dated May 21st 1698, on pp. 405-406 and the English draft in Appendix II, p. 791.

On this matter and for some of my objections see in this volume *The Correspondence of John Locke*, p. 221 ss. and *The Rational evidence of the Unity of God in the Correspondence of John Locke*, p. 227 ss.]

FIRST LETTER OF JOHN LOCKE TO
PHILIP VAN LIMBORCH

Monsieur,

Mss. Locke
c. 24 f. 156ʳ Si mon nom est venu à la connoissance de ces habiles gens avec qui vous vous entretenez quelque fois, et s'ils daignent parler des mes Escrits dans les conversations que vous avez avec eux, c'est une faveur dont je vous suis entièrement redevable. La bonne opinion que vous avez d'une personne que vous voulez bien honorer de vôtre amitié les a prévenus en ma faveur. Je souheterois que mon *Essai concernant l'Entendement* fût écrit dans une Langue que ces excellents hommes pussent entendre, car par le jugement exact et sincère qu'ils porteroient de mon Ouvrage je pourrois compter sûrement sur ce qu'il y a de vray ou de faux et sur ce qu'il peut y avoir de tolérable.

Il y a sept ans que ce Livre a été publié. La première, et la seconde édition ont eû le bonheur d'être généralement bien reçuës: mais la dernière n'a pas eû le même avantage. Après un silence de cinq ou six années on commence d'y découvrir je ne sçais quelles fautes dont on ne s'étoit point apperçu auparavant, et ce qu'il y a de singulier, on prétend trouver matière à des controverses de Religion dans cet Ouvrage où je n'ai eû dessein de traiter que des questions de pure spéculation Philosophique.

J'avois resolu de faire quelques additions, dont j'ai déjà composé quelques unes qui sont assex amples, et qui auroient pû paroître en leur place dans la quatrième Edition que le Libraire se dispose à faire. Et j'aurois volontier satisfait à votre désir ou au désir d'aucun de vos amys en y insérant les preuves de l'unité de Dieu qui se présentent à mon esprit. Car je suis enclin à croire que l'Unité de Dieu peut être aussi évidemment démonstrée que son existence; et qu'elle peut être establie sur des preuves qui ne laisseront aucun sujet d'en douter. Mai j'aime la Paix, et il y a des gens dans le monde qui aiment si fort les criailleries et les vaines contestations que je doute, si je doit leur fournir de nouveaux sujets de dispute.

[A l'egard de cette question qui vous a été faite par quelqu'un dans cette conférence, si je n'avois point dit quelque chose dans mon Livre touchant l'unité de Dieu, Vous aurez la bonté de luy faire sçavoir que je n'en ai rien dit, et cela pour deux raisons. La première parce que cela

était hors d'oeuvre, comme il le verra luy même, s'il voit jamais mon Ouvrage. La seconde parce que je n'ai point crû qu'il fût nécessaire de mettre cela en question. L'idée de Dieu sur laquelle j'ai raisonné, c'est celle d'un Etre Eternel tout Puissant et *Omniscient.* Ces attributs ‖ c. 24 f. 156ᵛ étant une fois reconnus en Dieu, nous conduisent aisément, si je ne me trompe, à l'unité de Dieu. Car si Dieu est tout puissant et *Omniscient,* je ne croy pas qu'il puisse entrer dans l'esprit d'une personne raisonnable, qu'il puisse y avoir deux Etres de cette nature.

Je ne veux pas appuyer sur l'opposition qu'il peut y avoir entre deux puissances lors qu'elles se rencontrent dans deux Etres Intelligens, qui existent indépendemment l'un de l'autre. Je ne veux pas presser non plus plusieurs autres difficultéz qui naîtroient de la supposition de deux Etres, tels que celui que cette idée de Dieu présente à l'Esprit.

Le raisonnement dont je me servirai présentement pour établir l'unité de Dieu, sera fondé sur la manière par laquelle nous venons à connoître qu'il y a un Dieu, car elle suffit, ce me semble, pour fair voir qu'il est absurde d'admettre plus d'un Dieu. Nous ne connoissons point Dieu par la considération directe de sa nature, et nous ne sçaurions le connoître de cette espèce de connoissance. Mais tout ce que nous pouvons connoître de luy, ne nous vient qu'à la faveur de quelques réflections obscures et imparfaites que nous sommes portéz à faire sur ce Souverain Etre par la considération des Créatures, c'est à dire que par les choses que nous voyons et que nous apparcevons, nous élevons nos pensées à celui qui les a faites.

Or si nous ne pouvons nous empêcher de penser qu'il n'y a qu'un Etre tout puissant qui puisse produire un Etre pensant (car je ne veux pas parler présentement de la Création de la Matière, ni de l'ordre et de la Beauté de ce Monde visible) je dois conclure que l'Etre qui m'a fait est tout puissant. Que si je suis parvenu une fois à découvrir l'existence d'un Etre tout puissant, il est contre la raison de supposer un autre Etre tout puissant, puis qu'un seul Etre tout puissant peut faire autant que cent. Enfin puis que nous ne cherchons à nous assurer de l'existence d'un Dieu, que pour régler le culte et l'obéissance que nous luy devons rendre, il est absurde lors que nous sommes assuréz de l'existence d'un Dieu, d'en admettre plusieurs, et de mettre par là sa Souveraineté et son honneur en question.

Mais peut être que ce sçavant homme qui m'oblige à vous parler sur cette matière, s'imaginera que cet argument est purement moral et que n'étant point fondé originairement sur la nature de la chose il n'est point demonstratif, mais tout au plus probable. Soit: Mais je ne laisse

211

f. 157ʳ pas de croire qu'un tel raisonnement doit suffir pour contenter toute ||
personne raisonnable, si l'on fait réflexion sur le peu d'étendu et sur
la foiblesse de nôtre Entendement dans cette vie.

Nos facultéz sont proportionées à l'usage que nous en pouvons faire
pour vivre dans ce monde et pour y servir Dieu en gens de bien πρὸς
ξωὴν καὶ εὐσεβές. Ce n'est que dans cette vue qu'elles nous ont été
données. Et dans le fonds je doute si jamais nos Esprits auront assez
d'étenduë et de lumière pour connoître Dieu tel qu'il est en luy même.
Quoy qu'il en soit, pour dire quelque chose de plus sur la question de
l'unité de Dieu, je croy qu'on m'accordera que Dieu est présent par
tout. S'il n'est point présent part tout, il ne sçauroit connoître ce qui
se fait dans d'autres parties de cet Univers différentes de celles où il est
renfermé, et il ne peut point remédier à ce qui y peut arriver contre ces
interêts ou au préjudice de cette partie qu'il a faite et sur laquelle il
préside, ce qui donneroit l'idée d'un Etre fort imparfait. Si donc Dieu
a une toute-puissance infinie, je croy qu'on peut prouver par là démonstrativement, ou peut s'en faut, qu'il ne peut y avoir qu'un Dieu.

Quoy que soit Dieu; quelle que soit sa nature, son Etre, ou sa Substance, il est certain que c'est quelque chose de réel, et de plus réel que
tous les autres Etres. Supposons donc que cet Etre réel existe dans
quelque point physique de l'Espace qu'on voudra supposer, je dis qu'il
s'ensuit démonstrativement de là qu'un autre Etre réel de la même
espèce ne sçauroit être dans le même point individuel de l'Espace, car
en ce cas là il n'y auroit qu'un seul être dans ce point, parce que là où
il n'y a aucune différence ni à l'égard de l'espèce, ni à l'égard du lieu,
il ne peut y avoir qu'un seul être.

Et qu'on ne s'imagine pas que ce raisonnement ne peut être bon
qu'à l'égard du corps et des parties de ma Matière, car on peut, je pense,
l'appliquer à ce qu'on appelle l'*Espace pur*, qui est ce qu'il y a de plus
éloigné de la matière. Car deux points physiques d'espace, ne peuvent
pas plutôt être reduits en un, que deux atomes physiques de matière
être reduits à un seul. La raison de cette impossibilité est fondée sur ce
que si deux points d'espace pouvoient être un, tout l'espace pouroit
être réduit en un seul point physique, ce qui est aussi impossible, qu'il
est impossible que toute la matière pût être réduite à un seul atome.
Pour moy qui ne connois pas ce que c'est que la substance de la
matière, je connois encore moins ce que c'est que la substance de Dieu,
mais je sçais pourtant que cette Substance est quelque chose, et qu'elle
doit exclure d'où elle est toutes les autres substances de la même
espèce, (s'il pouvoit y en avoir de telles). Si donc Dieu est immense

et présent partout, c'est pour moy une ‖ démonstration qu'il n'y a
qu'un Dieu et qu'il n'en peut y avoir qu'un seul.

Je me suis hazardé à vous faire part de mes pensées sur ce sujet,
comme elles se sont presentées à mon esprit, sans les ranger dans un
certain ordre qui pourroit servir peut être à les mettre dans un plus
grand jour si on leur donnoit un peu plus d'étenduë; mais je me serois
donné de la peine inutilement ayant à faire à une personne d'une aussi
grande pénétration que vous. Telles que sont ces pensées je vous prie de
me dire ce que vous en croyez, afin que selon le jugement que vous
en ferez je puisse pour ma propre satisfaction les examiner de nouveau
et leur donner plus de force que ma mauvaise santé et le peu de loisir
que j'ai ne me permettent de faire présentement, ou bien les abandonner
tout-à-fait comme ne pouvant être d'aucun usage].

Les remarques que vous me dites que d'habiles gens on faites sur le
Reasonableness of Christianity sont sans doute fort justes, et il est vray
que plusieurs Lecteurs ont été choquéz de certaines pensées qu'on voit
au commencement de ce livre, lesquelles ne s'accordent pas tout-à-fait
avec des Doctrines communément reçuës. Mais sur cela je suis obligé
de renvoyer ces Messieurs aux deux défenses que l'Auteur a faites de
son Ouvrage. Car ayant publié ce petit Livre, comme il le dit luy-même,
principalement afin de convaincre ceux qui doutent de la Religion
Chrétienne, il semble qu'il a été conduit à traiter ces matières malgré
luy, car pour rendre son Livre utile aux Déistes, il ne pouvoit point se
taire entièrement sur ces articles auxquels ils s'aheurtent dès qu'ils
veulent entrer dans l'examen de la Religion Chrétienne. Je suis

London, Oct. 97   Monsieur
                     Votre très humble et très obéissant
                     serviteur.

Vir amplissime,

Ne mireris quòd linguâ Gallicâ responsum à me sit acceptissimis tuis
Latinis 8. huius mensis mihi scriptis, liceat mihi me tibi excusare et
negotiorum multitudine quae otium negat, et linguae Latinae dissuetudine, quae expeditè scribere prohibet. Hanc meam epistolam aliis vel
praelegendam vel monstrandam ex tuis colligo: virorum praecellentium
censurae styli negligentiâ me objicere minimè decorum judicavi. Quic-

quid enim tua vel humanitas vel amicitia in me excusare solet, aliis vel nauseam vel certè non condonandam molestiam creare potest. Scripsi igitur quod dicendum habui linguâ vernaculâ festinatim, Galloque in suam linguam vertendam tradidi. Ex quo exorta est inter episcopum Wigorniensem (qui me quaesitâ causâ aggressus est) et me disputatio; gens theologorum togata in librum meum mirè excitatur, laudataque hactenus dissertatio illa, tota jam scatet erroribus (vel saltem continet latentia errorum vel scepseos fundamenta) piâ doctorum virorum curâ nunc demum detegendis. Ad unitatem Dei quod attinet, Grotii, fateor, in loco a te citato argumenta non abundè satisfaciunt. Putasne tamen quempiam, qui Deum agnoscit, posse dubitare numen illud esse unicum? ego sane nunquam dubitavi; etiamsi, fateor, mihi ex hac occasione cogitandi videtur altius aliquanto elevandam esse mentem, et à communi philosophandi ratione segregandam, si quis id philosophice, vel, si ita dicam, physice probare velit; sed hoc tibi soli dictum sit. Uxorem tuam dilectissimam liberosque officiosissime saluto.

SECOND LETTER OF JOHN LOCKE TO PHILIP VAN LIMBORCH

Monsieur,

La question que vous m'avez proposée, vient de la part d'une personne d'un génie si vaste et d'une si profonde capacité que je suis confus de l'honneur qu'il me fait de déferer si fort à mon jugement dans une occasion, où il luy seroit plus avantageux et plus sûr de s'en rapporter à luy-même. Je ne sais quelle opinion vous avez pû luy donner de moy, séduit par l'amitié que vous me portez; mais une chose dont je suis fort assûré, c'est que, si je ne consultois que ma propre réputation, j'éviterois d'exposer mes foibles pensées devant une personne d'un si grand jugement, et que je ne me hazarderois pas à regarder cet Article comme une Question à prouver, bien des gens étant peut-être d'avis qu'il vaut mieux le recevoir en qualité de Maxime, parce que, selon eux, il est mieux établi sur les fondemens ordinaires

que si l'on tâchoit de l'expliquer par des spéculations et des raisonnemens aux quels tout le monde n'est pas accoutumé. Mais je sais que
la Personne par qui je crois que cette Question vous a été proposée,
a l'esprit autrement tourné. Sa candeur et sa probité égalent sa science
et ses autres grandes qualitéz. S'il ne trouve pas mes raisons assez
claires ou assez convaincantes il ne sera pour cela porté à condamner
aussitôt mon intention, ni à mal juger de moy sous prétexte que mes
preuves ne sont pas aussi bonnes qu'il l'auroit souhaité. Enfin, moins
il trouvera de satisfaction dans mes raisonnemens, plus il sera obligé
de ‖ me pardonner, parce que, quelque convaincu que je sois de mes   f. 158ᵛ
foiblesse, je n'ai pas laissé d'obeïr à ses ordres.

J'écris donc simplement parce que vous le voulez l'un et l'autre;
et je veux bien, Monsieur, que vous fassiez voir s'ils vous plaît ma
Lettre à cet excellent homme, et aux autres personnes, qui se trou-
vèrent dans vôtre conference. Mais c'est aux conditions suivantes: la
première, que ces Messieurs me promettront de m'apprendre librement
et sincèrement leurs pensées sur ce que je dis. La seconde, que vous
ne donnerez aucune copie de ce que je vous écris à qui que ce soit, mais
que vous me promettez de jetter cette lettre au feu quand je vous
prierai de le faire. A quoy je serois bien aise que vous eussiez la bonté
d'ajouter une troisième condition, c'est que ces Messieurs me feront
l'honneur de me communiquer les raisons sur lesquelles ils établissent
eux mêmes l'Unité de Dieu.

La question dont vous me parlez, se réduit à ceci, *Comment l'unité
de Dieu peut être prouvée?* ou en d'autres termes, *Comment on peut
prouver qu'il n'y a qu'un Dieu?*

Pour résoudre cette question il est nécessaire de savoir, avant que de
venir aux preuves de l'unité de Dieu, ce qu'on entend par le mot de
Dieu. L'idée ordinaire et à ce que je croy, la véritable idée qu'ont de
Dieu, ceux qui reconnoissent son exsistence, c'est qu'il est *un Etre
infini, éternel, incorporel et tout parfait.* Or cette idée ‖ une fois   f. 158ʳ
reconnuë, il me semble fort aisé d'en déduire l'unité de Dieu. En effet
un être qui est tout parfait, ou pour ainsi dire, parfaitement parfait,
ne peut être qu'unique, parce qu'un être tout parfait ne sçauroit
manquer d'aucun des attributs, perfections ou dégrez de perfections,
qu'il luy importe plus de posseder que d'en être privé, car autrement il
s'en faudroit d'autant qu'il ne fût entièrement parfait.

Par exemple, avoir du pouvoir est une plus grande perfection que
d'en avoir point; avoir plus de pouvoir est une plus grande perfection
que d'en avoir moins, et avoir tout pouvoir (ce qui est être tout-puissant)

215

c'est une plus grande perfection que de ne l'avoir pas tout. Cela posé, deux Etres tout-puissans sont incompatibles; parce qu'on est obligé de supposer que l'un doit vouloir nécéssairement ce que l'autre veut, et en ce cas-là, l'un des deux dont la volonté est nécéssairement déterminée par la volonté de l'autre, n'est pas libre, et n'a pas, par conséquent, cette perfection là, car il est mieux d'être libre, que d'être soumis à la détermination de la volonté d'un autre. Que s'ils ne sont pas tous deux réduits à la nécessité de vouloir toujours la même chose, alors l'un peut vouloir faire, ce que l'autre ne voudroit fût fait, auquel cas la volonté de l'un prevaudra sur la volonté de l'autre, et ainsi celui des deux, dont la puissance ne sauroit seconder la volonté, n'est pas tout-puissant; car il ne peut pas faire autant que l'autre. Donc l'un des deux n'est pas tout-puissant. Donc il n'y a ni ne sauroit y avoir deux tout-puissans, ni par conséquent deux Dieux.

f. 159^v (Par la même idée de perfection nous venons à connoître, que Dieu est *omniscient*. Or dans la supposition de deux Etres distincts qui ont un pouvoir et une volonté distincte, c'est une imperfection de ne pouvoir pas cacher ses pensées. Mais si l'un des deux cache ses pensées à l'autre, cet autre n'est pas *omniscient*, car non seulement il ne connoît pas tout ce qui peut être connu, mais il ne connoît pas même ce qu'un autre connoît.

On peut dire la même chose de la toute-présence de Dieu: Il vaut mieux qu'il soit par tout dans l'étendüe infinie de l'espace que d'être exclus de quelque partie de cet espace, car s'il est exclu de quelque endroit, il ne peut pas y opérer, ni savoir ce qu'on y fait, et par conséquent il n'est ni tout-puissant, ni *omniscient*.

Que si pour anéantir les raisonnemens que je viens de faire, on dit que les deux Dieux qu'on suppose, ou les deux cent mille (car par la même raison qu'il peut y en avoir deux il y peut en avoir deux millions, parce qu'on n'a plus aucun moyen d'en limiter le nombre) si l'on oppose, dis-je, que plusieurs Dieux ont une parfaite toute-puissance qui soit exactement la même, qu'ils ont aussi la même connoissance, la même volonté et qu'ils existent également dans le même lieu, c'est seulement multiplier le même Etre, mais dans le fonds et dans la vérité de la chose on ne fait que réduire une pluralité supposée à une véritable

f. 160^r unité. Car de supposer ‖ deux Etres intelligens, qui connoissent, veulent, et font incessamment la même chose, et qui n'ont pas une existence separée, c'est supposer, en pa. oles, une pluralité, mais poser effectivement une simple unité. Car être inséparablement uni par l'entendement, par la volonté, par l'action, et par le lieu, c'est être

216

autant uni qu'un être intelligent peut être uni à luy-même; et par conséquent, supposer que là, où il y a une telle union, il peut y avoir deux Etres, c'est supposer une division sans division, et une chose divisée d'avec elle-même.

[Considérons un peu plus à fonds la Toute-préşence de Dieu. Il faut de toute nécéssité que Dieu soit tout-présent, à l'infini; à moins qu'il ne soit renfermé dans quelque petit coin de l'Espace, sans que nous sachions, ni pourquoy, ni comment, ni par qui, ni en quel lieu: je dis un petit coin, parce qu'une certaine partie déterminée de l'espace, de quelque étendüe qu'on la suppose, est fort peu de chose si elle est comparée à l'Espace infini. Or si Dieu a une Toute-puissance infinie, c'est, je croy, une preuve qui approchera de la démonstration, qu'il ne peut y avoir qu'un Dieu. Quelle que soit la nature, l'être ou la substance de Dieu, là où Dieu est, il y a certainement quelque chose de réel et qui est plus réel que tous les autres Etres. Supposons donc que cet Etre réel existe dans tel point Physique de l'Espace qu'on voudra supposer, je dis qu'il s'ensuit démonstrativement de là, qu'un autre Etre réel de la même espèce, ne sauroit être dans le même point individuel de l'Espace; car en ce cas-là, il n'y auroit qu'un seul Etre dans ce point parce que là où il n'y a aucune différence ni à l'égard de l'espèce ni à l'égard du lieu, il n'y peut y avoir qu'un seul Etre. Et qu'on ne s'imagine pas que ce raisonnement ne peut être bon qu'à l'égard du corps et des parties de la Matière; car on peut, je pense, l'appliquer fort bien à ce qu'on appelle l'*Espace pur*, qui est ce qu'il y a de plus éloigné de la Matière. Car deux points physiques d'Espace ne peuvent pas plûtôt être réduits en un seul, que deux Atomes physiques de la Matière être réduits à un seul Atome. La raison de cette impossibilité est fondée sur ce que, si deux points d'espace pouvoient être réduits en un, tout l'Espace pourroit être réduit en ‖ un seul point physique; ce qui est aussi impossible, f. 160ʳ qu'il est impossible que toute la Matière pût être réduite à un seul Atome.

Pour moy qui ne connois pas ce que c'est que la Substance de la Matière, je connois encore moins ce que c'est que la substance de Dieu; mais je sçais pourtant que cette substance est quelque chose, et qu'elle doit exclure d'où elle est, toutes les autres substances de la même espèce, (s'il pouvoit y en avoir de telles). Si donc Dieu est immense et présent par tout, c'est pour moy une démonstration qu'il n'y a qu'un Dieu, et qu'il n'y en peut avoir qu'un seul.]

217

Je me suis hazardé à vous écrire mes réflexions sur ce sujet, comme elles se sont présentées, à mon esprit, sans les ranger dans un certain ordre qui pourroit servir peut-être à les mettre dans un plus grand jour si on leur donnoit un peu plus d'étenduë. Mais ceci doit paroître devant des personnes d'une si grande pénétration, que ce seroit les amuser inutilement que développer davantage mes pensées. Telles qu'elles sont je vous prie de m'en écrire vôtre opinion et celle de ces Messieurs, afin que selon le jugement que vous en ferez, je puisse, pour ma propre satisfaction, les examiner de nouveau, et leur donner plus de force (ce que ma mauvaise santé et le peu de loisir qui me reste, ne me permettent pas de faire présentement) ou bien les abandonner tout-à-fait comme ne pouvant être d'aucun usage. [Je suis ...]

[Oates 2 April 1698]

THIRD LETTER OF JOHN LOCKE TO PHILIP VAN LIMBORCH

Oates, 21 may 1698

Monsieur,

Mss. Locke
c. 24 f. 164ʳ   Si ma santé ne me permettoit pas de satisfaire commodément l'envie que j'ai d'exécuter les ordres de ce grand homme qui reçoit si favorablement mes réflexions, toutes médiocres qu'elles sont, il est pourtant vray que je ne saurois la sacrifier pour une meilleure occasion que celle qui me porte à examiner le sujet où il m'a engagé, et qui me fournit le moyen de luy faire voir combien je suis prêt à luy obeïr. Mais je ne prétens pas qu'en cette rencontre il me soit obligé d'un tel sacrifice; car si je ne hazarde point ma réputation auprès de luy, je suis fort assuré que ma santé ne sera point intéressée par ce que je vais écrire. Ayant à faire à un homme qui raisonne si nettement, et qui a si bien approfondi cette matière, je n'aurai pas besoin de parler beaucoup pour me faire entendre. Son extrême pénétration luy fera sentir d'abord le fondement de la preuve que je vais proposer, de sorte que sans qu'il

soit nécéssaire que je m'engage dans de longues déductions, il pourra juger si elle est bien ou mal fondée.

Je ne puis m'empêcher de remarquer l'exactitude de son jugement par rapport à l'ordre qu'il a donné à ses propositions, et il est vray, comme il l'a fort bien remarqué, qu'en mettant la troisième à la place de la seconde, les Théologiens, les Philosophes, et Descartes luy-même, supposent l'unité de Dieu sans la prouver.

Si par la question qui me fût d'abord proposée, j'eusse compris comme je fais présentement, quel étoit le but de cet habile homme, je n'aurois pas envoyé la réponse que je vous ai envoyée, mais une beaucoup plus courte, et plus conforme à l'ordre de la nature et de la raison, où chaque chose paroît dans son meilleur jour.

Je croy que quiconque réfléchira sur soy-même, connoîtra évidemment sans en pouvoir douter le moins du monde, qu'il y a eû de toute éternité un Etre intelligent. Je croy encore qu'il est évident à tout homme qui pense, qu'il y a aussi un Etre infini. Or je dis qu'il ne peut y avoir qu'un Etre infini, et que cet Etre infini doit être aussi l'Etre éternel, parce que, ce qui est infini, doit avoir été infini de toute éternité; car aucunes additions faites dans le temps, ne sauroient rendre une chose infinie, si elle ne l'est pas en elle même, et par elle même de toute éternité. Telle étant la nature de l'infini ‖ qu'on n'en peut rien f. 164^V ôter, et qu'on n'y peut rien ajouter. D'où il s'ensuit que l'infini ne sauroit être séparé en plus d'un, ni être qu'un.

C'est là, selon moy, une preuve à priori que l'Etre éternel indépendent n'est qu'un; et si nous y joignons l'idée de toutes les perfections possibles, nous avons alors l'idée d'un Dieu eternel, infini, omniscient, et tout-puissant, etc.

Si ce raisonnement s'accorde avec les notions de l'excellent homme qui doit le voir, j'en serai extrèmement satisfait. Et s'il ne s'en accomode pas, je regarderai comme une grande faveur s'il veut bien me communiquer sa preuve que je tiendrai secrète, ou que je communiquerai comme venant de sa part, selon qu'il le jugera à propos. Je vous prie de l'assurer de mes très humbles respects. Je suis,

Monsieur

THE CORRESPONDENCE OF JOHN LOCKE

When in 1708, that is to say hardly four years after Locke's death, Awnsham and John Churchill who had already published much that Locke had written, published the first collection of his letters with the title *Some Familiar Letters between Mr. Locke and Several of his Friends*, it became clear that this correspondence might be important in order to have, not only a better understanding of the events of Locke's life and works and in general of the human and philosophical personality of the author of the *Essay on Human Understanding*, but also a deeper knowledge of the social, political and cultural environment of the time in which he lived.

The proof of that is the fact that John Churchill, heir and successor to Awnsham, thought it well worth while to republish those same Familiar Letters in the first complete edition of *Locke's Works*, which came out in London in 1714. He did this because he knew very well that the importance of Locke's correspondence, printed with his complete works would gain the thanks of the reader for the editor. "I cannot doubt of your thanks for the present I make you" one can read in the Preface *To the Reader* (III p. 499).

That it was a real present, as timely as it was welcome, it was soon shown by none other than Le Clerc, who had personal knowledge of Locke and the circle of the Dutch Remonstrants in which he had lived during his years of exile, and who had been Locke's first biographer.

Under the title "*Lettres diverses de Mr. Locke et de Mr. Limborch, contenant quelques remarques sur deux Livres intitulez Le Christianisme Raisonnable et Essai Concernant l'Entendement Humain*", Le Clerc in fact published some 23 of the letters from the correspondence between Locke and Limborch. These letters, which had already appeared in *Some Familiar Letters* were translated into French and inserted into Vol. II of the *Oeuvres Diverses* de Mr. Locke which was published in Amsterdam in 1732. "Les Lettres, roulant sur deux aspects très importants, l'Unité de Dieu et la liberté de l'homme", Le Clerc wrote in the *Avertissement*, p. X, "l'on peut considerer comme des eclaircissements utiles sur les matières les plus graves qui sont traitées dans l'*Essai concernant l'Entendement.*"

Since then there have been many partial editions of Locke's Letters among them the particularly important 98 letters published in London in 1830 by Lord King, *Original Letter of Locke; Algerson Sidney; and Anthony Lord Shaftesbury* [...], the outstanding collection of Ollion and De Beer appeared in the Hague in 1912 under the title *Lettres inédites de John Locke à ses amis Nicholas Toynard, Philippe Van Limborch et Edward Clarke* [...] which followed *Notes sur la Correspondence de John Locke* [...] Paris 1908 also by Ollion, who in addition to the 32 unpublished letters from Locke to Toynard added a list of 600 letters of Locke and his correspondents which at that time was believed to be the complete correspondence of Locke. Then came the publication of the letters between Locke and Clarke, edited by Rand, *The Correspondence of John Locke and Edward Clarke* [...] Oxford 1927, which was particularly important for a better understanding of Locke's writings on the value of currency, the *Essay on Human Understanding* and the *Thoughts on Education*. There followed other letters to illuminate this or that aspect of Locke's thinking or his relationship with this or that correspondent or even just to put on record some chance discoveries of the widely dispersed letters of Locke.

But it was precisely the incomplete and fitful way in which Locke's correspondence was published that drew attention to the need for a definitive edition of Locke's correspondence that would include all the available letters, both published and unpublished, especially after the acquisition by the Bodleian Library in Oxford of the Lovelace Collection and the fruitful research done on it by critics and biographers of Locke's.

To fulfill this need, which was even more felt at a time when there was a happy rebirth of the study of Locke, the Clarendon Press entrusted a complete edition of Locke's *Correspondence* to Esmond de Beer in 1956. De Beer had already given a magnificent proof of his unusual attitude to this type of work and of his rare capability as a scholar when he edited the six volumes of the *Diary of John Evelyn* (Oxford U.P.,1955).

In an article that appeared on the 16th of July, 1971 in the *Times Literary Supplement* (pp. 837-838) under the heading *The Correspondence of John Locke* Esmond De Beer informed the readers of the assignment he had been given by the Clarendon Press. "In 1956 I was invited by the Clarendon Press to edit the Correspondence; not only that in the Lovelace Collection but everything else that is available". He summarized the main criteria that he was following in his work: "I adopted a different arrangement [from] that used by Madame

222

Labrousse in her *Inventaire Critique* (1961) of Bayle's correspondence; it is to the Burke Checklist that I am indebted for grounding in the essential work of registering the letters" and he ended by hoping that "the letters are to be printed so far as possible".

It was only in March 1977, though dated 1976, that Vol. I of the *Correspondence of John Locke* edited by De Beer finally appeared in the Oxford edition of the *Complete Works of Locke (The Correspondence of John Locke*, ed. by E.S. De Beer, in eight volumes; volume I Letters nos 1-461. Oxford. At the Clarendon Press, 1976) which already contained the Peter H. Nidditch's masterly edition of the *Essay concerning Human Understanding;* the second volume (Volume II. Letters no. 462-848. Oxford 1976) of the correspondence quickly followed in April.

No less than twenty years of painstaking and patient work were needed so that De Beer could complete and pass the proofs of the first volumes of Locke's correspondence. These two volumes contained the first 983 letters out of a total of 3650 that have been preserved and which are therefore intended to be contained in the remaining eight volumes of more than 5000 pages.

These 3650 letters cover 50 years and more of Locke's life, that is to say they go from when he was a student at Christchurch College in Oxford until his death in 1704, and only a part has been published; the greater part has not. They were received or sent from Great-Britain, from France, from America, from Holland or from Indonesia. Most of them were written in English, many in French or Latin or in both languages, some were in Dutch or even in Greek. 1023 of these letters are in Locke's own hand or copies of the originals or quite definitely attributed to him. The remaining 2637 on the other hand were written to Locke by his correspondents, three of whom wrote no less than 20 letters each.

Yet, however boundless the *Correspondence* collected by De Beer may seem, especially when set beside the 600 letters listed by Ollion at the beginning of the century, there is no doubt that a part, perhaps not even a small part, has gone astray or has been destroyed by the owners of Locke's letters. There is reason to believe that Locke himself, because of that extreme prudence which rightly led Le Clerc to call him "plutôt timide que courageux" might have destroyed or asked others to destroy his letters or other people's whenever it seemed to him to be prudent to do so.

We have a clear proof of it in a letter from Locke to Limborch dated

2nd April 1698, where Locke explicitly asks the Arminian theologian " [...] Vous me prometez de jetter cette lettre au feu quand je vous prierait de le faire" (B.L. Mss. Locke c24F 158^r - 160^v, cit. f.158^v in *Three Letters from Locke to Limborch*, quot. ib.).

Of course one cannot say for certain if and which and how many letters among those missing from Locke's correspondence were destroyed for motives of prudence. For this reason De Beer quite rightly notes (Vol. I, *Introd.* p. XXXVI) "The question of destruction for political reasons can scarcely arise for the many demonstrable gaps from 1699 onwards". However, especially after the evidence quoted above, that does not exclude the suspicion that some letters – few or many hardly matters – may have been destroyed by Locke or at his wish.

Of the 3650 letters collected by De Beer, the first two volumes published, as it has been said already, 938 letters of Locke and his correspondents. These span more than 30 years, that is from 1650 to 1681, the years that go from Locke's adolescence to his maturity, from the first scholastic exercises at the well known Oxford college to the exile in Holland.

Those are the years in which Locke built his world of human relationships, of moral, cultural and political experiences and fixed the horizons of his thinking. All the same they are the most intense and fruitful years of Locke's life and literary career, a career that began when he was not yet thirty and which was revealed to the public only when he was on the brink of old age.

While he was still very young in 1660-62 Locke wrote two *Treatises on the Civil Magistrate;* between '62 and '64 when he was Censor of Moral Philosophy at Christ Church in Oxford he wrote the *Essays on the Law of Nature;* in '66 he made the acquaintance of Lord Ashley Cooper, the future Lord Shaftesbury, to whose uncertain political future his own was to be tied; in '67 he wrote the *Essay concerning Toleration* and in '78 the first drafts of the *Essay concerning Human Understanding;* between '75 and '79 he stayed for long periods in France where he got to know Toynard, busy at the time in trying to reach reconciliation of the Gospels, and with whom he began a voluminous correspondence which was destined to be the largest in the correspondence of Locke existing in the Bodleian Library; between '80 and '82 he wrote *Two Treatises of Government*, which were to lie for a long time among his secret papers and in the same years he made friends with Damaris Cudworth, the future Lady Masham, whose affectionate devotion would comfort him in his exile and bring tranquil-

lity to the philosopher's last years.

When Shaftesbury died in 1683, Locke took refuge in Holland, where he immediately got in touch with the circle of Arminians in Amsterdam and bound himself in staunch friendship with Limborch, theologian and spiritual head of the community of the Remonstrants. Locke was to receive much intellectual help and stimulation from his conversations with Limborch. In July 1684, during his exile in Holland while he was preparing the final lay-out of the *Essay on Human Understanding*, he wrote Clarke the letters advising him on the education of his children, letters which were to be published in 1693 with the title *Some Thoughts Concerning Education;* in the winter of 1685-86, on the eve of the revocation of the Edict of Nantes he was to write the *Epistola de Tolerantia* which would later be published by Limborch at Gouda after Locke himself had returned to England in 1689.

So, in the thirty years covered by the first two volumes of the *Correspondence,* Locke's major works were already written, such as the *Essay on Human Understanding,* the *Two Treatises on Government,* the *Epistola de Tolerantia* and the *Thoughts on Education,* without mentioning the many youthful works. That does not mean, let it be clearly said, that the 983 letters published in these two first volumes always offer clarification on the origins of Locke's works or information on his thinking, nor can one expect that of the letters that will appear in the volumes to follow. On the contrary, it is well to say at once that many of those 983 letters are irrelevant or can be overlooked; some of them are purely occasional and transitory and in any case of little or no use to anyone writing about Locke's biography or thought. All the same, there is no doubt that , taken all together, they furnish a most precious testimony to the man and his background; and it is well known that the more one knows the man and his world the better one understands the philosopher.

Knowledge of the man and the philosopher Locke is for the rest made very easy by the happy mediation of De Beer who provides the reader with the most useful explanations and information about each of Locke's correspondents, gives pertinent references and reminders of names and contents to the letters; he sets down the date – sometimes in accordance with the double calendar in use at the time – the places it was written from, and sent to, where the letter is to be found today, and the particulars of publication if the letter has already been printed; each letter is transcribed exactly as in the original manuscript, where that is possible and, when the letter is written in a language other than

225

English or French, it is given a careful translation in English.

The principles already set out in the article in *The Times Literary Supplement* and followed in the edition of Locke's correspondence are here amply described by De Beer in the course of a long introduction, where among other bibliographical aids, he also tells of the present state of Locke's correspondence and points out some of the essential moments of his biography to which the correspondence refers or indirectly relates.

With regard to the *Introduction*, we limit ourselves to saying that we are in complete agreement with De Beer (I. *Introd.* p. 24) in holding that the *Epistola de Tolerantia* was not written *to* Limborch but *for* Limborch as we have already noted in the *Introd.* to our critical edition of Locke's famous *Epistola* (*Introd.* pp. XXXVI-XXXVII). We also agree with De Beer (*op. cit.* I, *Introd.* pp. XXXIII-XXXVII) in thinking that it was only in 1690 that Locke admitted to Churchill that he was the author of the *Letter Concerning Toleration* published anonymously by Popple in 1689; even if it seems to us more likely that Locke would have revealed to the editor that he had written the *Letter* not when he handed over the *Second Letter* but rather when he handed over the *Second Edition Corrected* of the first *Letter Concerning Toleration* (cf. *The Socinianism of Locke*, p. 144).

When the publication of *Locke's Correspondence* is completed – and this can be foreseen within a reasonably short period of time – the scholar will at last have available in the eight volumes that will make up De Beer's exemplary edition, a work that most intimately reveals Locke's human and philosophical personality and an extremely rich picture of the age in which he lived; an age that coincides, as De Beer recalls (I *Introd.*, p. XV), with that which Paul Hazard called the crisis of the European conscience; an age here re-lived through the fascinating evocation of figures humanly alive in the very discreetness of Locke's relationship as a correspondent with Limborch, Le Clerc, Clarke, Tyrrell, Toynard and Lady Masham, all intimately connected with the world of Locke's emotions and culture and therefore indissolubly linked with his name and his fortunes.

But there is no need for the edition of the *Correspondence* of John Locke in the *Clarendon Edition of Locke's Works* to be finished to testify to the gratitude towards De Beer which John Churchill confidently expected when he published the *Familiar Letters* in the first edition of Locke's *Works*.

London, Spring 1978

THE RATIONAL EVIDENCE OF THE UNITY OF GOD
IN THE CORRESPONDENCE OF LOCKE

With exemplary constancy and punctual regularity, E. De Beer keeps on publishing Locke's copious correspondence, some already in print, but most previously unpublished. *The Correspondence of John Locke*, ed. by E.S. De Beer, in eight volumes, vol. VI, Oxford 1981. From 1976, when vol. I was issued, to this day, De Beer has published six of the eight expected volumes, that is 2664 letters by Locke and his correspondents, exchanged in about 50 years.

This last published volume, vol. VI, contains 265 letters, covering the period between 1697 and 1700.

At that time, Locke had already published his main works and was now engaged in defending them from the unremitting and persistent criticism, whether anonymous or otherwise, directed, on religious grounds, against the *Reasonableness of Christianity* as well as against the *Essay*, which appeared, and indeed were, the former in particular, undoubtedly of Unitarian and Socinian inspiration. And we know that Locke, "plutôt timide que courageux", as Le Clerc remembers him, did not like it at all to be taken for Unitarian, least of all for Socinian or atheist, as he was said to be, in an age when belief in the Trinity was decreed by law. Consequently, despite the anonymity of the *Reasonableness*, Locke obstinately refuted, point by point, the objections and accusations moved to him by Edwards, amongst others for demoting Christ to a Messiah, as well as those expressed by Stillingfleet, Bishop of Worcester, who was uncovering the Socinian matrix of the *Essay* in Locke's criticism of the concept of substance. Nevertheless, in issuing Locke's letter to Molineux, dated 22 February 1697 (vl. VI, n. 2202 p. 4 ff.), where Locke lamented the attacks levelled against him by Stillingfleet in a Sunday sermon, De Beer wrongly interprets the Bishop's covered inference, confusing him — according to a deep-rooted conviction — with Dr. Sherlock who, undoubtedly, was not that "great man" meant by Locke. So much so that a few years after the same Locke did not take any notice of the *Discourse* in which Sherlock took a stand in the anti-Trinitarian dispute.

To this dispute must be connected also the more eagerly awaited and more interesting letters of this vol. VI, those exchanged between Locke and the Dutch theologian Philippus van Limborch, Arminian of Unitarian belief, who, for himself and on behalf of common friends, insistently asked Locke to declare his position on the Unity of God and to offer rational evidence of it. The letters in question are those dated 29 October 1697 (n. 2340, vl. VI, p. 243), 24 February 1698 (n. 2395, vl. VI, p. 320 ff.) and 21 May 1698 (n. 2443, vl. VI, p. 405 f.); these letters are written in French, rather than in Latin, as Locke was accustomed to do when corresponding *currente calamo* with Limborch, neither knowing each other's language. Owing to the delicacy of the matter, Locke preferred to think and write in his own language, letting then Coste translate it in French, which Limborch and his friends could understand easily. However, fearful of having said too much about a subject upon which he preferred to speak little, when he was about to send the first letter, Locke deleted its middle, more interesting and novel section, reducing it to a very minor thing.

He did the same with the second letter, dated 21 February (but actually, according to a note in Locke's hand. of the 2 April 1698), deleting a large part of obvious anti-Cartesian inspiration.

These two letters, in Coste's original manuscript, and the other on the same subject, together with two drafts in Locke's handwriting, are in the Bodleian Library in Oxford. I made them the object of a study and published them for the first time, in their entirety (v. M.Montuori, *Tre lettere di Locke a Limborch sull'Unità di Dio*, in Atti dell'Accademia Pontania, n.s.v. XXIII 1974, p. 33 of the coll., repr. above *Three Letters from Locke to Limborch*, cit.). In these letters, Locke, despite fears and after-thoughts, decided to give that rational evidence of the Unity of God which he had intended to include in a new edition of the *Essay* (letter 2340, vl. VI, p. 243) but never did to avoid, as he apologetically explained to Limborch, adding new fuel to the arguments of his adversaries. "Je doute", Locke writes (cit.) "si je doit leur fournir de nouveaux sujets de dispute."

But even if omitted for peace's sake (*j'aime la paix*, cit.let.) in a work destined to have vast cultural circulation, such as the *Essay*, it cannot be denied that Locke nevertheless revealed to Limborch, who personally did not need it, and to friends in his entourage, the rational foundations of his Unitarian belief, thus confirming both the close ties with Dutch and English anti-Unitarian followers (see here, *The Socinianism of Locke*, cit.) and the well-motivated accusations

voiced by Edwards, by Stillingfleet and by all those who had discovered his essential Unitarianism. Instead, De Beer, in issuing these same letters, and although knowing my arguments as regards Locke's evidence given to Limborch on the subject of the Unity of God (v.vl. VI, app. II p. 783), suggests that "the doctrine of the Trinity is not concerned" (p. 206), the question being simply, in his opinion, of evidence of the Unity of God as against the "plurality of gods, as in heathen belief" (ib). De Beer's statement really is surprising.

And was it necessary, to deny the plurality of those "dei falsi e dugiardi," to have recourse to such secretness both from the person on whose behalf Limborch asked Locke to furnish evidence of the Unity of God, that "vir magnificus" who, for his part, did not wish his name to be revealed "nomen (...) suum (...) celatum voluit" (vl. VI letter n. 2318 p. 206), and from Locke who, in turn, asked "vous ne donnerez aucune copie de ce que je vous écris à qui ce soit, mais (...) vous me promettez de jetter cette lettre au feu, quand je vous prierai de le faire." (vl. VI, letter n.2395, p. 321). Was it necessary, in fact, that in order to deny the plurality of the pagan gods Locke should expose himself to an explicit declaration of Unitarian faith: "Putasne tamen quempian, qui deum adnoscit posse dubitare numen illud [Deum] esse unicum? Ego sane numquam dubitavi?" (vl. LVI, letter 2400, p. 245). And is it conceivable that Locke should have intended to add to the IV book of the *Essay*, after and as a conclusion of the evidence of the existence of God, that which denied the plurality of the pagan gods? It will therefore be appropriate to state again that Locke had been deeply influenced by the English and Dutch Unitarian and Socinian company which he frequented, and in particular by that same Limborch, spiritual head of the Dutch Arminians, hence radically and avowedly Unitarian (cfr. *The Socinianism of Locke*, cit.). So much so that, whilst writing the *Reasonableness*, he also wrote a series of notes in anti-logical form, afterwards published by Lord King in *Life of John Locke* (...) 2 vols. London 1830, under the title, given by Locke himself of *Adversaria Theologica* (vl. II pp. 186-195), where, rather than a comparison between the sources for or against the Trinity, Locke is searching for a textual confirmation of the concept of Unity which he had already reached and to which he sincerely subscribed (cf. *Three Letters from Locke to Limborch*, cit.). It should suffice to remember that in the antilogy *Christus Deus Supremus – Christus non-Deus Supremus*, Locke, distinguishing the Son from the Father, denies the Son consubstantiality with the Father: "He [Christus] is not equal to God." The

Father is greater than he [Christus]." (cit. p. 190). Briefly, Christ is for Locke only the Messiah and the Trinity a dogma contrary to the Scriptures' very evidence.

John Edwards was therefore perfectly right when, openly calling Locke "the gentleman who wrote *Human Understanding* and *Education,*" remarked that anyone affirming that every Christian must only believe "that Jesus is the Messiah" denied, at the same time, "the Holy Trinity: Father, Son and Holy Ghost", thus revealing himself "all over Socinianized" (J. Edwards, *Some Thoughts concerning the several causes and occasion of Atheism* [...], London 1695, p. 113).

Evidently, De Beer has not examined in depth — nor could be expected to do so in a brief editorial note — this complex and delicate subject which profoundly influenced the character of Locke's human and philosophical personality such as it is fixed in the historiographic tradition. If this is mentioned here, it is only to avoid that others may incur in the same error, and without belittling in any way De Beer's laudable effort, which is rendering accessible to scholars Locke's immense volume of correspondence and making it possible for them to penetrate in the deepest recesses of his thoughts.

London, summer 1981

INDEX OF NAMES

151, 158, 159, 160, 161, 162, 164, 182, 188, 189, 208, 228
Courcelle, Ethienne de, XVIII
Cranston, M., XV, XVII, XVIII, XIX, XXIII, XXV, XXIX, XXXIII, XXXIV, 123, 124, 129, 131, 132, 134, 136, 139, 143, 144, 152, 153, 176, 178, 180, 185, 206
Crippa, R., 124, 176 180

Dal Pra, M., 191
Daranda, P., 136
De Beer, E.S., 177, 182, 185, 208, 209, 222, 223, 224, 225, 226, 227, 229, 230
De Boer, T.V., XVIII
De Marchi, E., 120, 147, 148
Descartes, R., 178, 192, 193, 194, 195, 201, 206
Diana, 29
Dibon, P., XXIX, 194
Dordrecht, Synod of, XIV, XXV, XXVII, 127, 194

Ebbinghaus, J., XXXI, L, 119, 120, 128, 136, 140, 147, 149, 156, 157, 158, 162, 168
Edward VI, King, 53
Edwards, J., XXXI, 124, 175, 176, 177, 180, 188, 189, 191, 227, 229, 230
Elizabeth I, Queen, 53
Elliott, O.D., VII
Emims, 75
England, XVI, XVII, XVIII, XIX, XXI, XXII, XXVII, XXVIII, XXIX, XXXII, XXXIII, XXXVI, XLI, 119, 126, 135, 140, 143, 153, 154, 183, 191, 223, 225
Episcopius, XVIII, XIX
Esau, 75
Euphrates, 77
Europe, 71, 126, 155, 195

Feversham, Lord, XVII
Firmin, Th., 119, 131, 134, 135, 153
Florence, 120
Fontainebleau, Edict of, XV
Formigari, L., 120, 147
Fox Bourne, H.R., XV, XVIII, XIX, XXI, XXV, XXX, XXXI, XXXIII, XXXIV, XLV, 124, 131, 134, 136, 157, 176, 177, 178, 196
France, XVI, XIX, XXVII, 223, 224
Furly, B., 152, 153, 154

Geneva, 45, 69, 101
Gieben, J.C., II
Gomarus, F., XXV, XXVII
Gouda or Tergouw, XVIII, XX, XXVII, XXIX, XXXI, XXXII, XXXIV, XXXV, XXXVII, XXXIX, XL, XLI, XLII, XLIII, XLVII, 119, 121, 122, 126, 127, 132, 147, 151, 152, 154, 163, 172, 225
Gough, J.W., XXXIV, 120, 147, 149, 150, 151, 153, 154, 156-158, 162-166,

XLVIII, 124, 126, 127, 131, 136, 137, 138, 140, 141, 143, 147, 150, 152, 153, 154, 158, 167, 175, 180, 181, 182, 183, 184, 185, 186, 187, 188, 190, 191, 194, 195, 196, 197, 199, 200, 205, 206, 207, 208, 210, 221, 223, 225, 226, 228, 229
Locke, J.
– Dr. Van der Linden, XVIII
– Philantropus, XLIV
London, XXXI, XXXII, 123, 124, 134, 136, 147, 152, 154, 178, 192, 196
Louvois, Francois-Michel Le Tellier, marquis de, XVI
Luke, Apostle, 7
Lyme, R., XVII

Mabbolt, J.D., 180
Manship, S., 145, 175, 176, 190
Marchand, P., XXI
Mary, the Bloody, 53
Martin, Mr., 130
Martinetti, P., 191
Masham, Damaris Lady, XV, XIX, XXI, XXII, XXIII, XXV, XXVI, XXVII, 136, 172, 206, 224, 226
Matthew, Apostle, 25
Meliboeus, 65
Minogue, V., VII
Moabites, 75
Molineux, W., 177, 179, 227
Monmouth, Duke of, XVI, XVII, XVIII
Montuori, M., 148, 228
Moreri, L., XVIII, XXI, XXXI, XXXVIII, 126, 137, 193
Moses, 73
Muir, J., II

Nantes, Edict of, 126, 150, 169, 225
Naples, 119
Newton, Sir Isaac, 134
Nidditch, P.H., 223
Nottingham, 126

Ogonowski, Z., 148
Ollion, H.L., 222, 223
Oxford, XXII, XXXII
– Bodleian or University Library of, XXXII, XLIII, XLIV, XLVI, 122, 123, 130, 134, 140, 151, 163, 175, 189, 200, 208, 224, 228

P.A.P.O.I.L.A., explanation of, XXI
Pays-Bas, 138
Pellizzi, V.C., 160, 192
Pembroke, Earl of, XXII
Penn, W., 128